A BRIEF INTRODUCTION TO
QUR'ANIC EXEGESIS

A BRIEF INTRODUCTION TO QUR'ANIC EXEGESIS

Ali Suleiman Ali

THE INTERNATIONAL INSTITUTE OF ISLAMIC THOUGHT

THE INTERNATIONAL INSTITUTE OF ISLAMIC THOUGHT
P.O. BOX 669, HERNDON, VA 20172, USA
www.iiit.org

LONDON OFFICE
P.O. BOX 126, RICHMOND, SURREY TW9 2UD, UK
www.iiituk.com

ISBN 978-1-56564-688-9 *limp*
ISBN 978-1-56564-699-5 *cased*

Printed in Malta by Gutenberg Press Ltd

CONTENTS

FOREWORD

بسم الله الرحمن الرحيم

In the Name of God, Most Gracious, Most Compassionate

> ...And We have sent down unto you (also) the Message; that you may explain clearly to men what is sent for them, and that they may give thought.
>
> (*An-Nahl* 16:44)

THE QUR'AN is the final revelation to mankind. It is the first source of Islamic law (*Sharʿī*). It is addressed first and foremost to mankind for guidance in all aspects of life, spiritually, politically, economically, socially etc. It is the light that illuminates man's straight and right path. Hence, from the time of the Prophet Muhammad (ṢAAS)* to the present day, Muslims have dedicated their lives to studying the Qur'an, pondering over its teachings, deducing beneficial lessons, analyzing the events that take place on earth in the light of this ever-lasting divine fountain. As a result of these endeavors, we have inherited an impressive corpus of knowledge about Islam.

The Qur'an is indeed the mother of all Islamic sciences. It can be correctly and fairly said that all the Islamic sciences, from the Hadith, (the sayings, actions and tacit approval of the Prophet Muhammad) and the principles of Islamic Jurisprudence (*uṣūl al-fiqh*) to Arabic grammar (*naḥw*) and rhetoric (*balāghah*), all carry the imprint of the Qur'an. Thus, knowledge concerning the evolution of *tafsīr* as the science of Qur'an interpretation (or Qur'anic exegesis) is highly

* ṢAAS – *Ṣalla Allāhu ʿAlayhi wa Sallam*: May the peace and blessings of Allah be upon him; said whenever the name of Prophet Muhammad is mentioned or whenever he is referred to as the Prophet of Allah.

important and beneficial not only to Muslims but also to non-Muslims.

This book aims to introduce students of sciences of *tafsīr* to the historical development of Qur'anic interpretation from the time of the Prophet Muhammad to the present day. The work highlights the nature, characteristics, and methodology of the Prophet's *tafsīr*. But it also discusses the *tafsīr* of the Prophet's Companions (*Ṣaḥābah*) as well as the *tafsīr* of the *Tābiʿūn*, that is to say, the generation that followed the Companions, including the status, characteristics, and methodologies of their *tafsīr*.

The various compilations of different types of *tafsīr* that emerged as well as their authors have been included in this work. The two major types of *tafsīr*, *al-tafsīr bi al-ma'thūr* and *al-tafsīr bi al-ra'y* have been dealt with. The book also sheds lights on some new trends in *tafsīr* in the contemporary world, highlighting some differences between classical works and modern ones.

Furthermore, the work has been designed to be brief and descriptive not analytical. This is because the chief objective has been to provide readers with basic information regarding the evolution of *tafsīr*, some major Qur'anic interpreters (*mufassirūn*) and their works. It is hoped that this brief introduction will be of great interest to the students of *tafsīr* and that it will encourage them to pursue research in the subject matter dealt with.

Where dates are cited according to the Islamic calendar (hijrah) they are labelled AH. Otherwise they follow the Gregorian calendar and labelled CE where necessary. Arabic words are italicized except for those which have entered common usage. Diacritical marks have been added only to those Arabic names not considered modern. English translations taken from Arabic references are those of the author.

Since its establishment in 1981, the IIIT has served as a major center to facilitate serious scholarly efforts. Towards this end it has, over the decades, conducted numerous programs of research, seminars and conferences as well as publishing scholarly works specialising in the social sciences and areas of theology, which to date number more than four hundred titles in English and Arabic, many of which have been translated into other major languages.

We would like to thank the author, as well as the editorial and production team at the IIIT London Office, and all those who were directly or indirectly involved in the completion of this book. May God reward them for all their efforts.

January, 2017

CHAPTER I

Historical Overview

SUMMARY

1. Qur'anic Exegesis as a whole is introduced with a basic definition of terms, what it means and how it has developed down the centuries.
2. An introduction to the most prominent exegetes and their works has been given listing key *tafsīr* titles.
3. The Qur'an clearly has many layers of meaning and other vast elements (verse 59:21 states "Had We sent down this Qur'an on a mountain, verily, thou wouldst have seen it humble itself and cleave asunder for fear of Allah"). But the question is do we as human beings have access to that meaning? Qur'anic exegesis involves understanding/elucidating/interpreting each verse. Do we take the clear, obvious meaning or do we try to look beneath the surface and unveil more hidden ones? Do we have the ability to do so, should we do so given our limited capacities, should we only adhere to what we know from Prophetic traditions?
4. What methodological standards should be adopted in Qur'anic exegesis? Should we rely on hadith and the Companion's comments only? Or, accounting for the time-space factor, adopt some level of reasoning, and/or rational understanding in interpretation of text?

These and other questions integral to Qur'anic exegesis have followed Muslims down the centuries. It has led to exegetes praising each other, criticizing each other, and even opposing each other. This chapter gives a brief overview of the issues involved.

THE SCIENCE OF *Tafsīr* aims to explain the meanings of Allah's word as revealed in His Sacred Book, the Qur'an, to His Messenger Muhammad, and is usually rendered as Qur'anic 'interpretation' or exegesis. It is one of the major Islamic sciences. The Arabic root *f-s-r* means to unveil, to uncover,[1] and traditional or classical Muslim scholars state that the verbal noun *tafsīr* is derived from *fassara* meaning to explain. The terms, *fassara*, *tafsirah*, and *tafsīr* all denote explanation, elucidating, exposition, and unveiling.

Tafsīr, literally meaning 'explanation', and *ta'wīl*, interpretation, are two terms usually used by scholars as synonymous or interchangeable to denote Qur'anic interpretation or exegesis. Both of these terms are derived from transitive verbs, although the term *tafsīr* is used more for its intensive signification.[2] According to Arabic lexicographers, the word *ta'wīl* is a derivation of either *awwala* (to return, or to arrive at the final end) and/or *iyālah* (the *maṣdar* meaning verbal noun of *āla*, to arrange or to shape).

The Difference Between *Tafsīr* and *Ta'wīl*

According to Muḥammad ibn Muḥammad al-Maturidī (d. 333 AH), *tafsīr* is the explanation of the ultimate meaning of the text that unveils what God exclusively intended by the text, while *ta'wīl* applies to upholding the more likely interpretation when the text has more than one possible meanings.[3] Ḥusayn ibn Muḥammad al-Rāghib al-Aṣfahānī (d. 502 AH) stated that *tafsīr* is more comprehensive than *ta'wīl* and is used more commonly to mean the explanation of words and isolated terms. *Ta'wīl* is often used to elucidate meanings and sentences and is most used in theological texts or books, whilst *tafsīr* is used in theological texts and other areas (such as the sciences of the Qur'an and Islamic jurisprudence).[4] Al-Suyūṭī for his part reported that *ta'wīl* is information about the actual intended meaning, while *tafsīr* is information about the indication of the meaning.[5] Other scholars understand *tafsīr* as an explanation of the Qur'an based on the transmitted traditions from the Prophet, his Companions and *Tābiʿūn*, whereas they consider *ta'wīl* as personal knowledge, which goes beyond the apparent meaning. The following example may help in clarifying this point. We read in verse 110:1-3:

> When comes the help of God, and victory, and thou dost see the people enter God's Religion in crowds, celebrate the praises of thy

> Lord and pray for His forgiveness: For, He is Oft-returning (in Grace and Mercy).[6]

The *tafsīr*, or meaning of these verses, is the apparent meaning as indicated in the translation. The *ta'wīl* of the verses, however, is the way ʿAbd Allāh ibn ʿAbbās interpreted them. He stated that this chapter or the verses together foreshadowed the impending passing of the Prophet Muhammad. Under this personal interpretation, the Prophet is a messenger and his mission had come to an end with the acceptance of Islam by the people in Arabia. Thus, he had to return to God, Who sent him.

However, Abū ʿUbaydah Muʿammar ibn al-Muthannā (d. 210 AH) and al-Ṭabarī differ with the above-cited definitions of *tafsīr* and *ta'wīl*. To them, there is no difference between the two terms, which they regard as synonymous.[7] The term *tafsīr* – according to my own finding – when used to mean the explanation of the Qur'an was developed towards the second half or the end of the first Islamic century. Perhaps, ʿAbd Allāh ibn ʿUmar was the first person known to have used the word *tafsīr* to mean interpretation of the Qur'an when he said "*mā yaʿjibunī jarā'at ibn ʿAbbās ʿalā tafsīr al-Qur'ān fal ān qad ʿalemtu annahu 'ūtiya ʿilm*" ("I do not like or I do not admire ibn ʿAbbās' daring on Qur'anic commentary but now, I know he has been given knowledge."[8] Indeed, we find no mention of this term in the Qur'an and the Hadith to mean the explanation of the meaning of the Qur'an. The Qur'an, on the other hand, used the word *tafsīr* in one place (25:33) to mean 'explanation': "*wa lā ya'tūnaka bimathalin illa ji'nāka bi al-ḥaqqi wa aḥsana tafsīran*" ("and no question or example do they bring to you but We reveal to you the truth and the best explanation (thereof)"). The terms that both Qur'an and Hadith use for Qur'anic interpretation are *bayān*, *tabyīn*, *ta'wīl*, and *qawl*. The following passages of the Qur'an and Hadith support my statement:

> It is for Us to collect it and to promulgate it: But when We have

promulgated it, follow thou its recital (as promulgated): Nay more, it is for Us to explain it (and make it clear) "*bayanahu*." (Qur'an 75:17-19)

The word *bayānah* is used to mean explanation or clarification.

and We have sent down unto you (also) the Message; that you may explain clearly "*litubayyina*" to men what is sent for them... (Qur'an 16:44)

In this verse, the word *litubayyina*, the verbal noun (*maṣdar*) of which is *tabyīn* refers to the clarification or elucidation of the Qur'anic verses.

Verse 3:7 of the Qur'an states, "but no one knows its hidden meanings (*ta'wīl*) except God." The word *ta'wīl* means the actual meaning or interpretation. In a popular hadith, Prophet Muhammad asks Allah to grant Ibn ᶜAbbās knowledge of both the understanding of *al-dīn* (religion, Islam) and the Qur'an: "*Allāhumma faqqihhu fī al-dīn wa ᶜallimhu al-ta'wīl*," meaning: "Oh God, grant him knowledge about Islam and teach him the explanation or interpretation of the Qur'an."[9]

In al-Tirmidhī's collection of Hadith, one narration reads: "*man qāla fī al-Qur'ān bi ra'yihi fal yatabawwa' maqᶜadahu min al nār*,"[10] that is to say, "Whosoever interprets the Qur'an using his own opinion, let him take his seat in the Hell fire." The term *qāla* (currently meaning 'to say') in the context of the hadith, refers to the interpretation of the Qur'an. Furthermore, both the Prophet and the Companions allegorically interpreted some Qur'anic verses. Yet, their interpretations are being called *tafsīr*, not *ta'wīl*. This, I assume, is because many scholars of *tafsīr*, if not the majority, have not seen any differences between the two meanings.

The use of these terms in the Qur'an and Hadith leads us to postulate that a number of Qur'an interpreters (*mufassirūn*), including scholars such as al-Ṭabarī, al-Zamakhsharī and others used the words *bayān*, *ta'wīl* and *qawl* in the title of their books because of these terms' connection with the Qur'anic explanation. Al-Ṭabarī's voluminous work is entitled *Jāmiᶜ al-Bayān ᶜan Ta'wīl Āyat al-Qur'ān*, and al-Zamakhsharī's famous book of *tafsīr* is entitled "*Al-Kashshāf ᶜan Ḥaqā'iq al-Tanzīl wa ᶜUyūn al-Aqāwīl fī Wujūh al-Ta'wīl*.

The Prophet Muhammad and *Tafsīr*

The Prophet Muhammad was the first exegete or interpreter of the Qur'an (*mufassir*). But he did not, however, explain the whole of the Qur'an word for word because many of the verses were clear to the people of his time by virtue of their being Arabs who understood their own language. Generally, his explanations of Qur'anic scriptures occurred on one of three occasions: when a particular passage could not be comprehended through a typical understanding of Arabic; when the literal meaning of a verse, according to Muslim scholars, was not intended by God; or when a Companion asked for clarification of certain verses. For example, ᶜUbādah ibn al-Ṣāmit asked the Prophet about the meaning of *bushrā* (glad tidings) in Qur'anic verses 10:63-64 which state: "Those who believe and (constantly) guard against evil [that is those who have *taqwā*]. For them are glad tidings [*bushrā*], in the life of the present and in the Hereafter; no change can there be in the words of Allah. This is indeed the supreme felicity." The Prophet replied: "you have asked me something none of my Ummah (the Muslim community) has ever asked before you." *Bushrā* the Prophet explained, meant in this verse a good dream that a man sees or which is seen on his behalf.[11]

The Qur'anic command pertaining to the time of breaking the fast during the month of Ramadan states: "and eat and drink, until the white thread of dawn appear to you distinct from its black thread" (2:187). To comply with this regulation, ᶜUday ibn Ḥātim, who did not understand this figure of speech, kept a white and black thread specifically to see when the early light of dawn would allow him to differentiate the threads in order for him to begin fasting for the day. The Prophet Muhammad explained to him that the white and black thread mentioned in the Qur'anic verse referred to the early morning light of the horizon contrasting with the darkness of the sky.[12]

Tafsīr After the Passing of Prophet Muhammad

The Muslims living immediately after the death of the Prophet recognized certain Companions' skills and capabilities in terms of Qur'anic knowledge. Before he died, the Prophet proclaimed their superior status concerning the Qur'an in three ways. First, he used to send them to other cities to teach the Qur'an and Islam. For example, he sent Muṣʿab ibn ʿUmayr to Madinah before the general hijrah or 'migration' of the Muslims from Makkah to Madinah.[13] Similarly, ʿAlī ibn Abī Ṭālib (d.39 AH) and Muʿadh ibn Jabal (d.18 AH) were sent to Yemen at different times to instruct the new Muslims about Islam and invite non-Muslims to accept it.[14]

Secondly, the Prophet would praise certain Companions such as ʿAbd Allāh ibn Masʿūd (d. 32 AH), Ubay ibn Kaʿb al-Khazrajī al-Anṣārī (d. 21 AH), Zayd ibn Thābit (d. 45 AH) and Muʿādh ibn Jabal for their skill in reciting the the Qur'an properly and thoroughly.[15]

Thirdly, he would ask certain Companions to give fatwas (legal opinions) in his presence.[16] For example, on different occasions, he requested Abū Bakr al-Ṣiddīq (d. 13 AH), ʿUmar ibn al-Khaṭṭāb (d. 23 AH), ʿUthmān ibn ʿAffān (d. 34 AH), and ʿAli ibn Abī Ṭālib to do so in his presence. After the death of the Prophet, Muslims turned to these Companions and others to learn about the Qur'an and its *tafsīr*. Other Companions noted for their exegetical ability were Abū Mūsa al-Ashʿarī (d. 44 AH), ʿĀ'ishah bint Abū Bakr al-Ṣiddīq (d. 58 AH), Abū al-Dardā' ʿUwaymir ibn Zayd (d. 32 AH), and ʿAbd Allāh ibn al-Zubayr (d. 73 AH).

After the death of the Prophet and with the spread of Islam, Muslims settled in the formerly non-Muslim lands and took upon themselves the responsibility of propagating the faith and teaching Qur'anic recitation and interpretation. Subsequently, four distinct schools of Qur'anic interpretation and recitation (*qirā'ah*) emerged and were identified by the areas in which they became prominent: Makkah, Madinah, Kufah (in the area of present day Iraq), and al-Shām (present day Palestine, Syria and Lebanon).

The Makkan School

According to Ibn Taymiyyah (d. 728 AH), the Qur'anic interpretation of the Makkah school was the best because its proponents were students of Ibn ʿAbbās, the principal teacher of the Makkan school of *tafsīr*.[17] Most of the knowledge he acquired with regards to interpretation, Hadith and other sciences came through the prominent Companions. That was because he was only thirteen years of age when the Prophet died. His teachers included ʿAlī ibn Abī Ṭālib, Ubay ibn Kaʿb, Zayd ibn Thābit, and ʿUmar ibn al-Khaṭṭāb.Praise for Ibn ʿAbbās from various contemporaries of the Prophet abounds in Islamic literature and he was given honorific titles such as the *ra's al-mufassirīn* (the leading Qur'an interpreter) and *ḥabr hādhihi al-ummah* (the learned or chief scholar of the Muslim community).

After the assassination of ʿAlī ibn Abī Ṭālib, whom Ibn ʿAbbās supported and fought for throughout the Caliph's stormy tenure, Ibn ʿAbbās returned to Makkah, his place of birth. He dedicated himself, until his death in Taif some twenty years later, to the teaching of the Qur'an and its interpretation, history, jurisprudence (fiqh), Hadith, Arabic, and poetry. His classrooms were the mosque and his house, and by all accounts his eloquence was superb and persuasive. Indeed students from different cities would travel to Makkah to study under him, with his teaching circles always full, and his numerous students going on to transmit his knowledge after him. The most prominent of them were: ʿIkrimah al-Barbarī (d. 105 AH), Saʿīd ibn Jubayr (d. 95

AH), and Mujāhid ibn Jabr (d. 104 AH). Mujāhid has received the greatest acclaim, for it is reported that he went through the Qur'an verse by verse three times with Ibn ʿAbbās,[18] although this does not mean that he did not disagree with his teacher's interpretation and so have his own opinion regarding interpretation of some verses.

The Iraqi School

According to Ibn Taymiyyah, al-Suyūṭī and others, ʿAbd Allāh ibn Masʿūd (d. 32 AH), was the founder of the Iraqi School of *tafsīr*.[19] ʿAbd Allāh, the sixth person to accept Islam and one of the first scribes of the Qur'an, was born in Makkah and died in Madinah. He was one of the four Companions whom the Prophet recognized for their excellent recitation of the Qur'an. Ibn Masʿūd claimed to have learned seventy chapters of Qur'an directly from the Prophet.[20] His contemporaries highly praised his knowledge of *tafsīr*, Hadith, and *Qirā'ah* to the extent that Abū Mūsā al-Ashʿarī (d. 52 AH) said to those who came to him with certain queries, "do not ask me anything as long as ibn Masʿūd is among you." After the Prophet's death and prior to the time when Ibn ʿAbbās came to be recognized as the most scholarly in *tafsīr*, no one took offense to Ibn Masʿūd's claim to being the most Islamically learned in Kufah. He is known for stating: "If I knew anyone with greater knowledge of the Book of God than me, I would go to him; there is no verse but that I know where and when it was revealed."[21] Ibn Masʿūd became the founder of the Kufah School when Caliph ʿUmar sent him there as an advisor to the Kufa governor and to teach Islam to the general population. Among his many students, the most prominent were Masrūq ibn al-Ajdaʿ (d. 63 AH), ʿAlqamah ibn Qays (d. 63 AH), and al-Ḥasan al-Baṣrī (d. 110 AH).

The Madinan School

The main teacher of this school was Ubay ibn Kaʿab ibn Qays al-Khazrajī al-Anṣārī (d. 21 AH), who was of Jewish origin, and who was born in Madinah and died there. Ubay was one of the first people of Madinah to accept Islam before the migration of the Prophet to Madinah. He participated in all the Prophet's wars. Ubay was one of the four Companions whose recitation of the Qur'an was praised by the Prophet. He recommended to the Companions to learn the Qur'an from him. He also memorized the whole Qur'an and gave fatwas during the Prophet's life time. According to Ibn Saʿd, the Prophet said that Ubay was the best reciter of the Qur'an in the Prophet's community."[22]

Ubay's contemporaries, such as Abū Bakr al-Ṣiddīq, ʿUmar ibn al-Khaṭṭāb, and ʿUthmān ibn ʿAffān, acknowledged his Qur'anic knowledge. Both Abū Bakr and ʿUthmān appointed Ubay to the committee that codified the Qur'an.[23] It is recorded that ʿUmar ibn al-Khaṭṭāb announced: "Whoever wants to learn the Qur'an, let him go to Ubay."[24]

After the death of the Prophet Muhammad, Ubay dedicated himself to teaching the Qur'an and its interpretation in Madinah. Students from al-Shām and other cities came to Madinah specifically to learn from him.[25] Ubay continued to teach the Qur'an and *tafsīr* till his death. Among the prominent students who transmitted Ubay's knowledge was his son, Ṭufayl ibn Ubay (d. 85 AH).

The School of Al-Shām

The principal teacher of this school was ʿUmayr ibn Zayd ibn Qays al-Khazrajī (d. 32 AH) who converted to Islam in the third year after the hijrah, and was popularly known as Abū al-Dardā'. During his tenure in al-Shām, where he later died, he taught the Qur'an in the Umayyad mosque. Abū al-Dardā' was a famous scholar and an ascetic (*zāhid*). He was one of the few Companions who compiled a complete hand-written Qur'an copy during the Prophet's lifetime.[26]

There were a number of important scholars from this school. One of the most prominent was ʿAbd al-Raḥmān ibn Ghannām al-Anṣārī (d. 78 AH)[27] who was sent to al-Shām by ʿUmar ibn al-Khaṭṭāb to teach the Qur'an and the Sunnah.[28] Another prominent student of this school was Rajā' ibn Ḥaywah al-Kindī (d. 131 AH). A third student was ʿUmar ibn ʿAbd al-ʿAzīz ibn Marwān (d. 101 AH), the eighth Umayyad Caliph. He was recognized as an authority in jurisprudence, Qur'anic sciences and Hadith, and acquired a great reputation for asceticism (*zuhd*) and being a just (*ʿādil*) leader.[29]

Tafsīr: From Early Interpreters to Modern Times

The Era of the Tābiʿūn

By the middle of the first century AH, the prominent Companions who were interpreters of the Qur'an had died, except Ibn ʿAbbās who died in 68 AH. In this period, *tafsīr* was taught by scholars using their independent reasoning, based on the sound principles of sciences of *tafsīr* or sound understanding of the Arabic language, (*tafsīr bi al-ra'y*) and the transmission by the students of the Companions, the *Tābiʿūn*. Among the most outstanding were Mujāhid ibn Jabr,[30] Saʿīd ibn Jubayr,[31] ʿIkrimah al-Barbarī,[32] ʿAlqamah ibn Qays,[33] Masrūq ibn al-Ajdaʿ,[34] Muḥammad ibn Kaʿab al-Quraẓī,[35] Abū al-ʿĀliyah Rāfiʿ ibn Maḥram[36] (d. 90 AH), Zayd ibn Aslam (d. 13 AH),[37] Rajā' ibn Ḥaywah (d. 131 AH)[38], and ʿAbd al-Raḥmān ibn Ghannām (d. 78 AH).[39] Each of these scholars learned from many Companions, although each of them associated himself with one Companion over a period of many years and, ultimately, became known as a student of that particular Companion. For instance, Mujāhid ibn Jabr, Saʿīd ibn Jubayr, and ʿIkrimah were known as students of Ibn ʿAbbās, while ʿAlqamah ibn Qays and Masrūq ibn al-Ajdaʿ were known as students of Ibn Masʿūd.

During this time some new trends in Qur'anic interpretation began to emerge, which resorted to the individual authors' personal opinion, with no precedence in the Prophet's tradition or that of his Companions, which led, in some instances, to interpretations that contradicted those of the Prophet and his Companions. The word *ra'y* is a verbal noun which means opinion, belief, analogy, and exertion. Technically, it is independent opinion, that is used to denote the interpretation of the Qur'an by exerting the mind in understanding the word of God based on the sound knowledge of the Arabic language and the implementation of the principles of *al-tafsīr*. This type of *al-tafsīr*, however, is divided into two parts: *al-Ra'y al-Maḥmūd* or *al-Mamdūḥ* (praiseworthy), and *al-Ra'y al-Madhdmūm* (blameworthy). The subject of *al-ra'y* (both praiseworthy and blameworthy) as well as that of *isrā'iliyyāt* (body of narratives originating from Jewish and Christian traditions) will be discussed in more detail in following chapters.

Blameworthy *al-ra'y* was also used to interpret the meanings of the Qur'an in such a way that later on it was termed 'sectarian *tafsīr*'. Furthermore, story tellers (*quṣṣāṣ*) became more involved in this period of Qur'anic interpretation using incredible imagination and drawing from legendary sources, with perhaps, Mujāhid ibn Jabr being the best example to cite here. For example, his interpretation of Qur'anic verses 75:22–23: "*wujūhn yawma'idhin nāẓiratun ilā Rabbihā nāẓiratun*" ("Some faces, that Day, will beam (in brightness and beauty); looking towards their Lord") contradicted that of the Prophet. Whilst according to the authentic Hadith of the Prophet and his Companions's *tafsīr*, these verses refer to the face of Allah that Muslims will see with the naked eye on the Day of Judgement, Mujāhid explains the word (*nāẓirah*) as Muslims will be expecting a reward from God, meaning ergo that Muslims will not see Allah on the Day of Judgement. Despite this Mujāhid's interpretation was later adopted by the Muʿtazilites and became identified with them instead of being linked to Mujāhid, its author.[40]

Other prominent scholars, notably, al-Ḥasan al-Baṣrī (d. 110 AH) and Qatādah ibn Duʿāmah were accused of using sectarian arguments in their *tafsīr*.[41] With the aforementioned trends mainly using *Isrā'iliyyāt* sources (both Jewish and Christian) and relying on subjective opinion (*al-ra'y*) without referring to the Prophetic tradition or to his Companions in explaining some Qur'anic passages, some scholars exercised great caution vis-à-vis the interpretations of Mujāhid, ʿIkrimah, Zayd ibn Aslam, and others. They believed that *ra'y* and *Isrā'illiyāt* had become incorporated into their *tafsīr*.[42] Other scholars such as al-Qāsim ibn Muḥammad ibn Abū Bakr (d. 106 AH), a grandson of Abū Bakr al-Ṣiddīq, and ʿUbayd Allāh ibn Ḥafṣ (d. 280 AH), a grandson of ʿUmar ibn al-Khaṭṭāb, abstained altogether from Qur'anic interpretation to avoid such accusations.[43]

One of the prominent authors of these scholars' period was Muqātil ibn Sulaymān. His outstanding work *Al-Wujūh wa al-Naẓā'ir* is believed to be the first complete work on *al-ra'y* (a detailed account of it will be given in chapter three). The *tafsīr* of this period is classified as being "the best" and "the worst," with the best referring to that *tafsīr* which does not contain *al-ra'y*, and the worst referring to that which is based entirely on *al-ra'y*. Among the best works are those of Ibn ʿAbbās, Mujāhid and others; among the worst are those of al-Dhaḥḥāk and Abū Ṣāliḥ.[44]

Tafsīr After the Era of the *Tābiʿūn*

By the end of the second century AH, the students of the Companions of the Prophet, the *Tābiʿūn*, had died. No interpreter of that period had produced works devoted exclusively to Qur'anic interpretation. It has been claimed that Muājhid wrote a complete *tafsīr* of the Qur'an. During the latter half of the second century AH, various scholars began compiling works on the Qur'an according to their specialties and interests. *Tafsīr* emerged as one such specialty. Scholars or traditionists such as Shuʿbah ibn al-ʿAjjāj (d. 160 AH), Ibn al-Ward (d. 160 AH),[45] Wakīʿ ibn al-Jarrāḥ (d. 197 AH),[46] and Sufyān ibn ʿUyaynah ibn Maymūn (d. 198 AH),[47] paid special attention to the narration of *tafsīr* attributed to the Prophet, his Companions and the *Tābiʿūn*. Grammarians and linguists wrote authoritative works on the Qur'an demonstrating their expertise. Some of these works include *Maᶜānī al-Qur'ān*, by Abū Zakariyyā Yaḥyā ibn Ziyād al-Farrā' (d. 207 AH), and *Majāz al-Qur'ān*, by Abū ᶜUbaydah ibn Muᶜammar ibn al-Muthannā al-Taymī (d. 204 or 224 AH).[48] Al-Farrā's work contained a small amount of Qur'anic interpretation from the Prophet, his Companions and the *Tābiᶜūn*.[49]

According to Ibn Khallikān, a person called Ibrāhīm ibn Ismāᶜīl asked Abū ᶜUbaydah about some meanings of the Qur'an. After Abū ᶜUbaydah had explained the meanings requested, Abū ᶜUbaydah committed himself to writing a book explaining the meanings of the Qur'an.[50] The completed work approaches the Qur'an from linguistic and grammatical perspectives and also includes explanations of difficult words known as *gharīb*. He used poetry extensively as part of his explanations. The work was published in one volume edited by Fuat Sezgin in 1959.

These approaches, as well as the methodologies used by grammarians and linguists and by the traditionists flourished until the end of the third century and the early fourth century AH. Hence, *tafsīr* literature became separated from the main body of Hadith literature. Both came to be established as independent sciences.

After the separation of *tafsīr* literature from the main body of Hadith, each became an independent science with its own literature and concerns. Hadith literature, for instance, is concerned with transmitted reports on the Prophet's actions and sayings only.

These reports were the subject of intense research during the first two and a half centuries of the Islamic era. They were collected into many written compilations and gradually six of these became recognized in most, if not all, Sunni circles as the most authentic. The six books are technically called *al-Kutub al-Ṣittah* (the authentic six books of Hadith) and are:

1. *Al-Jāmiᶜ al-Ṣaḥīḥ* by Abū ᶜAbd Allāh Muḥammad ibn Ismāᶜīl al-Bukhārī.
2. *Ṣaḥīḥ Muslim* by Abū al-Ḥasan Muslim ibn al-Ḥajjāj al-Qushayrī.

3. *Sunan Abū Dāwūd* by Abū Dāwūd Sulaymān ibn al-Ashʿath al-Sijistānī.
4. *Al-Jāmiʿ al-Ṣaḥīḥ* or *Sunan al-Tirmidhī* by Abū ʿĪsa Muḥammad ibn ʿĪsa al-Tirmidhī.
5. *Sunan al-Nasā'ī* by Abū ʿAbd al-Raḥīman ibn ʿAlī ibn Shuʿayb al-Nasā'ī.
6. *Sunan Ibn Mājah* by Abū ʿAbd Allāh Yazīd ibn Mājah.

Tafsīr literature deals with the transmission of reports regarding the Prophet's explanation of the Qur'an, as well as those of the Companions and the *Tābiʿūn*, together with linguistic, rhetoric, juridical and theological considerations. These reports and considerations were the subject of intense study after the separation between Hadith and *tafsīr* had taken place. *Tafsīr* literature was eventually divided into two major types technically known as *al-tafsīr bi al-ma'thūr* and *al-tafsīr bi al-ra'y*. *Al-tafsīr bi al-ma'thūr* works include books such as the *Jāmiʿ al-Bayān ʿan Ta'wīl Āyāt al-Qur'ān* by Muḥammad ibn Jarīr al-Ṭabarī, *Al-Muḥarrir al-Wajīz fi Tafsīr al-ʿAzīz* by ʿAbd al-Ḥaqq ibn Ghālib ibn ʿAṭiyyah, and *Tafsīr al-Qur'ān al-ʿAẓīm* by ʿImād al-Dīn Ismāʿīl ibn Kathīr. Examples of *al-tafsīr bi al-ra'y* works are *Al-Tafsīr al-Kabīr*, also known as *Mafātīḥ al-Ghayb*, by Muḥammad ibn ʿUmar Fakhr al-Dīn al-Rāzī, *Al-Baḥr al-Muḥīṭ* by Athīr al-Dīn ibn Yūsuf Abū Ḥayyān, and *Al-Kashshāf ʿan Ḥaqā'iq wa Ghawāmiḍ al-Tanzīl wa ʿUyūn al-Aqāwīl fī Wujūh al-Ta'wīl*, by Abū al-qāsim Muḥmūd ibn ʿAmr ibn Muḥammad al-Zamakhsharī.

CHAPTER 2

Tafsīr in the Third and Fourth Centuries (AH)

SUMMARY

1. An incredibly huge volume of work exists on Qur'anic exegesis. Although certain scholars and their works have stood the test of time, and stand in greater prominence to others, to make sense of all this sea of literature as a whole, scholars have tried to categorize it.
2. The two major categories for understanding Qur'an commentaries according to scholars are *al-tafsīr bi al-ma'thūr* (tradition-based commentary) and *al-tafsīr bi al-ra'y* (opinion-based commentary).
3. The distinctions are important and under them many countless works on *tafsīr*, that is Qur'anic commentaries, have appeared, defined in turn by sub-categories. These sub-categories can be classified in simple terms i.e. Sunni, Shia, Sufi etc. as outlined or under more complex ones i.e. a) *ikhtiṣār al-asānīd*, b) the age of specialization, and c) *tafsīr al-bidʿah*. Under these categories, we have sub-sub categories of linguistics, law, grammar, mystical interpretation, and others etc. Each sub category and sub-sub category is defined by key scholastic works which typify it.
4. As well as sub-categories we also have different intrinsic approaches in Qur'anic exegesis or methodologies which have been utilised. Some are rigorous focusing on complete chains of hadith transmission, others more interpretive to the point of being considered *bidʿah*. The general idea seems to be that more classical, authentic commentaries follow Qur'anic exegesis based on rigorous methodologies using sound traditions (*al-tafsīr bi al-ma'thūr*) and the more interpretative (and therefore less regarded) commentaries follow less rigorous approaches based on opinion (*al-tafsīr bi al-ra'y*).
5. As each Qur'anic commentary was written it naturally had at its disposal the body of work that had already been published before it, and to a lesser or greater degree would therefore have been influenced by it. To simplify timelines the general historical period has been classified as a) the era from the Prophet to the Successors, then b) up to al-Ṭabarī (who wrote one of the first extremely comprehensive works and which is the earliest major running commentary of the Qur'an to have survived in its original form) and then c) the third and fourth centuries, the focus of this chapter, when Qur'anic exegesis further evolved. From there we move up to our modern times and orientalism which saw scholars surface such as Hungarian born Ignaz Goldziher considered the founder of modern Islamic studies in Europe.

IN THE THIRD AND FOURTH centuries AH the writing of *tafsīr* evolved. The transmission of *tafsīr* with a complete chain of transmission (*isnād*) became popular and began to attract the attention of theologians and lexicographers as a specialization in one aspect of Qur'anic exegesis. Thus, they began to produce *tafsīr* commentaries dominated by a notable distinctive feature. Relevant but non-extant works include exegeses by Abū ʿAbd Allāh Yazīd ibn Mājah (d. 273 AH) [1], ʿAbd al-Raḥmān ibn Abī Ḥātim (d. 304 AH)[2], and Al-Ḥusayn ibn Dāwūd al-Masīsī known as Sunayd. According to Ibn Taymiyyah, the works of these particular traditionists were solely based on the sayings of the Prophet, the Companions, and the *Tābiʿūn*.[3]

Among the remarkable works completed by lexicographers and linguists were *Tafsīr Gharīb al-Qur'ān by* Ibn Qutaybah (d. 276 AH), and *Al-Mufradāt fī Gharīb al-Qur'ān* by al-Rāghib al-Aṣfahānī (d. 502 AH), the latter believed to be the best work in this field. These works dealt with the lexical difficulties of the Qur'anic words. During this period Abū Jaʿfar Muḥammad ibn Yazīd al-Ṭabarī appeared with a methodology and approach distinct from his contemporaries. Al-Ṭabarī's *tafsīr*, *Jāmiʿ al-Bayān ʿan Ta'wīl al-Qur'ān*, is generally acknowledged to be the most comprehensive work of *tafsīr* by Muslim and non-Muslim scholars.[4] And in his *Al-Tafsīr wa al-Mufassirūn*, al-Dhahabī (a contemporary) also claimed the methodology adopted by al-Ṭabarī in the work to be unprecedented. These two claims were challenged by Ibn Ḥazm.[5]

Important Developments After *Al-Ṭabarī*

After the fourth century AH, three main developments occurred in the field of Qur'anic commentary. In al-Suyūṭī's terms, these were a) *ikhtiṣār al-asānīd* meaning the shortening of the chains of narration (which were accompanied by unverified statements), b) the age of specialization, and c) *tafsīr al-bidʿah* (heretical interpretation), that is the emergence of unorthodox exegesis.[6]

There is another category, not mentioned by al-Suyūṭī, which is *Naẓm al-Durar fī Tanāsub al-Āyāt wa al-Suwar*. This concerns the relationship between the surahs of the Qur'an on the one hand, and the relationship between the verses in each surah on the other. Although some scholars like al-Zarkashī in his *Al-Burhān fī ʿUlūm al-Qur'ān*, al-Rāzī in his *Al-Tafsīr al-Kabīr*, and others touched upon the subject matter in brief.

a) Ikhtiṣār al-Asānīd and the Use of Unreliable Information

The shortcutting of a chain of narration is known in the science of Hadith as *ikhtiṣār al-asānīd*. Instead of repeating the name of each teacher or reporter in a given chain of narration (*isnād*), Muslim scholars began to omit the full *isnād* which went against the methodology of Islamic scholarship because this tendency did not provide for the verification of the sources of information. It was, therefore, common and easy to quote or adopt a report from nonexistent or unreliable sources. Consequently, many texts were written of such poor scholarship and standard that their authors made no distinction between accurate and inaccurate data. In addition, authors did not distinguish scholarly interpretations from the rest.[7]

A major *tafsīr* work that is representative of others concerning *ikhtiṣār al-asānīd* and the use of unverified information is *Tafsīr al-Kashf wa al-Bayān ʿan Tafsīr al-Qur'ān* authored by the historian al-Thaʿālibī (d. 427 AH). It is largely composed of detailed accounts of stories, without critical attention paid to their veracity, that is whether the information contained is true or false.[8] In addition to some which are sound, al-Thaʿālibī also narrates a number of hadith, which are weak and fabricated, without distinguishing between the two. He claims to have sourced his information from around one hundred books and statements that he received from around three hundred scholars.[9]

Al-Thaʿālibī informs us in his Introduction that the *tafsīr* was written in response to a request from some people, and that he wanted, therefore, to write a comprehensive, authentic, brief, understandable, and well organized work of *tafsīr* as opposed to one containing long chains of narrators, repeating various narrations with unnecessary lines of transmitters, such as al-Ṭabarī's whom he criticized. Nonetheless, al-Thaᶜālibī himself includes a significant number of stories and *Isrā'iliyyāt*, in addition to judicial issues, grammatical decisions, and traditions emanating from the Prophet, the Companions, and the *Tābiᶜūn*. In fact so critical was Ibn Qayyim (d. 701 AH) of al-Thaᶜālibī for narrating weak traditions that he produced an edited version of this author's *tafsīr*.[10]

b) The Age of Specialization

Al-Suyūṭī and others consider the period from the fifth century upward as that of the age of specialization in *tafsīr* because experts produced Qur'anic interpretation from the perspective of their field of specialization only, with greater emphasis on grammatical, jusristic, and theological analysis. The word specialization as used here should not be understood in its modern context. It should be rather understood as a reference to the most dominant element appearing in the work from beginning to end. The extent to which a particular element dominates the work, determines its specialization.

(i) *Grammatical Tafsīr*

Among the representatives of grammatical interpretation were *Maᶜānī al-Qur'ān* by al-Zajjāj (d. 316 AH),[11] *Al-Wasīṭ fī Tafsīr al-Qur'ān al-Majīd*, and *Al-Wajīz fī Tafsīr al-Kitāb* by al-Wāḥidī (d. 468 AH), and *Al-Baḥr al-Muḥīṭ* by Abū Ḥayyān (d. 745 AH). The discussion that follows focuses upon the latter because it was considered to have been the first comprehensive and the most important work on grammatical *tafsīr*.[12]

Abū Ḥayyān Muḥammad ibn Yūsuf ibn ᶜAlī ibn Yūsuf Ḥayyān al-Andalusī began writing his *tafsīr* at the age of fifty-seven. He stated that he wrote his book to please God. His methodology and approach was to first explain each verse word by word followed by a grammatical and linguistic discussion. When a verse had more than one meaning, he would mention it, and then proceed to discuss the occasion upon which a particular verse had been revealed. This would be followed by a presentation of both the accepted and rejected variant readings of a passage including a discussion of their grammatical aspect. A textual reading was considered rejected if it contradicted the canonical text put forth by the Caliph ʿUthmān ibn ʿAffān or was contrary to the accepted Arabic language use.[13]

Finally, Abū Ḥayyān would quote statements from the *Tābiʿūn* (the generation after the four Caliphs). When a passage pertained to judicial matters, he repeated the opinion of each of the heads of the four Sunni legal schools of thought: Imāms Abū Ḥanīfah, Mālik ibn Anas, Muḥammad ibn Idrīs al-Shāfiʿī, and Aḥmed ibn Ḥanbal.[14]

(ii) *Juristic Tafsīr (Tafsīr of Fiqh or Islamic Law)*

Juristic *tafsīr*. There are three main juridical interpretation texts with the same name. They are: *Aḥkām al-Qur'ān* by Abū Bakr ibn ʿAlī al-Rāzī known as al-Jaṣṣāṣ (d. 370), *Aḥkām al-Qur'ān* by Abū al-Ḥasan ʿImād al-Dīn ʿAlī ibn Muḥamad ibn ʿAlī, al-Ṭabarī, known as al-Kiyā al-Hurāsy (d. 504), and *Aḥkām al-Qur'ān* by Muḥammad ibn ʿAbd Allāh ibn Muḥammad al-Maʿārifī known as al-Qāḍī Abū Bakr ibn al-ʿArabī (d. 543). Although the authors dealt generally with every chapter of the Qur'an, they gave the *tafsīr* of only those verses which concern legal aspects.[15]

Another common feature of these authors was their bias towards their particular schools of thought. Al-Jaṣṣāṣ was a Ḥanafī, al-Kiyā al-Hurāsy was a Shāfiʿī, and Ibn al-ʿArabī was a Mālikī. Again, each of their works contained some of the traditions emanating from the Prophet Muhammad, the Companions, and the *Tābiʿūn*, as well as some grammatical and linguistic discussion. Al-Jaṣṣāṣ's approach was to arrange his work according to the juristic literature of *uṣūl al-fiqh*. He discussed each issue under a separate section (*faṣl*) or chapter (*bāb*).

He included parts of the Qur'an to explain Qur'anic verses and also hadith to support his school of thought.

Ibn al-ᶜArabī, on the other hand, would mention the name of the Qur'anic chapter he intended to explain followed by the total number of verses it contained which were related to juristic matters. He would then number the legal matters pertaining to some verses by stating, for example, that there are five juristic issues in the first verse and ten others in the second verse, etc. Similarly, he would incorporate passages of the Qur'an as al-Jaṣṣāṣ did.

Another prominent interpretation worthy of mention in this regard is *Al-Jāmiᶜ li-Aḥkām al-Qur'ān* by the jurist Abū ᶜAbd Allāh Muḥammad al-Qurṭubī (d. 671 AH).

The contemporary Egyptian scholar Muḥammad al-Dhahabī wrote that al-Qurṭubī was an encyclopedia and that his work was among the greatest exegeses from which the common person could benefit. It was well organized and extremely usable.[16] Modern scholars have classified his commentary under Jurisprudence.[17] Worth noting, however, is that sometimes al-Qurṭubī was so involved in the area of legal issues that he discussed problems that were not relevant to the particular verses he was interpreting.

Furthermore, he stated in his introduction that he had decided to devote the rest of his lifetime to Qur'anic interpretation and to use all his strength to produce a *tafsīr* that would encompass linguistics, variant Qur'anic readings as well as grammar; and that he would rebuke the opinions of perverse men (those who twist the meanings of the Qur'an). He added that he would refer to many hadiths, to the Companions and to the *Tābiᶜūn* in support of his views on judicial issues.[18]

(iii) *Theological Tafsīr*

The foremost comprehensive work representative of a *tafsīr* written from the perspective of theology was *Al-Tafsīr al-Kabīr* also known as *Mafātīḥ al-Ghayb* by Muḥammad ibn ᶜUmar Fakhr al-Dīn al-Rāzī

(d. 606 AH), who was a legal theorist, theologian and exegete. The work consists of 32 volumes. Al-Rāzī gives a detailed account of the existing theological arguments, including discussions on the issues of the relationships or coherence (*munāsabāt*) between Qur'anic verses as well as between the Qur'anic chapters (*suwar*). The author discusses at length the theological propositions and arguments that criticize the Muᶜtazilites' doctrine. When he comes to the verses dealing with juristic matters, his interpretation inclines toward the al-Shāfiᶜī *madhhab* which was his own school of thought

Al-Rāzī also touched upon grammatical and philological issues, Hadith, and the traditions from the Companions and *Tābiᶜūn*. It is generally believed that al-Rāzī died before completing his book and that it was completed by his student Aḥmed ibn Muḥammad ibn Abī al-Ḥāzm al-Makkī Najm al-Dīn al-Makhzūmī al-Qummī (d. 672 AH). He followed his master's methodology and style so faithfully that it is impossible to distinguish between the two.[19] A third person may have been involved in completing the *tafsīr*. His name was Shihāb al-Dīn Khalīl al-Khawli al-Dimashqī (d. 639 AH). Although the work has been praised for its importance in the field of Qur'anic interpretation, Abū Ḥayyān, al-Suyūṭī and others on the other hand have criticized al-Rāzī's commentary. They believed it contained too many theological arguments and other elements, to the extent that a reader could possibly find everything but interpretation.[20] This view, in my and others' opinion, is an exaggeration. One finds in al-Rāzī's *tafsīr* all the elements of *tafsīr* that al-Ṭabarī's *Jāmiᶜ al-Bayān*, as well as Ibn ᶜAṭiyyah's, Ibn Kathīr's, and all major *tafsīr* literature's work contain.

Naẓm al-Durar fī Tanāsub al-Āyāt wa al-Suwar

While Qur'anic interpreters (*mufassirūn*) compiled their works based on their specialties, Abū al-Ḥasan Burhān al-Dīn Ibrāhīm ibn ᶜUmar al-Biqāᶜī introduced a new, or more comprehensive element which some previous scholars had only briefly touched upon to enrich the field of *tafsīr*. And he produced a pioneering work using this approach entitled *Naẓm al-Durar*. It is obvious from the work's introduction that al-Biqāʿī's main focus was the issue of the coherence between both *āyāt* (verses) and *suwa*r (chapters). This is where the essence of *ʿilm al-munāsabāt* lies, according to al-Biqāʿī. For him the latter meaning trying to understand coherent themes in the Qur'an whose beginning and end are coherently connected.

Al-Biqāʿī, praised himself for possessing various Islamic sciences, beneficial books and sound opinions. He described his own book as *kitāb al-ʿajā'ib* (book of wonders), an unprecedented high quality work. Indeed, this scholar acknowledged the works authored before him as well as books that discussed the importance of *ʿilm al-munasabāt* (relationships between the Qur'anic verses) such as al-Zarkashī's *Al- Burhān fī ʿUlūm al-Qur'ān*. Among the books dealing with the topic of coherence in the Qur'an, he mentioned, *Al-Muʿlam bi al-Burhān fī Tartīb Suwar al-Qur'ān* by Abū Jaʿfar as well as the work of Aḥmad ibn Ibrāhīm ibn al-Zubayr al-Thaqafī (d. 585), the work of Imam Abū ʿAbd Allāh Muḥammad ibn Sulayman (well known as ibn al-Naqīb) and also al-Rāzī's *tafsīr*.

However, for al-Biqāʿī, none of these works dealt extensively with the issue of coherence in the Qur'an. For example, the work of Ibn al-Zubayr tackled only the question of the relationships (*munāsabāt*) between the chapters of the Qur'anic verses, whereas al-Zarkashī's book dealt with the issue of *munāsabāt* in only four pages. As for al-Rāzī's *tafsīr*, he did not confine his work to only *munāsabāt*, but also covered issues related to subtlety in the Qur'an. Ibn al-Naqīb's sixty volumes did not cover all the verses of the Qur'an as far as the *munāsabāt* are concerned.

Al-Biqāʿī debated with himself as to the title of his *tafsīr*. After initially naming it *Naẓm al-Durar fī Tanāsub al-Āyāt wa al-Suwar*, he decided that the most appropriate title would be *Fatḥ al-Raḥmān fī Tanāsub Ajzā' al-Qur'ān* before opting for *Turjumān al-Qur'ān wa*

*Mubdi*ᶜ *Munāsabāt al-Qur'ān*. However, in spite of all the alternatives, he ended up keeping the original title, *Naẓm al-Durar*.

His methodology was that generally speaking, before discussing any surah, al-Biqāᶜī would state its purpose saying "*maqṣūduhā...*" (its purpose is...). He would then go on to discuss the surah's name, why this name was given, what its meaning was, and, if the surah had more than one name, would mention it with an explanation. Then he discussed the meaning of *Bismi Allāh al-Raḥmān al-Raḥīm*. Here, we note an amazing phenomenon. For he does not simply discuss *Bismi Allāh al-Raḥmān al-Raḥīm* on its first occurrence but from the beginning of surah one through to surah 114, al-Biqāᶜī qualifies the term 'Allah' with different attributes, the word *al-Raḥmān* with different attributes and the word *al-Raḥīm* with yet different attributes.

To illustrate this statement, here are a few examples. In the beginning of the first *Bismi Allāh al-Raḥmān al-Raḥīm* in surah 1 (*al-Fātiḥah*), he states: "*Bismi Allāh al-Qayyūm alladhī lā ya*ᶜ*zub shay'* ᶜ*an* ᶜ*ilmihi al-Raḥmān alladhī* ᶜ*ammat raḥmatuhu al-mawjūdāt, al-Raḥīm alladhī tammat ni*ᶜ*matuhu bi takhṣīṣ ahl walāyatih bi-arda al-*ᶜ*ibadāt*" (in the name of Allah, the Self–Subsisting Who keeps up and maintains all life, Nothing can escape from His knowledge, the Compassionate Whose compassion encompasses all creation; and the Merciful Whose favor is overwhelming in choosing for his servants the most immaculate worship).

In the *Bismi Allāh* at the beginning of surah 2, he states "*Bismi Allāh naṣab ma*ᶜ*a kawnihi bāṭina dalā'il al-hudā, al-Raḥmān alladhī afāda bi-raḥmatihi* ᶜ*alā' sā'ir khalqihi, al-Raḥīm alladhī khaṣṣa ahl wuddihi bi al-tawfīq,*" (In the name of Allah, He showed the way to guidance. The Merciful, who showered His mercy upon His creation. The Compassionate, who exclusively granted success to His lovers). After this unique style, he follows up with discussion on the relationship between the previous surah and the following one, and finally, he discusses the *tanāsub*, that is to say, the relationships or coherence among the verses. One of the remarkable features of al-Biqāqᶜī's methodology is that, when he comes to *āyāt* that pertain to legal matters he generally ignores the opinions of the *fuqahā'* (jurists) and gives his own interpretation. However, he quotes from the Hadith and from the Companions' statements for substantiation.

c) Emergence of Unorthodox Exegesis – Tafsīr Variations

This is the third of al-Suyūṭī's categories, which he called *tafsīr al-bidᶜah* (heretical interpretation). I have chosen to designate it as '*tafsīr* variations.' Following the assassination of ᶜUthmān ibn ᶜAffān, the third Caliph, and the religio-political conflict faced by the Muslims, three main groups emerged: the Alids (supporters of ᶜAlī ibn Abī Ṭālib), the Umayyad (the supporters of Muᶜāwiyah ibn Abī Sufyān), and the Kharijites. The Sunni and Shia divide also resulted.

The three parties mutually accused each other of being false Muslims. This on-going issue is reflected in the texts of the protagonists in general and in *tafsīr* works in particular. Al-Ṭabarī's *Jāmiᶜ al-Bayān* is one of the *tafsīrs* that represent the Sunni points of view. Sunni scholars such as al-Ṭabarī, Ibn Taymiyyah, al-Suyūṭī, and others have classified most, if not all, of the *tafsīrs* written by the Shia, the Muᶜtazilities and the Sufis as *tafsīr al-bidᶜah* (interpretation that has no Islamic precedence in the Qur'an or more particularly, in the Sunnah of the Prophet). On the other hand, al-Qāḍī ᶜAbd al-Jabbār (d. 410 AH), al-Zamakhsharī, and others have retaliated by claiming that such Sunnis were unintelligent and un-realistic, that they were false Muslims and hypocrites.[21]

(i) *The Shia*

Shia *tafsīr* developed in parallel to that of the Sunnis. However, there are two major distinctions between them. First, some Shia believe that the Qur'an primarily speaks to their imam ᶜAlī ibn Abī Ṭālib and his eleven descendants, for it is part of Shia belief that it is they who inherited the knowledge of the Prophet Muhammad and previous Prophets. The Sunnis, on the other hand, believe that the Qur'an is addressed to all mankind in general. Second, the Shia believe or consider the twelve imams to be the only legitimate authorities on the Qur'an after the Prophet. The Sunnis believe that the Prophet, the Companions and any qualified Muslim are legitimate authorities.[22]

Muhammad Ayyub a contemporary Islamic scholar and lecturer at Temple University, Philadelphia, notes that the *tafsīr* of Abū al-Ḥasan ʿAlī ibn Ibrāhīm ibn Hāshim al-Qummī (d. 328 AH), known as *Tafsīr al-Qummī*, is an example of early Shia work representing the Shia point of view.[23] Al-Qummī's text, says a partisan Sunni Monograph, frequently accuses the Companions and the Sunnis of literally altering the text of the Qur'an. For this and other reasons it labels them as non-Muslims, unbelievers, hypocrites, etc.[24] Nonetheless, the Shia, in general, have regarded Qummī's work as a reliable and trustworthy authority.

Abū ʿAlī al-Faḍl ibn al-Ḥasan al-Ṭabarsī (d. 548 AH) wrote *Majmaʿ al-Bayān fī Tafsīr al-Qur'ān* and took a liberal approach to moderate the Shia position relative to the Sunnis. Thus, he quotes hadith from *Ṣaḥīḥ al-Bukhārī* a Sunni hadith collection and a text the Shia in general reject, and also uses narrations from both those Companions who were praised by the Shia and those who were not. Sometimes, he even prefers someone else's opinion over that of ʿAlī ibn Abī Ṭālib's. For example, concerning verse 56:10: "And those Foremost (in Faith) will be Foremost (in the Hereafter)" ("*wa al-sābiqūn al-sābiqūn*"), al-Ṭabarsī mentions that whilst ʿAlī ibn Abī Ṭālib stated the term "foremost" to refer to those who are first in congregation to say the five daily prayers, others explain the term as referring to Muslims who are foremost in the various good deeds that Islam calls them to do. So, foremost is not limited to those first in congregation for Salah but includes all the various categories of good deeds and people that have been mentioned in the Qur'an.[25]

Furthermore, in his introduction, al-Ṭabarsī indicates that the reason he had written his *tafsīr* was because Sunni scholars alone had written comprehensive and intelligent *tafsīr* and had elucidated the deep and hidden meanings of the Qur'an. He describes Shia *tafsīr* in contrast as being very simple and brief, without giving full lines of transmission, and lacking detailed discussion. The only exception being Muḥammad ibn al-Ḥasan al-Ṭūsī's (d. 460 AH) who produced *Al-Tibyān al-Jāmiʿ li Kull ʿUlūm al-Qur'ān*. But nevertheless this work according to al-Ṭabarsī, suffered from linguistic and grammatical errors, a lack of reliable information and was poorly structured, it did not contribute to a better understanding of the Qur'an and, according to al-Ṭabarsī, failed to win the intellectuals' appreciation.[26]

Al-Ṭabarsī's approach consists in explaining the whole Qur'an word by word, in the chronological order of the Qur'anic revelations over the 23 years in which it was revealed. Before explaining each surah, he clearly states to which of the two Qur'anic revelation phases (Makkan or Madinan) the surah belongs, and also indicates if the whole or part of the surah was revealed in Makkah or Madinah. Then he follows up with the traditions of the Prophet, and those of the Companions and *Tābiʿūn*, while mentioning the virtue of the surah in general. Afterwards, he proceeds to present the various *qirā'āt* (variant readings of the Qur'an) and begins to interpret verses applying his linguistic skills, and pointing out the grammatical impact on the meaning. He then goes on to mention the circumstances in which the verse was revealed as well as the *tanāsub* (relationship) between the preceding and the following verses.

When he comes across a verse pertaining to judicial matters, he frequently mentions the opinion of the *Shīʿah imāmiyyah* (the major Shia sect), trying to support their viewpoints. Sometimes he quotes the Sunni perspective too.

(ii) *Tafsīr of the Muʿtazilites*

The *tafsīr* of the Muʿtazilites as previously mentioned was branded by the traditionalists as *bidʿah* because they believed that the Muʿtazilites twisted some of the words of the Qur'an to support or fit their own perspectives. We previously mentioned, for instance, verse 75:22-3:

"Some faces, that Day, will beam (in brightness and beauty); looking towards their Lord" wherein it is believed that Muslims will literally see God with their own eyes in Paradise. According to the Muʿtazilites, the verse means that Muslims will be expecting a reward from God. Verses relating to the attributes of God are interpreted contrary to the traditional *tafsīr* of the Prophet and his Companions.[27]

The Muʿtazilites, however, wrote many *tafsīr* books expressing their points of view and exposing what they believed to be the mistakes of the traditionalists.

The Muʿtazilites hold that the traditionalists misunderstood them or misinterpreted their views. Hence, one of their great scholars, al-Qāḍī ʿAbd al-Jabbār, wrote his *tafsīr* entitled *Tanzīh al-Qur'ān ʿan Al-Maṭāʿin* (Defending the Qur'an against Slander) to elaborate on the distinction between *muḥkam* and *mutashābihāt* and to point out the mistakes of the traditionalists.[28]

The most comprehensive existing *tafsīr* in which the Muʿtazilites doctrine is brilliantly demonstrated is *Al-Kashshāf* by al-Zamakhsharī (d. 467 AH).[29] The work was highly praised as much as it was bitterly criticized. In his introduction, al-Zamakhsharī mentions three reasons for writing the *tafsīr*:

1. He was asked by a group of al-Muʿtazilites who admired his knowledge to write a commentary of the Qur'an for them. They were so emphatic about the need for him to offer a course that they asked some dignitaries to intercede with al-Zamakhsharī on their behalf.
2. The *amīr* of Makkah, Imam Sharīf Abū al-Ḥasan ibn Ḥamzah, who belonged to the Prophet's family, also asked him to write a *tafsīr*.
3. He, al-Zamakasharī, wanted to please God so that he would be saved from the Hell fire. It took him a little over two years and two or three months to finish writing *Al-Kashshāf*, and even described it a poem:

> Verily, there are countless works of *tafsīr* in this world; but you cannot find one like *Al-Kashshāf*. If you are looking for guidance you have to persist in reading it. Ignorance is just like sickness, and *Al-Kashshāf* is like a cure.[30]

Muslim scholars have both praised and condemned *Al-Kashshāf*. Abū Ḥayyān states that Ibn Bashkuwal believed *Al-Kashshāf* to be very precise and deep, but its author twisted the meaning of some verses in favor of his Muᶜtazilite doctrine. However, Abū Ḥayyān himself expresses great appreciation of al-Zamakhsharī's *tafsīr*.[31] Ibn Khaldūn (d. 808 AH) commented on it, saying: "it was one of the best *tafsīrs* as far as philology and literary aspects are concerned.[32] Taj al-Dīn al-Subkī (d. 735 AH) stated that *al-Kahshāf* was a great book in its field, and its author a leading scholar in his field, but that he was nevertheless a heretic innovator (*mubtadiᶜ*) who publicly declared his *bidᶜah*.

Al-Zamaksharī's approach is not unique for his time, and he uses the same methods as his contemporaries. For the most part, at the beginning of surahs he states the place of revelation, Makkah or Madinah, to which the surah belongs. Occasionally, he follows this with a discussion on Qur'an and its recitation methods. He then proceeds with a detailed, grammatical, linguistic or philological and rhetorical discussion. When he comes across verses pertaining to judicial issues he briefly touches upon them, and sometimes mentions the jurists' point of view. In other instances, he quotes the traditions of the Prophet, of the Companions, and those of the *Tābiᶜūn*. Also, when dealing with verses that relate to theological propositions, he clearly presents various arguments, applying his language skills to support the Muᶜtazilite perspective. For example, and once again, the traditional interpretation of verse 75:22-23: "Some faces, that Day, will beam (in brightness and beauty); looking towards their Lord" is that Muslims shall see God with their physical eyes in Paradise.[33] The Muᶜtazilite position is that God can never and will not be seen. So, al-Zamaksharī interprets the words "*ilā Rabbihā nāẓirah*" as "expecting and hoping in Allah's mercy"[34] because, according to him, it is impossible, physically speaking, to ever see God. Because of such an interpretation, Goldziher and others went along with the traditionalists' opinion and considered al-Zamaksharī's *tafsīr* as both *bidᶜah* and one of the best representations of the Muᶜtazilite point of view.[35]

Despite being a Muᶜtazilite representative al-Zamaksharī's analysis of the Qur'an from a grammatical, linguistic and rhetorical perspective is so well done that Ibn Khaldūn, Abū Ḥayyān and others declare *Al-Kashshāf* to be one of the best *tafsīrs* for philological, rhetorical, and grammatical interpretation. Finally, among the dominant features of al-Zamaksharī's methodology is "*fa in qāla*." This refers to his style in raising assumptive questions where he often says "*idhā qulta, qultu*" (if you say so and so, I say).

(iii) *Tafsīr of the Ṣūfīs*

Sufi *tafsīr* is mystical in nature and heavily influenced by philosophical thought. The Sufis believe the Qur'an to have two meanings: an apparent meaning (*ẓāhir*) and an inner, hidden one (*bāṭin*). They assert that general people only know the outer meaning while the inner meaning is known to the Sufis alone. Thus, much of Sufi *tafsīr* clearly contradicts both the plain meaning of the language and the meaning given by the Prophet, the Companions, their Successors (*Tābiᶜūn*) and the Traditionalists. For example verses 55:19-20: "He has let free the two bodies of flowing water, meeting together: Between them is a Barrier which they do not transgress." The two seas to most, if not all Sunni Muslims, are salt-water ocean and the fresh water that meet. Ibn ᶜArabī (d. 638 AH), a prominent Sufi Shaykh interpretes the two seas to be the soul and body of a person.[36] Another example, concerns verse 73:8: "But keep in remembrance the name of thy Lord and devote thyself to Him whole-heartedly." Ibn ᶜArabī states this to mean "remember the name of your Lord, for

He is you."[37] This bold assertion is a clear counter statement to *Sūrah al-Ikhlāṣ* (112), "Say: He is Allah, the One and Only; Allah, the Eternal, Absolute; He begetteth not, nor is He begotten; And there is none like unto Him." It also contradicts the verse of the Throne (*Āyatu al-Kursy, Sūrah al-Baqarah*: 2:255) as well as other parts of the Qur'an. Fundamentally, this statement about God is the outcome of misguided knowledge. Due to such interpretations, scholars such as al-Dhahabī and Ibn Taymiyyah have regarded the Sufi *tafsīr* as a heresy.[38]

Another *tafsīr* which reflects the Sufi perspective is *Ḥaqā'iq al-Tafsīr* by Abū 'Abd al-Raḥmān Muḥammad ibn al-Ḥasan ibn al-Azdī, also known as al-Sulamī (d. 412 AH).[39] The work of al-Sulamī was very controversial. Some scholars bitterly criticized it, while others praised it.[40] The late modern Egyptian *tafsīr* scholar, Muhammad Husayn al-Dhahabi, read the manuscript and found that it comprised whole chapters of the Qur'an, but it did not cover all the verses. Based on Dāwūdī's report in his *Ṭabaqāt al-Mufassirīn*", it can be said with assurance that *Ḥaqā'iq al-Tafsīr* was solely of the Sufi point of view.

Consequently, some Muslim scholars such as al-Wāḥidī (d. 468 AH) stated, "If al-Sulamī believes that *Haqā'iq al-Tafsīr* is *tafsīr*, then he has committed apostasy ("*faqadd kafar*")."[41]

Abū Bakr Muḥyī al-Dīn Muḥammad ibn ʿArabī ibn Muḥammad (d. 638 AH) is regarded by many both in his time and today as the epitome of Sufism and its greatest figure. He was given the title of *al-Shaykh al-Akbar* "the greatest master" and *al-'Ārif bi-Allāh* "the knower of God." He remains the most controversial Sufi figure. It has been a popular belief that the author of the famous *tafsīr* work known as *Tafsīr Ibn ʿArabī* was Ibn ʿArabī, however, the late Egyptian scholar Muhammad Abduh queried this believing it to be the work of ʿAbd Al-Razzāq al-Qashānī al-Bāṭinī. Furthermore, Muhammad Husayn al-Dhahabi not only supported Muhammad Abduh's claim but, on the basis of the manuscript available in Cairo, was categoric that the work was by al-Qashānī. Certain scholars have also stated that it is now proven beyond doubt that the *tafsīr* was not written by Ibn ʿArabī.[42]

Ibn Taymiyyah, Dhahabī and other scholars bitterly criticized Ibn ʿArabī because of this *tafsīr* work, while scholars like Muḥammad ibn Yaʿqūb al-Shirāzī al-Faīrozābādī (d. 812 AH) and al-Suyūṭī were among the scholars who defended him.

Although the real *tafsīr* of Ibn ʿArabī has not reached us, we do have some of his Qur'anic interpretations contained in certain of his published works, such as *Al-Futūḥāt al-Makkiyyah* and *Fuṣūṣ al-Ḥikam*. For example, consider verse 71:28: "O my Lord! Forgive me, my parents, all who enter my house in Faith, and (all) believing men and believing women." Ibn ʿArabī interprets "parents" as intellect and nature, "house" as heart, "believing men" as intellect, and "believing women" as soul.[43]

(iv) *Al-Tafsīr al-Ishārī (Indication or Allegorical Interpretation)*

This method of interpretation is termed *al-tafsīr al-Ishārī* (interpretation by indication or allegory) because it looks beyond the apparent meanings of the Qur'an. It is one which infers meanings that are not visible to anyone, its exponents allege, but those whose heart God has opened. Its proponents base their interpretation upon certain *tafsīr* of the Companions of the Prophet. One frequently given example in this respect is Ibn ʿAbbās's *tafsīr* of *Sūrah al-Naṣr* (110: 1-3) which states:

> When comes the Help of God, and Victory, And thou dost see the people enter God's Religion in crowds, Celebrate the praises of thy Lord, and pray for His Forgiveness: For He is Oft-Returning (in Grace and Mercy).

Since Ibn ʿAbbās interpreted the verse as a special indication of the Prophet's impending death, and because it is regarded both as an accurate interpretation of the text by mainstream Muslims and as an interpretation that, obviously, does not concern an 'outer' meaning, it has become a supporting proposition for the legitimacy of allegorical interpretation. Another reference for this type of *tafsīr* is ʿUmar ibn al-Khaṭṭāb's understanding of verse 5:3: "This day have I perfected your religion for you, completed My favour upon you, and have chosen for you Islam as your religion." Because ʿUmar ibn al-Khaṭṭāb understood the verse as an indication of the start of the decline of the quality of Islam as practiced by its adherents,[44] in addition to the obvious meaning of the verse, some allude to this as another justification for allegorical *tafsīr*.

A third example is from Ālūsī concerning the meaning of verse 11:105-6. The verse states: "The day it arrives, no soul shall speak except by His leave: of those (gathered) some will be wretched and some will be blessed. Those who are wretched shall be in the Fire: There will be for them therein (nothing but) the heaving of sighs and sobs". According to Ālūsī "shall be in the fire" is "*nār al-ḥirmān ʿan al-murād*" (the fire of being denied a goal, desire or want). He further stated that the "fire" in this verse is not the fire of Hell, but rather "*ʿadhāb al-nafs*" (punishment of self).[45]

Scholars have differed as to the legality of *al-tafsīr al-Ishārī*. Some have rejected it on the grounds that it is based on sheer opinion. Others like Muḥammad ibn Abū Bakr Shams al-Dīn ibn Qayyim al-Jawziyyah (d. 751 AH), accept it provided that five principles are adhered to: a) that there is no disagreement with the obvious meaning of the verse and the derived allegorical meaning, b) that it is a sound meaning in itself, c) that in the wording, there is some indication to warrant the derived allegorical meaning, d) that there are close connections between it and the obvious, outer meaning, and finally, e) that it should not be claimed that the derived allegorical meaning is the only intended meaning.

According to al-Zarkashī *al-tafsīr al-ishārī* is not the kind of *tafsīr* that one acquires through learning, rather, it is the outcome of a mystical experience that one feels while reciting the Qur'an.[46]

The best considered example of *al-Tafsīr al-Ishārī* is a work authored by ʿAbd al-Karīm ibn Hawāzin ibn ʿAbd al-Malik ibn Ṭalḥah ibn Muḥammad al-Nīsābūrī, known as al-Qushayrī (d. 465 AH), and entitled *Laṭā'if al-Ishārāt.* Al-Qushayrī was regarded as *the* Sufi shaykh of his time, and also a moderate Sufi personality. He had mastered the traditional Islamic sciences such as Hadith and fiqh, as understood by non-Sufi scholars, never claimed to have received knowledge from the unseen, nor believed interpretation to be devoid of traditional or linguistic substantiation,[47] Other Sufis considered him a scholar of mysticism. Because he did not write material that was considered extreme, his *tafsīr* was the only one or one of the Sufi *tafsīr* works that escaped stringent criticism. Indeed, *Laṭā'if al-Ishārāt* was praised by both traditionists and *Ṣūfīs*.

Al-Qushayrī's work is a complete *tafsīr*. It discusses each surah as a unit in addition to explaining all of the verses of the whole Qur'an. Each surah of the Qur'an which begins with "In the name of God, Most Gracious, Most Merciful" is covered, including surah nine (which note does not begin with this statement). Al-Qushayrī does not consider each surah's introductory phrase *'Bismi Allāh'* to be an independent introduction to each surah but rather a part of the surah. In addition, he believed each one to have different meanings from the others, and each a significant mystical implication.[48] He begins each surah by explaining its unique meaning before explaining each verse individually, sentence by sentence. In doing so, he first presents the apparent meaning or the meaning as understood by the traditionists, then he moves on to its mystical meaning according to the moderate Sufis. This sequence is not rigidly followed though in his work, which can be described as typical of moderate Sufi works. He sometimes touches slightly on grammatical issues and totally ignores juristic ones.

Here is an example of Al-Qushayrī's interpretation of "*Bismi Allāh al-Raḥmān al-Raḥīm* (In the name of God, Most Gracious, Most Merciful." He interprets the term "*al-ism*," (the name) as the reader should strive to elevate himself to ascend to the rank of those who have elevated themselves to the status of *al-mushāhadā*t 'witnesses (of the truth). He further adds that whoever does not strive to elevate himself, will not feel the ecstasy that one should feel upon reciting the verse, and will fail to honor the purity of the relationship that is inherent between the state of the reciter/witness of the truth and the verse.[49]

Orthodox Reaction to the Variations of Interpretation and al-Ra'y

The emergence of *tafsīr* variations was strongly criticized by traditionists such as Ibn Taymiyyah, al-Dhahabī, Ibn Kathīr, al-Suyūṭī and others. They believed such interpretations by so-called *mubtadiᶜah* (practitioners of un-Islamic unorthodox, blamable innovation) to be nothing but distortions of the interpretation of the Prophet, those of his Companions and those of the Successors. Thus, they launched uncompromising attacks on *tafsīr* variations. In addition, the traditionists advocated that Muslims should write and read traditional *tafsīr* works only and warned against *al-ra'y* (intellectual reasoning) that is devoid of sound Arabic usage and grounding. They used four different sources to substantiate their views: the Qur'an, Hadith, the Companions' reports, and those of the Successors. Among the Qur'anic, verses quoted to support their position is verse 7:33:

> Say: the things that my Lord hath indeed forbidden are: shameful deeds, whether open or secret; sins and trespasses against truth or reason; assigning of partners to Allah, for which He hath given no authority; and saying things about Allah of which ye have no knowledge.

According to traditionists the structure and clear meanings of the verse indicate that stating things about Allah without having the correct and necessary knowledge is a great sin similar to the sins mentioned at the beginning of the verse. Therefore, any interpretation not corroborated by the Prophet is prohibited. [50]

Then there is the following verse 16:44: "and We have sent down unto you (Muhammad) (also) the Message; that you may explain clearly to men what is sent for them, and that they may give thought." The idea here, as understood by the traditionists, is that the Prophet Muhammad is the only person who has been given authority by God to explain the Qur'an. Thus, no one can give *tafsīr* by recourse to his own independent opinion.

The orthodox also frequently quote the following hadith to support their view: "Whoever explains the Qur'an according to his personal opinion, shall take his place in Hell."[51] In another narration, "whoever said anything about the Qur'an based on his own opinion, even if it is correct, is wrong."[52] They quote Abū Bakr al-Ṣiddīq's well known comment: "What earth will bear me and what sky will shadow me if I say anything based on my own opinion when explaining the Qur'an?"[53] They also cite Saᶜīd ibn al-Musayyib (d. 94 AH) who whenever he was asked about *tafsīr* stated, "We do not say anything about the Qur'an."[54] According to Masrūq ibn al-Ajdaᶜ: "Be careful with *tafsīr* ("*ittaqū al-tafsīr*"), for, indeed, it is a narration about God."[55]

Some proponents of the traditional approach to *tafsīr* have claimed that the Qur'an cannot be understood without the Prophetic Hadith. The call for traditional interpretation exclusively and against all use of rational endeavor is not intellectually justifiable in their view. Certain jurists, grammarians, and theologians including Abū Ḥāmid al-Ghazālī, Ibn ᶜAṭiyyah, al-Qurṭubī, and Abū Ḥayyān challenged this view with uncompromising, sharp, and forceful responses using the same sources employed by their opponents. In response to the traditionalists reference to Qur'anic verse

16:44, Ibn ʿAṭiyyah argued that although the Prophet was given responsibility to explain the Qur'an, his interpretation was given according to the necessities of his time and for the people of that particular period. Following his death, the time-space factor might require further intellectual exertion to clarify generalities in the Prophet's interpretation. This, the argument proceeded, would necessitate resort to scholastic reasoning (*ra'y*) and is permissible provided the basic rules of *tafsīr* are applied.[56]

Al-Bayhaqī (d. 458 AH) questioned the authenticity of the hadith "Whoever explains the Qur'an according to his personal opinion, shall take his place in Hell," adding if the hadith were authentic it could be a prohibition only on opinions that do not adhere to the basic rules of *tafsīr*.[57]

According to al-Ghazālī the hadith had two probable meanings or indications, either that it limited *tafsīr* to the Prophet only, which he believed was not the case because the Prophet did not explain the whole of the Qur'an, or that it might mean something else. He added that if the first assumption were correct, then verse 4:83 should be taken into account as well: "When there comes to them some matter touching (Public) safety or fear, they divulge it. If they had only referred it to the Messenger, or to those charged with authority among them, the proper investigators would have Tested it from them (direct). Were it not for the Grace and Mercy of Allah unto you, all but a few of you would have fallen into the clutches of Satan". Al-Ghazālī contended in reference to the verse that proper investigation cannot be done without using *ra'y*.

As for Abū Bakr al-Ṣiddīq's statement "What earth will bear me and what sky will shadow me if I say anything based on my own opinion when explaining the Qur'an?"[58] Ibn ʿAṭiyyah allowed for two possibilities, either that Abū Bakr had said this at the very beginning of his *khilāfah* to prevent Muslims from engaging in *tafsīr* haphazardly; or that when he first became Caliph, this was his initial opinion (that *tafsīr* should not be made on the basis of reasoned opinion, *al-ra'y*, alone), but, as time passed, he realized that the use of *ra'y* was unavoidable in *tafsīr*. Thus, when he was asked about the meaning of "*kalālah*," mentioned in Qur'anic verse 4:12, he said, "I answer on the basis of my own view (*al-ra'y*). If it is correct, thanks be to God. If it is wrong, however, it is from me and the devil, and God is innocent of it."[59]

As for some of the *Tābiᶜūn*'s refraining from engaging in *tafsīr*, al-Zarkashī compared their attitudes to that of the Prophet's Companions. He pointed out that certain eminent Companions, such as al-Zubayr ibn al-ᶜAwwām, ᶜUthmān ibn ᶜAffān, and Ṭalḥah ibn ᶜUbayd Allāh avoided narrating hadith or ascribing sayings to the Prophet not to avoid giving independent opinion, but out of piety only. Therefore, the same could be said of the *Tābiᶜūn*'s stands vis-à-vis *tafsīr*.[60]

The defenders of the use of *ra'y* in *tafsīr* also used the Qur'an to substantiate their position. Among the frequent examples quoted was verse 38:29 whereby Allah invites men to ponder over and draw meanings from His words: "(Here is) a Book which We have sent down unto thee, full of blessings, that they may mediate on its Signs, and that men of understanding may receive admonition" (38:29). They also quote verse 47:24 which states: "Do they not then earnestly seek to understand the Qur'an...?" The point made here is that, if using opinion in understanding the Qur'an was prohibited, there would be no purpose for the revelation of these verses.

The proponents of *ra'y* cite the famous hadith in which the Prophet clearly encouraged his followers to engage in ijtihad: "whoever makes ijtihad and he is right, will earn two rewards. If, however, he is wrong, he will earn only one reward."[61]

As a result of these arguments between traditionalists and theologian-jurists, the classical *tafsīr* was divided into two major categories: *al-tafsīr bi al-ma'thūr* and *al-tafsīr bi al-ra'y*. Naturally, the *tafsīr* literature was also divided into two.

The Major Categorizations of *Tafsīr*

Al-Tafsīr bi al-Ma'thūr

The word *ma'thūr* is a passive participle derived from the root verb *athara*, meaning 'to trace', to mark. The verb *athara* also means to transmit, to report, to pass along, etc. Thus, *ma'thūr* means that which is transmitted, handed down. *Al-Tafsīr bi al-ma'thūr* is, generally speaking, understood to be the Qur'anic interpretations derived by the Prophet, by the Companions and by the Successors. The major *tafsīr* works considered as representatives of *al-tafsīr bi al-ma'thūr* are:

1. *Jāmiᶜ al-Bayān* by al-Ṭabarī.
2. *Al-Muḥarrir al-Wajīz fī Tafsīr al-Kitāb al-ᶜAzīz*, by Ibn ᶜAṭiyyah.
3. *Maᶜālim al-Tanzīl* by al-Baghawī.
4. *Tafsīr al-Qur'ān al-ᶜAẓīm* by Ibn Kathīr.
5. *Al-Durr al-Manthūr*, by al-Suyūṭī.
6. *Baḥr al-ᶜUlūm* known as *Tafsīr Abu Layth al-Samarqandī*.

Al-Tafsīr bi al-Ra'y

The word *ra'y* is a verbal noun which means opinion, view, belief, and usually involves analogy and intellectual exertion. Technically, it refers to independent opinion that is used to derive Qur'anic interpretation by exerting the mind in understanding the word of God. It is usually based on the sound knowledge of the Arabic language and the implementation of the agreed principles of *tafsīr*. This type of *tafsīr*, however, is divided into two parts:

1. *Al-Ra'y al-Maḥmūd* or *al-mamdūḥ* (praiseworthy).
2. *Al-Ra'y al-Madhmūm* (blameworthy).

1. *Al-Tafsīr bi al-Ra'y al-Maḥmūd*
Al-ra'y al-maḥmūd is independent opinion that is based on the principles of *tafsīr* and the Arabic language, provided that the resulting interpretation does not conflict with the tradition of the Prophet or the general fundamentals of Islamic thought.

2. *Al-Tafsīr bi al-Ra'y al-Madhmūm*
Al-ra'y al-madhmūm is independent opinion that is neither based on the principles of Arabic nor on the Hadith and the Sunnah of the Prophet, the Companions' reports, or the *Tābiʿūn*'s statements. *Al-ra'y al-madhmūm* earned this classification because both traditionalists and traditionists believed that the purpose of producing such *tafsīr* was to promote *bidʿah*.[62] *Mafātīḥ al-Ghayb* by al-Rāzī and *Anwār al-Tanzīl* by al-Baydāwī (d. 685 AH) are among the important *al-tafsīr bi al-ra'y al-mamdūḥ*.

The *tafsīr* texts mentioned earlier in the section on *tafsīr* variations are considered to be *al-tafsīr bi al-ra'y al-madhmūm* by traditionalists and some jurists, such as Ibn Taymiyyah, al-Ghazālī, Ibn Kathīr and others. They believed these works of *tafsīr* had ignored the linguistic aspect as well as the Prophet, his Companions and the Successors' interpretations. They further believed that the authors of such texts were too educated to be unaware that they were misapplying and misinterpreting Qur'anic verses. They simply desired Qur'anic justifications for the teaching of the dogma to which they wished to give prominence.

Al-tafsīr bi al-ma'thūr and *al-tafsīr bi al-ra'y* continued to be the two major categories of the science of *tafsīr* until our modern time, when other trends and methodology in *tafsīr* emerged due to new social structures, diverse political systems, technological advancement, and science.

CHAPTER 3

Tafsīr Based on Tradition

Al-Tafsīr bi al-Ma'thūr

SUMMARY

1. *Al-Tafsīr bi al-Ma'thūr* is generally speaking understood as follows:
   - Qur'anic exegesis that has been handed down from the Prophet and his Companions
   - Qur'anic exegesis that can be traced back to the Prophet, and also to some degree which pertains to the occasions of the revelation *asbāb al-nuzūl*.
   - The explanation of the Qur'an given in the Qur'an itself, by the Prophet, and by his Companions.
   - The explanations of the Qur'an by other Qur'anic verses, by the Prophet, his Companions, and Successors.
2. The reason for these differences has to do with the concept of *ḥujjah*. *Ḥujjah* is usually translated as "binding proof" notwithstanding. Some scholars, however, defined *ḥujjah* as "to make something clear, to expose and explain and when it is presented before you, it becomes binding to act upon it because it is the decree of Allah."
3. Then there is an issue of who has greater authority or whose *tafsīr* is *ḥujjah*. Does the *tafsīr* of the Companions and the Successors have equal weight as the *tafsīr* of the Prophet? Is the *tafsīr* of the Successors to be considered equal to the *tafsīr* of the Companions? Indeed, some scholars like Ibn Taymiyyah believed that the *tafsīr* of the Companions is equal in authority to the exegesis of the Prophet. Others such as al-Ḥākim al-Nīsabūrī (d. 450 AH) and Ibn al-Ṣalāḥ hold that the *tafsīr* of the Companions is *ḥujjah* when it relates to *asbāb al-nuzūl*. As for the *tafsīr* of the Successors the majority of the scholars viewed it as non-*ḥujjah*. According to some reports Imam Aḥmad ibn Ḥanbal considered their *tafsīr* as a *ḥujjah*. For Ibn Qayyim the Successor's exegesis is *ḥujjah*.

This issue and the debate on whether the Prophet explained the entire Qur'an is explored.

Concept and Definition

THE TWO MAJOR CATEGORIES for understanding the Qur'an according to scholars and as mentioned earlier are *al-tafsīr bi al-ma'thūr* (tradition-based commentary) and *al-tafsīr bi al-ra'y* (opinion-based commentary). In reality, as will become apparent the division is not so clear cut as *ra'y* will inevitably be involved at some stage in *ma'thūr* tradition-based exegesis.

The word *ma'thūr* is a passive participle derived from the verbal noun *athara*. According to the Arabic lexicon, *athara* has a variety of meanings, ranging from to "trace," to "mark," to "report," and to "transmit." Thus, the phrase "*athara khuff al-baʿīr*" means "He made an incision in the foot of the camel in order to know and trace the foot print."[1]

The Qur'an used the term in different forms to indicate the same lexical meanings and more. In verse 48:29: "On their faces are their marks, (being) the traces of their prostration." The noun *athar* in this verse is used to mean 'traces' or 'marks'. Its meaning as 'trace' is also found in verse 36:12: "Verily We shall give life to the dead, and We record that which they send before and that which they leave behind (*wa āthārahum*), and of all things have We taken account in a clear Book (of evidence)."

In Hadith, the term *athar* is also used as in the lexical meaning. The Prophet said: "*inna ummatī yudʿawna yawma al-qiyāmah...min athar al-wuḍū'*," that is to say, on the Day of Judgment, my community or Muslims will be called (will be distinguished or be known)...from the traces of ablution."[2]

At the time of the Companions, the term was used to mean a hadith of the Prophet. For example, Ibn Masʿūd was once asked about the situation of a woman whose husband had died without consummation of marriage, and while the *mahr* (compulsory gift a groom gives to a bride before the wedding day) was not decided. He said, "Ask the Companions if any *athar* has been handed down in the matter."[3]

Ibn ʿAbbās advises the Muslims to, "Stick with the right path and *athar.*"[4] In the time of the *Tābiʿūn*, the hadith narrators (*muḥaddithūn*) and jurists employed the term to mean two things: that which is related to the Prophet and his Companions, and whatever is ascribed only to the Companions.[5] In the science of *tafsīr*, however, the term *athar* is technically understood in four different ways:

1. The Qur'anic interpretation that has been handed down from the Prophet and the Companions.[6]
2. The Qur'anic interpretation that can be traced back to the Prophet, and also to some degree which pertains to the occasions of the revelation (*asbāb al-nuzūl*).[7]
3. The explanations of the Qur'an given in the Qur'an itself, by the Prophet, and by his Companions.[8]
4. The explanations of the Qur'an by other Qur'anic verses, by the Prophet, his Companions, and Successors.[9]

Al-Ḥākim, Ibn al-Ṣalāḥ and others considered the *tafsīr* of the Companions's *tāfsīr* as *al-tafsīr bi al-ma'thūr* only if what the Companions narrated pertained to *asbāb al-nuzūl*. It is possible that they, unlike others, classified *asbāb al-nuzūl* as interpretation rather than just a useful tool to aid in understanding a verse in its immediate circumstances or context. Such knowledge is a prerequisite for a competent interpreter (*mufassir*). On the other hand, Ibn Taymiyyah and others agreed that *al-tafsīr bi al-ma'thūr* can include the use of one part of the Qur'an to explain another. But they failed to distinguish this from *ra'y* when they opposed *ra'y*. In fact, using the Qur'an to explain the Qur'an without injecting anything from the Prophet would appear to be *ra'y* or ijtihad anyway; and there is no clear statement in the Qur'an that certain verses are to be used to explain other verses. In the light of these definitions, it becomes apparent that the Companions' interpretation is included in three definitions, and the Successors' included in the fourth definition only.

The question that immediately comes to mind is the reason for including a Companion's and a Successor's interpretations, along with that of the Prophet, under the same definition concerning *athar* of the Companion.

The answer has to do with the concept of *ḥujjah*. *Ḥujjah* is usually translated in English as 'binding proof.' However, in his *Ḥujjiyyat al-Sunnah*, Abd al-Ghani Abd Al-Khaliq defined the term as "to make something clear, to expose and explain and when it is presented before you, it becomes binding to act upon it because it is the decree of Allah."[10]

Ibn Taymiyyah, Ibn Qayyim and others were of the opinion that a Companion's interpretation was equal in authority to that of the Prophet,[11] with both considered as *al-tafsīr bi al-ma'thūr*. Other scholars i.e. al-Ḥākim al-Nīsābūrī (d. 405 AH) and Ibn al-Ṣalāḥ viewed the Companions' interpretation differently. They regarded it as *ḥujjah* (proof, evidence) only when it pertained to *asbāb al-nuzūl*.[12] Some scholars including Ibn Qayyim, held that the *tafsīr* of the Successors was equal in authority to the Prophet and the Companions.[13] The argument of each group will be presented in detail when the Prophet's *tafsīr*, the Companions' and the Successors' will be discussed separately.

Discussed next is the Prophet's Hadith or his Sunnah in relation to Qur'anic interpretation.

Hadith, *Athar, Ma'thūr* and Qur'anic Exegesis

Use of Hadith in the Qur'an

In Arabic, the term 'hadith' literally means "new" as opposed to "old," and it refers to report, story, communication, conversation, talk, etc. – that is to say, news. The Qur'an uses this word normally to denote the linguistic meaning of story, communication, and conversation. Verse 79:15: "Has the story (hadith) of Moses reached you?" The term hadith here denotes story. In verse 68:44: "Then leave Me alone with such as reject this Message (hadith)..." In this passage hadith refers to the Qur'an itself. In verse 6:68: "When you see men engaged in vain discourse about Our signs, turn away from them unless they turn to a different theme (hadith)." Hadith here is used to mean general conversation.

Hadith in the Sayings of the Prophet

The Prophet used the term hadith as it has been used in the linguistic sense and in the Qur'an. In *Fatḥ al-Bārī*, one hadith reads: "The best hadith is the book of Allah." Another report from al-Bukhārī, narrates: "Whoever tries to eavesdrop on the hadith of people (people's private conversations) when they dislike his doing so..." with hadith used here to denote conversation, talk.[14]

Hadith in the Usage of the Muḥaddithūn

The *Muḥaddithūn* (scholars of Hadith) used the term hadith to denote that which was transmitted from or about the Prophet concerning his deeds, sayings, tacit approval or descriptions of his *Ṣifāt* (physical appearance). The *fuqahā'* (jurists) adhered to the same definition as the *Muḥaddithūn*, but they excluded the description of *Ṣifāt* from the definition. It is reasonable to assume that the jurists excluded *Ṣifāt* because its value did not fall into their sphere. Muslims are commanded by the Qur'an to follow the Prophet without reservation and to regard him as an example to be imitated; this means obeying him and following his behavior, which does not include his physical description.

The Terms Hadith and Sunnah

Sunnah is literally a way, rule, or manner, whether it be good or bad, and the Qur'an uses the term in the linguistic meaning to denote this literal sense. We read in 3:137: "Many were the Ways of Life (*sunan*) that have passed away before you: travel through the earth, and see what was the end of those who rejected Truth."

In his *Riyāḍ al-Sāliḥīn*, al-Nawawī reports a hadith in which the Prophet talks about the reward of introducing a good or a bad Sunnah: "Whoever introduces a *sunnah ḥasanah* (a good Sunnah) ... and whoever introduces an evil *sunnah*..." In this hadith, the word *Sunnah* is used to indicate both good ways or manners and bad ones. Sunnah as an Islamic term, or in the usage of subsequent generations, is restricted to the Sunnah of the Prophet according to the al-Shāfiʿī school of thought.

However, the terms Hadith and Sunnah were used interchangeably by the Prophet's Companions. Ibn Qayyim quotes ʿUmar ibn al-Khaṭṭāb as saying: "The users of *ra'y* (that is, those who would use their opinion on matters the Hadith has already dealt with) are the enemies of the Sunnah. It is hard for them to memorize the Hadith. Therefore, they are not able to understand Hadith. They could not bring themselves to say 'I do not know' whenever they were asked [about certain matters]. In this manner, they rejected the Sunnah."[15] For our purpose, and to avoid confusion, we will use both words interchangeably since such has been the practice of the classical and contemporary Muslim scholars.

The Prophet's Interpretation

It is natural to make this our starting point not only because the Prophet is the only direct connection with God but also because the Sunnah is the second authoritative source on all aspects of the Muslim faith. Muslims believe that the Prophet was divinely commanded to explain the Qur'an to mankind, not by his own reasoning, but through the words which Angel Gabriel had brought to him from God.

Three of the Qur'anic texts that were commonly cited to substantiate this position were verse 16:44: "and We have sent down unto you (also) the Message; that you may explain clearly to men what is sent for them." The second verse is 75:17-19: "It is for Us to collect it and to promulgate it. But when We have promulgated it, follow thou its recital (as promulgated). Nay more, it is for Us to explain it (and make it clear)." The third is 53:3-4: "Nor does he say (aught) of (his own) Desire. It is no less than inspiration sent down to him."

These and other verses indicate that the Prophet must be the first interpreter of the Qur'an. Did he provide interpretation for the whole Qur'an or not? There are three different opinions regarding the answer to this question. First, there are those who hold that the Prophet explained the whole Qur'an. In his *al-Tafsīr wa al-Mufassirūn*, al-Dhahabī states that certain prominent scholars such as Ibn Taymiyyah believe that the Prophet explained every single word of the Qur'an.[16] In his *Fatāwā*, he quotes the Qur'anic statement, "*litubayyina li al-Nās mā nuzzila ilayhim*" ("that you may explain clearly to men what is sent for them,") which expresses Allah's command to the Prophet to communicate the words of the Revelation as well as explanations of its meanings. These scholars also maintain that the Companions of the Prophet did not move on to learn any additional portion of the Qur'an before comprehending the full meaning of what they had already received from the Prophet. Hence, scholars such as Ibn Taymiyyah believe that this is evidence enough that the Prophet has explained the meaning of all the Qur'an to his Companions.

They also cite a statement ascribed to ʿUmar ibn al-Khaṭṭāb which states: "Among the last verses revealed was the verse of *ribā* (usury). However, the Prophet died before explaining it." From this, they inferred that the Prophet used to explain every single verse to the Companions. Otherwise, ʿUmar ibn al-Khaṭṭāb's specifically mentioning that the Prophet was unable to explain the verse because of his death serves no purpose. Finally, they maintain that people naturally try to comprehend important books and scientific knowledge, hence the Qur'an being far more important than anything else including the latter, they would not have simply memorized it without understanding it in full.[17]

Secondly, there are those such as al-Ṭabarī, al-Suyūṭī, al-Shāṭibī and others who believe that the Prophet gave the interpretation of only a few verses of the Qur'an. In support of this they cite the statement of the Prophet's wife, ʿĀ'ishah: "The Prophet explained but a few verses that the angel Gabriel had taught him."[18] Scholars of this opinion contend that if it is true that the Prophet did explain the whole of the Qur'an, then his singling out of Ibn ʿAbbās for God to bless him with *ta'wīl* of the Qur'an would have been superfluous (the Prophet made a *duʿā'* for Ibn ʿAbbās: "O Allah, bless him with understanding of the *dīn* of Islam, and teach him the meaning of the Qur'an," indeed, I found the Prophet did not make this *duʿā'* for any Companion). Al-Suyūṭī challenges those who dispute this opinion by presenting a list of the verses that he believed were actually explained by the Prophet.[19] But the supporters of this opinion argue in response that it is impossible that Allah would have ordered the Prophet to explain every verse in the Qur'an because this would leave no room for human reflection on it, something which God has urged both Muslims and non-Muslims to do.

Thirdly, there are those such as al-Zarkashī's disciples who believe that the Qur'anic verses which the Prophet explained were numerous. Unlike al-Suyūṭī, however, they do not list the verses which were explained by the Prophet, therefore failing to substantiate their claim with any concrete evidence.[20]

A quick glance at the supporting arguments which each side presents gives the impression that the questions are hopelessly confusing. But closer examination of the arguments reveals otherwise. To begin with, the Qur'anic phrase Ibn Taymiyyah brings forth to support this argument ("that you may explain clearly to men what is sent for them,") in my opinion does not necessarily imply the Prophet explained the totality of the Qur'an. It more likely implies the explanations of problematic verses as well as those that cannot be comprehended through the Arabic alone, such as the verses on fasting, pilgrimage, etc., which can only be understood through the

Sunnah (for example, how to perform salah). The same also can be said of the report regarding the Companions' way of learning the Qur'an. Even though they were careful to comprehend the meaning of the portion they memorized, such comprehension could come through private discussion among themselves or through individual meditation and reflection on the Qur'an. In fact, Muslims are urged more than once in the Qur'an and Hadith to reflect on the Qur'an as a way of understanding it. For example verse 38:29: "[All this have We expounded in this] blessed divine writ which We have revealed unto thee, [O Muhammad,] so that men may ponder over its messages, and that those who are endowed with insight may take them to heart."

In his *Matn al-Arbaᶜūn al-Nawawiyyah*, Imam al-Nawawī reports that the Prophet said:

> No people gather in one of the houses of Allah reciting the Book of Allah and studying it among themselves, without tranquility descending upon them, mercy enveloping them, the angels *surrounding* them, and Allah making mention of them amongst those who are with Him.[21]

Moreover, it cannot be inferred from what ᶜUmar ibn Khaṭṭāb stated concerning the verse on *ribā* that the Prophet used to explain every single verse of the Qur'an. Rather, it gives the the impression that this verse was somewhat confusing to ᶜUmar ibn Khaṭṭāb himself and would have been made clear by the Prophet had he not died shortly afterward. In fact ᶜUmar himself on other occasions expressed difficulty in understanding some verses of the Qur'an, such as the verse mentioning *kalālah* (4:176) for those who die and "leave no descendants or ascendants as heirs."[22]

It is noteworthy that in his *Fatḥ al-Bārī*, a commentary on al-Bukhārī's *Al-Jāmiᶜal-Ṣaḥīḥ*, Ibn Ḥajar al-ᶜAsqalānī collected 548 hadith in the chapter that discusses *tafsīr*.[23] Of these 548 only 100 hadith are not, from a technical point of view, repetitions or *muʿallaq*.[24]

In his concise and excellent study of *tafsīr* literature in the six authoritative collections, R. Marston Speight (who directed the Office on Christian/Muslim relations for the National Council of Churches for from 1979 to 1992) gives an account of 475 hadith in al-Bukhārī's chapter – not counting repetitions. He also lists 393 reports which *Jāmiʿ al-Tirmidhī* contains in regard to *tafsīr*. In the four books, he did not give a specific statistic, but sufficiently explained the attitude of each book towards the function of hadith as commentary on the Qur'an and what pertains to it, such as *asbāb al-nuzūl*, *al-aḥruf al-sabʿah* (literally seven versions but the exact meaning remains elusive) etc.[25]

CHAPTER 4

Tafsīr and Fatwas of the Prophet's Companions (*Ṣaḥābah*)

SUMMARY

The Companions of the Prophet are an important source in *tafsīr* and following the Prophet's death became in effect the first *mufassirs*. They did not explain the whole Qur'an, but more difficult parts, and their exegesis constitutes a first step in the science of *tafsīr*. Whilst this would seem to be an obvious statement, in scholastic terms there are various opinions as to:

a) what constitutes a Companion as opposed to anyone who lived during this time and witnessed Prophet Muhammad, and
b) to what extent the Companions's *tafsīr* has definitive authority, that is, in other words, it is considered binding.

The methodology the Companions used was first to consult the Qur'an, then the Sunnah, and if no explanation could be gained from this, to use personal interpretation based on the occasions of revelation of verses, and their knowledge of Arabic grammar. We begin by a discussion of the word *Ṣaḥābī* or *Ṣāḥib* (Companion), then deal with the arguments concerning the authority of the *Ṣaḥābah's tafsīr* before proceeding to present some examples of this.

Introduction

THE COMPANIONS became the most important interpreters of the Qur'an following the Prophet's death. They used a number of sources in their *tafsīr* including the statements of the Prophet and their own reasoning or understanding (ijtihad), as well as Arabic grammar. They were also aware of the circumstances in which the Qur'an was revealed, as well as the reasons of revelation and its place. Some of the most prominet in the field are the Four Caliphs, (Abū Bakr, ʿUmar, ʿUthmān and ʿAlī), as well as ʿAbd Allāh ibn Masʿūd,

ʿAbd Allāh ibn ʿAbbās, Ubay ibn Kaʿb, Zayd ibn Thābit, Abū Musā al-Ashʿarī and ʿAbd Allāh ibn al-Zubayr. ʿAbdullāh ibn ʿAbbās is considered the most knowledgeable of the Companions.

Definition of *Ṣāḥib* and *Ṣaḥābah*

The Arabic word *ṣāḥib* (adjective) is derived from the verbal noun (*maṣdar*) *ṣuḥbah*, which has many meanings all denoting the notion of companionship or submission. Thus, the phrase "*wa aṣḥabtuhu al-shay*'" means "I made something to be his companion."[1] Whilst the phrase "*fa asḥabtuhu al-nāqah*" (which is part of a hadith) means, according to Ibn Manẓūr, "the camel submitted and followed her owner."[2]

Ṣāḥib in Islamic historiography refers to a contemporary of the Prophet, someone who believed in him as a Prophet, kept his company, and died as such. Traditionists and jurists alike have their own definition of this term. Traditionists, including Ibn Ḥajar, Ibn Kathīr and others, define a *ṣāḥib* or *ṣaḥābī* as anyone who met Prophet Muhammad in reality (as opposed to seeing him in a dream) after he became a Prophet, and died as a believer in him, even if he or she did not transmit a single hadith from him.[3]

This definition does not seem to have satisfied the critical criteria of legal theorists (*uṣūliyyīn*) for whom a *ṣaḥābī* was not simply someone who met the Prophet, but far more, someone who acknowledged his prophethood, became his disciple, accompanied him over a long period of time, met with him frequently during that period, and learned from him.[4] The jurists' definition hence excluded from the rank of the *Ṣaḥābah* many people whom the traditionists considered to have that status, especially those people who saw the Prophet once during the only one pilgrimage he made to Makkah.

This difference between the two opinions is largely due to two reasons. First, the notion of ʿ*adālah* (justice/fairness), honesty, and uprightness have made it necessary for the jurists to be reserved in their definition of the term more than the traditionists because the former were more concerned with the legal ramifications of the term whilst the latter were concerned principally with Hadith transmission. Second, the traditionists did not go beyond the literal sense of the word, whilst the jurists went deeper to examine its application in *ʿurf* (usage/custom).

Arguments Concerning the *Ḥujjiyyah* (Binding Proof) of a *Ṣaḥābī's* Interpretation and Fatwa

Praise for the *Ṣahābah* in the Qur'an and Hadith have made Muslims of later generations hold the Prophet's Companions in high esteem, although in various degrees, ranging from absolute authority that puts their opinion on an equal footing with that of the Prophet, to mere reverence that is limited to honoring their pioneering role in Islam and their Companionship with the Prophet. This lack of consensus among Muslims regarding the legal status of the *Ṣaḥhābah* (to be discussed in greater detail) impacted to some degree Qur'anic interpretation and Islamic law. The Companions, whether during the Prophet's life or thereafter, had at times used their own opinion in the interpretation of both the Qur'an and Hadith. This effort on their part came to be known as *ra'y Ṣāḥib* (a Companion's opinion, saying, or fatwa), and its authority became the subject of controversy among Muslim scholars.[5] In his *Principles of Islamic Jurisprudence*, Muhammad Hashim Kamali has correctly presented the arguments in precise context as follows:

> The Sunni scholars are unanimously agreed on the 'Companions' *ijmāʿ* (Muslim scholars' consensus) as a binding proof and the most authoritative form of *ijmāʿ*. The question arises as to whether the fatwa of a single Companion should also be recognized as a binding proof and therefore be given precedence over fundamental principles such as *qiyās* (analogical reasoning) or the fatwa of another

mujtahid[6] (a person qualified to give authoritative opinions in religious jurisprudence).

Scholastic opinion falls into four major groups:

1. The saying of a Companion or his *tafsīr* is an absolute binding authority that takes priority over *qiyās* and everyone else's *tafsīr*. Among the proponents of this view are Imam Mālik, Imam Aḥmed ibn Ḥanbal, Ibn Taymiyyah, Ibn Qayyim, and others.[7]
2. The saying of a Companion is a binding authority only if it pertains to the occasions of the revelation or to that which cannot be subjectively discussed (*mā lā majāl li al-ra'y fīh*).[8]
3. The view that maintains that only the first two Caliphs's statements are absolutely binding.
4. The saying of a Companion is not a binding proof. This is the view of many jurists and theologians including Abū Ḥamed al-Ghazālī, Ibn Ḥazm, al-Āmidī, Muḥammad ʿAlī al-Shawkānī and others.[9]

Group 1: The saying of a Companion or his tafsīr is an absolute binding authority that takes priority over qiyās and everyone else's tafsīr

The first group invokes surah 9:100 as a main argument to support their view: "the first of those who forsook (their homes) and of those who gave them aid, and (also) those who follow them in (all) good deeds, well-pleased is Allah with them, as are they with Him." This refers to the first emigrants from Makkah and the people of Madinah called theAnsar who supported them in Madinah.

They maintain that the importance of this verse lies in the fact that God praised the Companions and those who followed them, individually or as a group. So, in their view, if anyone differs with one of them or does not accept his opinion(s), he will be excluded from the blessing of God. They thus conclude that the Companions' opinion is an absolute binding authority within Islamic law and we must follow their judgments or opinions.[10] Another verse invoked is: "You are indeed the best community that has ever been brought forth for [the good of] mankind" (3:110). What is inferred from this is that God is describing the Companions as being the best people ever to have been raised up for mankind,[11] thereby suggesting that their judgments and opinions are the best and must be accepted.

The proponents of this view also refer to several Hadith. One of these being: "*aṣḥābī ka al-nujūm: bi ayyihim iqtadaytum ihtadaytum,*" (my companions are like stars; whoever of you follows anyone of them will be guided to the right path). This hadith is not sound. Another hadith states: "*Khayr al-qurūni qarnī hādhā, thumma al-ladhīna yalūnahum, thumma a-lathīna yalūnahum,*" (the best generation is mine, then the succeeding generation, then the generation that follows).[12] These two hadith, mainly the former, indicate very clearly that anyone who follows any Companion is on the right path. This appears to uphold the authority of the Companions' opinion. One of the strongest arguments used by the exponents of this view is that God blessed the Companions with the companionship of the Prophet; they learned the whole Qur'an from the Prophet directly; they witnessed the revelation, and understood the circumstances in which it was sent down. Furthermore, they understood well the Prophet's methodology and mastered the Arabic language, which is the Qur'an's language.[13]

The two most outstanding advocates of this view are Ibn Taymiyyah and his faithful student Ibn Qayyim, who seriously challenged the opponents of this idea and defended their own position by presenting around forty-six arguments from the Qur'an, Hadith, the Companions' statements as well as simple logic.

Further Qur'anic evidence for this group includes verse 27:59: "Say: 'Praise be to Allah, and Peace on his servants whom He has chosen (*iṣṭafā*) (for his Message).'" For Ibn ʿAbbās, God's selected servants are the *Companions* of the Prophet, and according to Ibn Qayyim: "The actual implication of the word *iṣṭifā*' is purification from impurity which includes mistakes. Thus, the Companions are purified." He further adds: "Although the Companions differed on some issues, this neither contradicts their purity nor affects their claims, for no one can have true understanding of Islam better than them."[14] Additional textual support includes:

> And among them are men who listen to thee, but in the end, when they go out from thee, they say to those who have received Knowledge (*al-ʿilm*), "What is it he said just then?" Such are men whose hearts Allah has sealed, and who follow their own lusts. (47:16)

> God will rise up, to (suitable) ranks (and degrees), those of you who believe and who have been granted [true] Knowledge (*al-ʿilm*). (58:11)

Ibn Qayyim claims that the definite article "*al*" in the word *al-ʿilm* in these verses stands for *al-ʿahd*, which indicates that it was something specifically known to the audience. Ibn Qayyim interprets this term as referring to the Qur'an. Thus, he concludes that if the Companions were given such knowledge, they must be followed in all what they said or decided.[15]

A third piece of Qur'anic evidence Ibn Qayyim quotes in support of this view is verse 2:143: "Thus, have We made of you an Ummah justly balanced, that ye might be witnesses over the nations." The point that Ibn Qayyim makes here is that, Allah has made the Companions the chosen and upright people by granting them the status of witnesses over people on the Day of Judgment. The testimony that Allah accepts is one which is based on knowledge and thus confirms the soundness of the knowledge of the Companions. Therefore, the truth or real understanding never escapes the latter's circle. Hence, he concludes: "We say to whoever disagrees with the Companions that the Componions' opinion is better than yours."[16]

Ibn Qayyim refers to the following hadith: "Do not abuse my Companions for if any one of you spent gold equal to (Mount) Uhud (in Allah's Cause), you still would not be able to achieve what they have done, nay, not even half of it." Ibn Qayyim commented on this hadith saying: "If the reach of the Companions is better in the sight of God than gold equal to Mount Uhud, than how could Allah not have inspired them with correct understanding in their fatwas and [why would He] instead inspire one of the next generations with such knowledge? This is obviously impossible."[17]

The second hadith cited is: "Verily, Allah has selected or chosen and selected companions for me. Some of them he made my ministers, helpers, and in-laws." Therefore, according to Ibn Qayyim, it is impossible that Allah would take away correct understanding or opinion on matters from the very people He had chosen as the Prophet's ministers, helpers and in-laws.[18]

Evidence is also cited from the Companions's own statements such as that of ʿAbd Allāh ibn Masʿūd who states:

> Whoever is looking for models to follow should follow the Companions of the Prophet, because they were the most virtuous people of this community, deeper in knowledge, less involved in unnecessary things, more guided and in a better condition. Allah chose them to accompany His Prophet and to establish Islam. You should recognize their virtue and follow their footsteps for, verily, they were on the right path.

Ibn Qayyim comments on this, using the same argument as in his previous statements.

A second statement is from Ḥudhayfah ibn al-Yamān, who says to a group of Qur'an reciters (*qurrā'*):

> Oh you group of Qur'an reciters, follow the path of those who were before you. I swear by Allah that if you stand straight (stick to Islam),

you will be guided, and if you abandon the path of your predecessors, you will go far astray.[19]

Thirdly, there is the case of an incident that took place in the house of a Companion, Jundub ibn ʿAbd Allāh. A group of Muslims (whom Ibn Qayyim describes as Kharijites) came to Jundub and said to him: "We are inviting you to Allah's Book." He said: "You?" They replied: "Yes." He repeated, "You?" They repeated: "Yes." Then he said: "Oh you the most evil among the creatures of Allah, do you want to follow evil or to follow our Sunnah for guidance?" Ibn Qayyim states that it is known that anyone who thinks that the Companions can possibly make mistakes, and thereby disagrees with them in their fatwas, has not followed their Sunnah.[20]

Fourthly, when a Companion says something or gives a fatwa, we might share the same opinions with him or we might not, but we have to realize that, not all of what the Companions heard from the Prophet was reported. To substantiate his point, Ibn Qayyim asks: "Where are the hadith that Abū Bakr al-Ṣiddīq and the prominent Companions narrated?" Abū Bakr accompanied the Prophet from the time he became a Prophet until he died. But the number of Hadith narrated by Abū Bakr does not exceed one hundred. Thus, whatever they said concerning Islam is most likely what they heard from the Prophet. Furthering his arguments, he presented six categories under which a fatwa or opinion of a Companion may fall:

1. He might have heard a statement from the Prophet, but did not ascribe anything to him for fear of misquoting him;
2. He might have heard it from a Companion who had heard it from the Prophet;
3. He might have understood it from the Qur'an, although it was unclear to others;
4. He might have said something which the majority of the Companions agreed upon, although it was not narrated to us

except the statement of one person who initiated a particular opinion;

5. Since the Companions understood their language very well, understood the ultimate purpose of Islam, observed the behavior of the Prophet in dealing with different issues, they were thereby qualified to understand what the next generation could not understand and, therefore, their opinions and fatwas are binding and must be followed
6. He might have misunderstood the saying of the Prophet, although this, Ibn Qayyim contends, is not possible or realistic.[21]

Group 2: The saying of a Companion is a binding authority only if it pertains to the occasions of the revelation or to that which cannot be subjectively discussed (mā lā majāl li al-ra'y fīh).

The second group of scholars includes those who support the idea that a Companion's interpretation or his fatwa is binding only if what he narrates concerns the occasions of revelation. They believe whatever a ṣaḥābī narrates in that context cannot be held as mere opinion. Thus, whatever the Companions relate in this regard must be based on eyewitness accounts or something heard from the Prophet.[22]

Group 3: The view that maintains that only the first two Caliphs's statements are absolutely binding.

The third group based their argument on the hadith which commands: "stick to my Sunnah and the Sunnah of the four guided Caliphs." A similar hadith also enjoins: "Imitate these two persons after me; Abū Bakr and ʿUmar."[23]

Group 4: The view that maintains that the saying of a Companion is not a binding proof (ḥujjah).

The fourth group upheld their opinion by quoting many verses of which two are central to this opinion. The first is verse 4:59: "If you differ in anything among yourselves, refer it to God and His Messenger."

They point to the fact that in this verse God has commanded the Muslims to refer what they differ upon only to God and His messenger. Hence, if a Companion's opinion were to be binding, God would have mentioned it.[24]

The second is verse 47:24: "Do they not then earnestly seek to understand the Qur'an, or are their hearts locked up by them?" In this verse, God exhorts Muslims to ponder over the verses of the Qur'an. It is therefore this group's view that to consider the opinion of a Companion as binding (*ḥujjah*) would be a violation of this divine injunction.[25]

Abū Ḥāmid al-Ghazālī seems to be the most insistent on rejecting the opinion of a Companion as *Ḥujjah*. He even rejects the idea that if the four rightly guided Caliphs were unanimous on an issue it would become binding on the Ummah, believing this viewpoint to be null and void (*wa al-kull bāṭil ʿindanā*),[26] adding that any person who is subject to making mistakes cannot be infallible. Furthermore, he questioned: "How can two people, each rendering an infallible opinion, differ on the same issue?" that is, how could two binding proofs (*ḥujjah*) be contradictory on the same issue? He pointed out that the Companions did differ on many issues to the extent that their opinion cannot be harmonized in any way.[27] He also argued that the Companions recognized that their own opinions were not binding proof. If they believed their opinions were binding, they would not have allowed themselves to differ. Scholars who support this opinion even go so far as to say that considering a Companion's *tafsīr* or fatwa as binding proof is tantamount to suppressing the intellect.[28]

Finally, the implication of these theological arguments has two dimensions. One is religious, the other is intellectual. Al-Ghazālī states regarding the religious dimension that if the opinion of a Companion is a binding proof, then it becomes one of the basic principles of Islam. For this to occur, their binding character must be established in the same way as the other basic principles of Islam were, that is to say, through proof and argument from the Qur'an and the Hadith.[29]

Another dimension in this thorny issue is that if the opinion of a Companion is a binding proof (*ḥujjah*), then it arrogates to itself the authority to restrict the general implication of the Qur'an. The Ḥanbalī jurists al-Qāḍī Abū Yaʿlā and Abū Barakāt, both confirmed that if the opinion of a Companion is to be considered a *ḥujjah*, then it can restrict the general implication of the Qur'an.[30] Al-Shāṭibī for his part holds a similar opinion with minor differences.

The intellectual implication concerns restricting thinking. Al-Ghazālī and al-Āmidī state that if one accepts the opinion of a Companion as a binding proof, then this is tantamount to *taqlīd* (acceptance and adoption of a legal conclusion without examining the premises). This, they say, is contrary to the Qur'anic invitation to Muslims to reflect upon the Qur'an (verse 47:24 above) and analyze its information. Thus, the scholarly approach concerning the authority of a Companion's opinion involves intellectual inquiry and analysis.[31]

Abū Ḥayyān raised yet another scholastic issue when he stated: "If it were true that the Qur'an can be understood only by reference to the Companions' and the *Tābiʿūn's* interpretations, then there would be no need for further interpretation by the scholars who followed them."[32]

Qur'anic Interpretation by the Companions

There are ample verses in the Qur'an and Hadith which command Muslims to seek knowledge and teach it. Inspired by this command, the Companions became involved in *tafsīr*. For all their endeavors, they did not interpret the whole Qur'an, nor did they leave a compendium of their contribution. This was for four main reasons. First, it was not common for ordinary Arabs to write. Ibn al-Nadīm mentions that only 13 people in Makkah were literate when the Prophet Muhammad became a messenger. This is why he trusted his own memory.

Secondly, at the beginning of his Caliphate, ʿUmar ibn al-Khaṭṭāb discouraged writing anything other than the Qur'an for religious purposes, including the traditions of the Prophet. But later he allowed this. The point was to prevent confusion between the Qur'an and the Hadith, or to avoid people occupying themselves with the Hadith rather than the Qur'an.

Thirdly, the Qur'an is in Arabic, this being their language, the *Ṣaḥabah* understood the language better than the subsequent generation, so they had a better understanding of the Qur'an.

Fourthly, they dedicated their lives to propagating Islam; thus, most of their life was spent in defending and protecting Islam and giving people the ability to choose the religion they would like to follow. It follows that the Companions who actually engaged in *tafsīr* were very few. The same applies to their giving fatwas.

In his *Al-Iḥkām fī Uṣūl al-Aḥkām*, Ibn Ḥazm specifies that the number of the Companions, both male and female, who issued fatwas ranged between 133-139.[33]

Generally speaking, according to the existing sources, the prominent exegetes (*mufassirūn*) among the Companions were ten: The four Caliphs (Abū Bakr, ʿUmar, ʿUthmān and ʿAlī), ʿAbd Allāh ibn Masʿūd, ʿAbd Allāh ibn ʿAbbās, Ubay ibn Kaʿb, Zayd ibn Thābit, Abū Musā al-Ashʿarī and ʿAbd Allāh ibn al-Zubayr. The others who are recognized for their ability to produce interpre-tation are Anas ibn Mālik, ʿĀ'ishah bint Abū Bakr al-Ṣiddīq, the wife of the Prophet, Abū Hurayrah, ʿAbd Allāh ibn ʿUmar, Jābir ibn ʿAbd Allāh, and ʿAmrū ibn al ʿĀṣ.[34]

The interpretation which the first three Caliphs produced was minimal compared to what ʿAlī ibn Abī Ṭālib, ibn Masʿūd and Ibn ʿAbbās produced. Al-Suyuṭī asserted that the reason for the small amount of *tafsīr* from the first three Caliphs was due to the fact that they died earlier than ʿAlī and other *mufassirūn*. He also noted that even though Abū Bakr was the closest Companion to the Prophet and the first man to accept Islam, he narrated very little *tafsīr* from the Prophet,[35] perhaps for reasons associated with piety (out of fear to misquote the Prophet). It is also possible, but unlikely, that his *tafsīr* became lost; he died shortly after the Prophet. However, Abū Bakr's well-known statement "What heavens shall shade me and what earth shall shelter me, if I say anything concerning the Qur'an of which I have no knowledge," suggests that the first assumption is the most likely reason. In spite of the fact that the three Caliphs' *tafsīr* is minimal, they are still considered by Muslim scholars to be among the most prominent exegetes, if not the first and foremost. This is because Muslims hold in high esteem the Companions in general and the four Caliphs in particular for they were extolled in the Qur'an and by the Prophet.

We examine next the *tafsīr* of some of the Companions. These include the four Caliphs (Abū Bakr, ʿUmar, ʿUthmān, and ʿAlī) as well as four other prominent Companions who are highly acclaimed for their Qur'anic commentary: Ibn Masʿūd, Ubay ibn Kaʿb, ʿĀ'ishah Bint Abū Bakr al-Ṣiddīq and Ibn ʿAbbās.

Tafsīr of Abū Bakr al-Ṣiddīq

Abū Bakr had noticed some Companions abstaining from enjoining good and prohibiting evil on the basis of their understanding of Qur'anic verse 5:105 which states: "O you who have attained to faith! It is [but] for your own selves that you are responsible: those who go astray can do you no harm if you [yourselves] are on the right path." This verse does not mean that people should just worry about their own salvation, and not shoulder the task of bettering or guiding others who may be deviating. This is why Abū Bakr corrected their perception stating to them: "Oh people! You recite this verse and misinterpret it. I heard the Prophet say, if people see corruption taking place and do not do anything to stop it, then God will cover them with His punishment."[36] In another instance, Abū Bakr was asked about the meaning of the Qur'anic term *kalālah*. He replied: "I say [regarding its meaning], that in my opinion it refers to anyone who has passed away and has no father or son." On another occasion, Saʿīd ibn ʿImrān (a Companion) requested Abū Bakr to explain verse 41:30: "In the case of those who say, 'Our Lord is Allah', and, further, stand straight and steadfast..." Abū Bakr interpreted it by stating: "They are those who do not associate anything with Allah."[37]

In light of these three instances, it is noticed that Abū Bakr:

a) In the first example refers to a hadith of the Prophet in explaining the meaning of Qur'anic verse 5:105.
b) In the second example depends on his own opinion.
c) In the third example, he did not refer to the Prophet, nor did he state clearly his opinoin as he did in the case of *kalālah*. Perhaps he deduced his perspective from the Prophet's explanation of verse 41:30 that "most of the people who stated in this verse 'Our Lord is Allah' became disbelievers afterwards. Whoever says this until his death has stood upright. Some people profess Islam but reject it later. So those who die in the state of Islam are those who have stood upright."[38]

ʿUmar ibn al-Khaṭṭāb

Among the Companions ʿUmar appears to have taken more time in pondering the deepest meanings of the Qur'an and the one more inclined to get the Companions to engage intellectually in understanding it. This assumption is based on the following incidents.

Whilst the rest of the Companions were delighted, ʿUmar cried when verse 5:3 of the Qur'an was revealed: "This day have I perfected your religion for you, completed My favour upon you, and have chosen for you Islam as your religion." When the Prophet asked ʿUmar why he was crying, he replied, "Nothing has ever been perfected but that afterwards it decreases." The Prophet supported his statement by saying "You are correct."[39]

Al-Bukhārī narrates that one day ʿUmar sought the Companions' opinion regarding the meaning of Qur'anic verse 2:266 which states:

> Would any of you like to have a garden of date-palms and vines, through which running waters flow, and have all manner of fruit therein - and then be overtaken by old age, with only weak children to [look after] him - and then [see] it smitten by a fiery whirlwind and utterly scorched? In this way God makes clear His messages unto you, so that you might take thought.

They replied, "Allah knows best." At this, ʿUmar exclaimed: "Say we know or we do not know." Upon hearing this, Ibn ʿAbbās stated: "Oh commander of the believers! I have something in mind." ʿUmar said: "O son of my brother, do not underestimate yourself." Ibn ʿAbbās said: "[The verse] has set up an example for deeds." ʿUmar said, "What deeds?" Ibn ʿAbbās repeated "for a deed." ʿUmar said, "What type of deed?" Ibn ʿAbbās replied, "For a wealthy man who does good deeds out of obedience to Allah, and then Allah sends Satan to him where upon he commits sins till his good deeds are annulled."[40]

On a similar occasion to this, we see ʿUmar asking the Companions as to their understanding of verses 110:1-3 of the Qur'an which read: "When God's succour comes, and victory, and thou seest people enter God's religion in hosts, - extol thy Sustainer's limitless glory, and praise Him, and seek His forgiveness: for, behold, He is ever an acceptor of repentance". Some answered: "We are commanded to praise Allah and ask Him for forgiveness when He blessed us with victory." Others remained quiet. ʿUmar interrogates further: "Ibn ʿAbbās, do you agree with their interpretations?" Ibn ʿAbbās replies: "No. I say it is an indication of the death of the Prophet."[41]

Again, we find ʿUmar interpreting the word "*istaqāmū*" (stand straight and steadfast) in verse 41:30 of the Qur'an: "[But,] behold, as for those who say, 'Our Lord is Allah', and, further, stand straight and steadfast, ..." explaining it as: "I swear by Allah, they follow the straight path to Allah by obedience to Him and they do not swerve the way foxes do,"[42] meaning they do not take advantage of any loopholes.

In light of this presentation, we conclude that ʿUmar had been studying the Qur'an and using his reasoning to understand it, and seems not to have depended on the obvious meaning of the text.

ʿUthmān ibn ʿAffān

ʿUthmān was one of the Caliphs but we have very little *tafsīr* from him with regard to understanding and interpreting the Qur'an, the sources consulted hardly mentioning him. Even so, the little interpretation that exists attributed to him will be discussed later in the chapter when comparing *tafsīr* differences between the Companions.

ʿAlī ibn Abī Ṭālib

Among the four Caliphs, ʿAlī was the most prolific exegete. He seems to have been strongly self-confident in his knowledge of the Qur'an, and is reported to have declared:

> Ask me! I swear by Allah, you ask me nothing but I answer you. Ask me about the book of *Allah*, I swear by *Allah*, no verse was revealed but I know whether it was revealed during the night or during the day, on level ground or on a mountain."[43]

One of ʿAlī's interpretations concerns Qur'anic verse 9:124 which states: "Whenever there cometh down a surah, some of them say: 'Which of you has had his faith increased by it?'" ʿAlī interpreted the verse by stating:

> Faith appears as a small white spot in the heart. Whenever it increases, the white sport also increases until the whole heart becomes white. (On the other hand) Hypocrisy appears as a small black spot in the heart. Whenever it increases, the black spot also increases...[44]

A further instance of ʿAlī's interpretation concerns the completion of *niʿmah* in verse 2:150 which indicates: "...and that I may complete My favours [*niʿmatī*] on you, and ye may (consent to) be guided." Ali explains this to mean that one should die in a state of surrender to Allah (Islam). He elaborates further stating that *niʿmah* includes Islam, the Qur'an, the Prophet, covering someone's sins or shortcomings, good health and being self-sufficient.[45]

In his *tafsīr*, ʿAlī also used the Qur'an to explain other Qur'anic verses, which has led contemporary Qur'anic scholar, Muhammad Ibrahim Sharif, to assume that ʿAlī was the first *mufassir* to initiate a conceptual approach to *tafsīr* which is known in modern times as *al-tafsīr al-mawḍūʿī*.[46]

ʿAbd Allāh ibn Masʿūd

Al-Suyūṭī regarded the *tafsīr* received from Ibn Masʿūd to be more developed than that originating from ʿAlī ibn Abī Ṭālib. Ibn Masʿūd's biography indicates that he went over the meaning of the Qur'an thoroughly.[47] This assumption is implied by Ibn Masʿūd's observation when he states: "The most comprehensive verse in regard to good and bad morals in the Qur'an is verse 16:90 which points out that 'Allah commands justice, the doing of good, and liberality to kith and kin, and He forbids all shameful deeds, and injustice and rebellion...'"

If he had not studied the Qur'an comprehensively, how could Ibn Masʿūd have made such a statement? One instance of his interpretation concerns verse 2:121 which reads: "Those to whom We have sent the Book study it as it should be studied." Ibn Masʿūd explains '*those*' as referring to people who legalized that which the book of God had ordered to be legalized and abstained from that which the book of God had prohibited, and did not distort it.[48]

Masrūq ibn Ajdaʿ once stated: "I asked Ibn Masʿūd about injustice in judgment done by a judge?" to which he goes on to say Ibn Masʿūd responded by reciting verse 5:44, which warns that "If any do fail to judge by (the light of) what Allah hath revealed, they are (no better than) Unbelievers."

It appears that by referring to this verse, Ibn Masʿūd interpreted the failure to judge by what Allah has revealed to be injustice, and injustice itself to be that is to say, disbelief, and a rebellion against Allah's commandment.

Concerning verse 44:10, "Wait, then, for the Day when the skies shall bring forth a pall of smoke which will make obvious [the approach of the Last Hour]" Ibn Masʿūd uses the historical circumstance of the verse's revelation to derive it's meaning. He states:

> When the Quraysh agitated and rebelled against the Prophet, the latter invoked God, saying: "O Allah! Help me against them by afflicting them with seven years of famine like the seven years of Yūsuf." So the Quraysh were stricken by a year of famine during which they ate bones and dead animals. When the tribe pleaded with God, saying: "Our Lord remove the torment from us, really we are believers," Allah told the Prophet that if He put an end to their torment, they would revert to their ways. But the Prophet pleaded in their favor with his Lord who ceased their punishment. Later they reverted to their initial habits, where upon Allah punished them at the battle of Badr, which is what Allah's statement indicates.

In the light of this interpretation, it is clear that Ibn Masʿūd, exercised his own judgement to understand the text, as in the case of verse 2:121, going beyond what is obvious to derive a novel meaning. It is worth noting that in so doing, Ibn Masʿūd followed one of the Prophet's interpretation methods as shown in the case of Qur'anic verse 44:10. That method involving answering the question by referring to the Qur'an.

Ubay ibn Kaʿb

Ubay ibn Kaʿb was one of the best reciters of the Qur'an and the principal teacher of the Madinah school of *tafsīr*. He was also of Jewish background and thus it was expected that his Jewish education would be reflected in his exegesis as noted by scholars in the Islamic interpretations of Kaᶜb al-Aḥbār and ᶜAbd Allāh ibn Sallām. One of Ubay's interpretation concerns verse 2:213: "Mankind was one single nation...". Scholars have understood this verse in so many different ways, with some interpreting "one single nation" to mean Adam and Eve, and others as referring to the prophet Nūḥ and the people who were in the Ark with him. Still others have assumed that reference is being made to mankind in general by virtue of the verse connoting disbelievers,[49] etc. Ubay, however, interpreted the verse as referring to mankind being one single nation or community "only once." By this he meant that Allah had brought the souls of the children of Adam together before dispersing them on the earth. That is to say, mankind was one community when it was in the loins of Adam. He supports his view by reference to verse 7:172 which states:

> When thy Lord drew forth from the Children of Adam - from their loins - their descendants, and made them testify concerning themselves, (saying): "Am I not your Lord (who cherishes and sustains you)?"- They said: "Yea! We do testify!"[50]

On an another occasion, Ubay was asked by Muṣᶜab ibn Saᶜd, one of the *Tābiᶜūn*, whether verse 107:5: "Who are neglectful of their prayers," meant thinking about oneself while praying.[51] Ubay dismissed the suggestion remarking that all people did so, and we find him going on to explain that the verse referred to neglecting the accomplishment of salah on time.

At another time a man comes to Ubay stating: "A verse in the Qur'an made me uncomfortable." When Ubay inquires as to the verse in question the man recites verse 4:123: "It may not accord with your wishful thinking - nor with the wishful thinking of the followers of earlier revelation - [that] he who does evil shall be requited for it." Ubay explains to him that, "The verse means when a calamity befalls a believer, and he patiently tolerates it for the sake of Allah, he will have all his sins wiped out."[52]

Ubay's methodology does not differ from that of his contemporaries. We find that he used the Qur'an to explain other Qur'anic verses and he exercised his own judgement in explaining the meaning of the text.

ʿĀ'ishah Bint Abū Bakr al-Ṣiddīq

Among the wives of the Prophet, ʿĀ'ishah was the most knowledgeable. She has been listed third in terms of narrating the Prophet's hadith. Her nephew, ʿUrwah ibn al-Zubayr narrated many of her interpretations as shown by the following exchanges between them both. The first instance concerns verse 2:158 which clarifies issues around Hajj rituals. It states:

> Behold! Safa and Marwa are among the Symbols of Allah. So if those who visit the House in the Season or at other times, should compass them round, it is no sin on them (*fa lā junāḥa ʿalayhi an yaṭṭawafa bihimā*). And if any one obeyeth his own impulse to good, – be sure that Allah is He Who recogniseth and knoweth.

ʿUrwah ibn al-Zubayr narrates that he asked ʿĀ'ishah, "Tell me about the sayings of Allah 2:158." Before ʿĀ'ishah responded as to her understanding he said: "There is no blame on anyone who does not walk between *al-Ṣafā* and *al-Marwah*." ʿĀ'ishah replied, "Woe to what you said oh my nephew. If your interpretation was correct the verse would have been *"fa lā junāḥa ʿalayhi an lā yaṭṭawafa bihimā"*. There is no blame on anyone who does *not* walk between *al-Ṣafā* and *al-Marwah*. This verse was revealed in connection with the *Anṣār* who before Islam, used to assume *Ihlāl* (or *iḥrām* for Hajj) in the area of Mushallal for their idol *Manāt* that they used to worship. Those who assumed *Ihlāl* for *Manāt*, used to hesitate to perform *ṭawāf* between *al-Ṣafā* and *al-Marwah* after embracing Islam regarding it as sinful to do so.[53]

In another instance related by al-Bukhārī, ʿĀ'ishah was asked by ʿUrwah as to the meaning of verse 12:110. He remarks: "Did (the apostles mentioned in the verse) suspect that they were betrayed by Allah or that they were treated as liars by their people?" ʿĀ'ishah answers him: "They suspected that they were treated as liars by their people."

ʿUrwah went on: "But they were sure that their people treated them as liars and it was a matter of suspicion." She replied: "Yes, 'upon my life' (*laʿamrī*), they were sure about it." ʿUrwah said to her: "So they (apostles) suspected their Lord of such a thing?" adding "What about this verse then?" Ā'ishah said, "It is about the apostles' followers who believed in their Lord and trusted their apostles, but the period of trials was prolonged and victory delayed until the apostles thought that their followers treated them as liars. There upon Allah's help came to them."[54]

Again, ʿUrwah asks ʿĀ'ishah's interpretion of verse 4:127:

> And they will ask thee to enlighten them about the laws concerning women. Say: God doth instruct you about them: And (remember) what hath been rehearsed unto you in the Book, concerning the orphans of women to whom ye give not the portions prescribed, and yet whom ye desire to marry...

ʿĀ'ishah replies:

> These verses have been revealed regarding the case of a man who has an orphan girl under his care, who shares with him all his property, even a date palm (garden), but he dislikes to marry her and dislikes to give her in marriage to somebody else, who would share with her the portion of the property due to her. For this reason, that guardian prevents that orphan girl from marriage.[55]

In the light of this brief presentation it can be concluded that ʿĀ'ishah used three different methods in Qur'anic interpretation. The first concerns her language skills, as illustrated in her correction of ʿUrwah's understanding of verse 2:158 wherein she states, "if what you have said is correct, the verse would have been *fa lā junāḥa ʿalayhi an* ***[lā]*** *yaṭṭawafa bihimā.*" In the first part of this statement, the particle *'lā'* stands for negation whereas in the latter part the *'lā'* (in bold) is not mentioned in the Qur'anic verse. Secondly, she uses her knowledge of traditional Arab culture as in the case of verse 2:158. Thirdly, she uses her knowledge of the circumstances of the revelation, as noted in her explanation of verse 4:127.

ʿAbd Allāh ibn ʿAbbās

When the Prophet died, Ibn ʿAbbās was about thirteen or fourteen years of age. However, he has been generally recognized as the most prominent exegete among the Companions. Muslim scholars believed that this was due to the Prophet's well-known prayer in his regard: "O God, grant him the knowledge of this religion (Islam) and teach him the interpretation the Qur'an."[56] As a result of his exegesis, Ibn ʿAbbās received praise from various contemporaries of the Prophet who called him invariably *tarjumān al-Qur'ān* (the best interpreter of the Qur'an), *ra's al-mufassirīn*, (head or leader of the exegetes), *ḥabr hādhihi al-ummah* (scholar of the Ummah), and so on. A negative consequence of Ibn ʿAbbās's popularity as an authority has been the false ascription to him of numerous hadith and exegetical texts. According to al-Suyūṭī there were countless numbers of such hadith (*Mā lā yuḥṣā kathrah*), and according to al-Shāfiʿī: "No more than one hundred hadith have come authentically from Ibn ʿAbbās."[57]

In his *Al-tafsīr wa al-Mufassirūn*, al-Dhahabī mentions the reason for this attribution of fabricated *tafsīr* reports to Ibn ʿAbbās as being due to his membership of the Prophet's House, and the fact that he was related to those from whom Muslims wanted to obtain their blessing. And because of Ibn ᶜAbbās's status, even a complete book entitled *Tanwīr al-Miqbās* was attributed to him. The work was compiled by Abū Ṭāhir Muḥammad ibn Yaᶜqūb Al-Fayrūzābādī Al-Shīrāzī (d. 817), and has been published several times in Egypt and Pakistan by *al-Maktabah al-Fārūqiyyah*. In reality, Ibn ᶜAbbās's *tafsīr* as reported in al-Ṭabarī's *Jāmiᶜ al-Bayān*, in al-Bukhārī's *al-Jāmiᶜ al-Ṣaḥīḥ*, in Ibn Kathīr's *Tafsīr al-Qur'ān Al-ᶜAẓīm*, and in other sources is different from Ibn ᶜAbbās's alleged *tafsīr* (interpretation) in *Tanwīr al-Miqbās*. Thus, I incline towards *Tanwīr al-Miqbās* cannot possibly representing the *tafsīr* of Ibn ᶜAbbās. For example, all Qur'anic surahs except one (surah *al-Tawbah*) begin with the *Basmala* (In Name of Allah, The Most Merciful, The Most Compassionate).[58] However, no interpretation attributed to Ibn ᶜAbbās concerning the meaning of the *Basmala* exists except in *Tanwīr al-Miqbās* which reportedly has him stating: The letter '*bā*' stands for '*bahā'u Allāh, bahjatuh; balā'uh, barakātuh*' (the magnificence of God, His delight, His trials, and His blessings). The letter '*sīn*' stands for '*sanā'uh, sumuwwuh*', and *ibtidā'u ismihi al-samīᶜ* (God's sublimity, His highness and the beginning of His lofty name and All-Hearing). As for the letter '*mīm*', it stands for '*mulkuh, majduh, minnatuh ᶜalā ᶜibādih*' (God's dominion, His glory, and His favors to His servants).[59]

Interpretations of such verses were not mentioned in any of the major *tafsīr* works. In his *Fatḥ Al-Qadīr*, al-Shawkānī mentions a weak or fabricated hadith from a Companion by the name of Abū Saᶜīd al-Khudurī (d. 16) who is supposed to have narrated the following hadith: The Prophet said that Jesus's mother sent him to a school to learn. The teacher asked Jesus to write down *bismi Allāh*. Jesus inquires: "what is *bismi Allāh*?" The teacher responds: "I do not know." Then Jesus states the letter '*bā*' stands for '*bahā'u Allāh*,' (the magnificence of God), the letter '*sīn*' stands for '*sanā'uh*' (God's sublimity) and the letter '*mīm*' stands for '*malakūtuh*' (God's kingdom).[60]

These interpretations are representative of the Sufi's allegorical interpretations (*ta'wīlāt*). And these type of allegorical interpretations appear in *Tanwīr al-Miqbās* at the beginning of most chapters which start with what are known as *al-ḥurūf al-muqaṭṭaᶜah*, the abbreviated letters. However, al-Ṭabarī, al-Shawkānī and others have reported Ibn ᶜAbbās to have stated, regarding the meanings of the abbreviated letters, that they are the greatest names of God. When he was asked about their meanings he did not give any specific interpretation.[61]

An analysis of *Tanwīr al-Miqbās* reveals that all the narrations it contains go back to Muḥammad ibn Marwān (d. 186),[62] Muḥammad ibn al-Sā'ib al-Kalbī,[63] and ᶜAlī ibn Abū Ṣāliḥ.[64] This chain of narration is technically known as *silsilat al-kadhib* (the chain of fabricated narrations).[65] Due to the rejection of this chain, it can safely be stated that *Tanwīr al-Miqbās* is not from Ibn ᶜAbbās.

However, some questions remain without answer: If the work is falsely attributed to Ibn ᶜAbbās, who is its originator? Why did he ascribe it to Ibn ᶜAbbās? And more importantly, what was his purpose in doing so? We can only speculate.

In answer to the first perhaps it was Abū Ṭāhir al-Fayrūzābādī who might have been the original author. As to why, it is assumed to advocate this type of mystical *tafsīr*, and finally as to the purpose, simply to give the text more credence.

Another *tafsīr* which has been ascribed to Ibn ᶜAbbās is that of *Masā'il Nāfiᶜ*[66] (the questions of Nāfiᶜ). This book consists of around two hundred questions which Nāfiᶜ ibn al-Azraq allegedly asks Ibn ᶜAbbās. The story goes that one day whilst Ibn ᶜAbbās was sitting inside the sacred Mosque in Makkah, answering people's questions concerning the meaning of various portions of the Qur'an, Nāfiᶜ and his friend Najdah ibn ᶜUwaymir approach him, with Nāfiᶜ stating: "We have come to ask you about some meanings of the Qu'ran, but we want the answers to be supported by Arabic poetry." Nāfiᶜ reportedly puts before Ibn ᶜAbbās two hundred questions which Ibn ᶜAbbās is said to have replied to, quoting supporting verses from poetry.

This story has been generally accepted by scholars such as Abu al-ʿAbbās Muḥammad ibn Yazīd al-Mubarrid (d. 285), Ibn Ḥajar al-ʿAsqalānī, al-Suyūṭī, Fuad Sezgin, and modern Egyptian scholar Aishah Abd al-Rahman bint al-Shati. The latter read the different manuscripts of *Masā'il* and compared them. While recognizing the problems involved in the text and its *isnād* (chain of transmission), she nevertheless seems to be convinced that the text is genuinely from Ibn ʿAbbās. According to al-Shati: " Ibn ʿAbbās's answers (to Ibn al-Azraq) were presented in the linguistic exegetical literature and in the comprehensive works on the Qur'anic sciences." She concluded her studies with the following note: "The purpose of presenting *Masā'il ibn al-Azraq* [*Masā'il Nāfiʿ*] here, as I mentioned previously, is to address the issue of the Qur'anic miraculous inimitability through the narration of Ibn ʿAbbās's interpretation of the Qur'anic words in *Masā'il ibn al-Azraq*.[67]

On the other hand, Western scholars such as Goldziher, Wansbrough and Andrew Rippin considered the *Masā'il* to be legend or fabrication. Goldziher, who does not present critical analysis to support his rejection, nevertheless describes the *Masā'il* as "ein lehrreiche legende angesetzt" (a scholarly legend).[68] Wansbrough believed the *Masā'il* to be a skilful forgery attributed to Ibn ʿAbbās. In support of this contention he consulted certain Islamic sources, such as *al-Jāmiʿ al-Ṣaḥīḥ*, *Ṣaḥīḥ Muslim*, *Sunan al-Tirmidhī*, and *al-Itqān*, finding in doing so that poetry was only occasionally cited for lexical explanation. In al-Bukhārī's *Masā'il* only one line of poetry was cited in connection with the Qur'anic description (9:114) of Prophet Ibrahīm as "*la-awwāh*" (tender-hearted). In *Ṣaḥīḥ Muslim*, a single verse was adduced, Qur'anic verse 7:31, and in *al-Tirmidhī*, none in an exegetical sense. He concluded that *Masā'il* exhibits an exegetical method considerably inferior to Ibn ʿAbbās's standard.[69] As for Rippin, he relied on Wansbrough's conclusion and declared *Masā'il* a fiction designed to lend the so-called Ibn ʿAbbās *tafsīr* more credence.[70]

And he is not alone. In his *Gharīb al-Qur'ān li Ibn ʿAbbās: Dirāsah Ijtimāʿiyyah lughawiyyah*, Tahir al-Mannai Muhammad Rashad al-Hamzawi also declared *Masā'il* to be a fabrication and even doubted that Ibn ʿAbbās and Nāfiʿ had ever met.

There is further argument to support the issue of fabrication. Al-Mubarrid notes that Nāfiʿ allegedly questioned Ibn ʿAbbās at length, until his patience ran out. At this point, the famous poet ʿUmar ibn Abī Rabīʿah arrives, greets Ibn ʿAbbās and sits down. Ibn ʿAbbās asks Ibn Abī Rabīʿah to recite some of his poems. He recites about eighty verses. Nāfiʿ listening angrily suddenly exclaims: "Oh God. O, Ibn ʿAbbās, we came from a distance to ask you about Islam and you turn your face away listening to foolishness from this young Qurayshī?" Ibn ʿAbbās replies "By God, I have not listened to foolishness." Nāfiʿ responds: "Did he (ʿUmar) not say: '*ra'at rajulan amma idhā al-shams ʿāraḍat fa yaḍḥā wa amma bi al-ʿashiy fa yakhṣar*' (she saw a man, when the sun appears he becomes ignominious and as for at night he suffers from the cold and it pains)?" Ibn ʿAbbās replies: "No he did not say *fa-yakhzā* (to abash), but he said, *fa yad-hā wa bi al-ʿashiy fa yakhsar*". At this point Nāfiʿ asks in amazement: "Did you memorize all of the verses?" "Yes," answers Ibn ʿAbbās adding, and "If you would like to hear all of them I will recite them." When Nāfiʿ replies he would Ibn ʿAbbās recites all the eighty verses.[71]

One has a right to be sceptical, for the number of the questions involved, two hundred, and the manner in which Nāfiʿ is asked throws into question the entire credibility of the story. We could only take it seriously if: a) Nāfiʿ had been well versed in *tafsīr* and the Arabic language; b) had memorized the whole Qur'an or a large portion of it; c) had in advance prepared for the two hundred questions; and d) had a strong memory, which he did not because he misquoted ʿUmar ibn Abī Rabīʿah's last verses mentioned above.

Furthermore, al-Mubarrid mentions that Nāfiʿ plagiarized the two hundred verses of Ibn ʿAbbās's *istishhādāt* (to quote a word or a text for supporting something). Meaning that, if what al-Mubarrid claims is true, then Nāfiʿ must have memorized all the two hundred verses at the time Ibn ʿAbbās recited them, since it is known he (Nāfiʿ) did not write them down. Now, if Nāfiʿ could not memorize properly ʿUmar ibn Abī Rabīʿah's eighty verses, as mentioned above, how could he have memorized these two hundred verses? Hence, we are inclined to doubt the authenticity of the story and are forced to conclude that the *Masā'il* seems to be fiction designed to give more credence to Ibn ʿAbbās's exegesis.

We now present some of Ibn ʿAbbās's exegsis as documented in some major *tafsīr* and hadith works.

In *Fatḥ al-Bārī*, there is an account of a man[72] once appearing before Ibn ʿAbbās and putting forward to him the following: "I find in the Qur'an certain things which seem to me contradictory. For example, Allah says in verse 23:101: 'Then, when the trumpet [of resurrection] is blown, no ties of kinship will on that Day prevail among them, and neither will they ask about one another.' Yet, Allah says in verse 37:27: 'but [since it will be too late,] they will turn upon one another, demanding of each other [to relieve them of the burden of their past sins].' Similarly, in verse 4:42, Allah says: 'Those who were bent on denying the truth and paid no heed to the Apostle will on that Day wish that the earth would swallow them: but they shall not [be able to] conceal from God anything that has happened.' Yet again, we read in verse 6:23: 'Whereupon, in their utter confusion, they will only [be able to] say: "By God, our Sustainer, we did not [mean to] ascribe divinity to aught beside Him!"' According to this verse, the idolaters will hide some facts. Moreover, in verse 79:27: '[O Men!] Are you more difficult to create than the heaven which He has built?' God mentions the creation of the heavens before the creation of the earth. Furthermore He says in verse 41:9–10: 'Say: Is it that ye deny Him Who created the earth in two Days? And do ye join equals with Him? He is the Lord of (all) the Worlds. He set on the (earth), mountains standing firm, high above it, and bestowed blessings on the earth, and measure therein all things to give them nourishment in due proportion, in four Days, in accordance with (the needs of) those who seek (Sustenance).' He mentions in this verse the creation of the earth before the sky. Meanwhile, He says in verse 4:56: 'Verily, God is Almighty, All-Wise,' while in verse 4:23, He says, 'for Allah is Oft-forgiving, Most Merciful,' and in verse 4:58, 'verily, God is All-Hearing, All-Seeing.' It seems to me that the meaning is Allah was Oft-Forgiving and not any more."

The man then asks Ibn ᶜAbbās to clarify his confusion. Ibn ᶜAbbās answers him thus: "As for verse 23:101 ('Then, when the trumpet [of resurrection] is blown, no ties of kinship will on that Day prevail among them...'), this will occur on the first blowing of the trumpet. The trumpet will be blown where upon all that is in the heavens and in the earth will swoon except those whom Allah will exempt. Then there will be no relationship between them, and at that time no one will ask one another questions. Then, when the trumpet is blown for the second time, they will turn to one another and ask questions. Concerning the statement that they never worshipped other deities besides Allah, and that they can hide no facts from Allah, Allah will forgive the sins of those who were sincere in their worship. As for the pagans, they will say (to each other) 'come, let's say we never worshipped other deities besides Allah,' but their mouths will be sealed and their hands will speak (the truth). At that time, it will be evident that no speech can be concealed from Allah and those who disbelieved (and disobeyed the Apostle) will wish that they were level to the ground, for they will not be able to hide facts from Allah. Concerning the idea that Allah created the earth in two days, and that He spread it (the earth), the spreading here means the bringing of water and pasture out of it. (Note this refers to verse 79:30: "And after that, the earth: wide has He spread its expanse"). He then created the mountains, the camels and the hills, and whatever is between them. Hence, (the earth and the heaven) came in two (other) days. Ibn ᶜAbbās states that the meaning of Allah's saying "He spread its expanse" and His saying "And He created the earth in two days" is that, earth and whatever is in it was created in two days. As regards His saying Allah was Oft-Forgiving, this is how Allah refers to Himself, but the contents of His saying is still valid; for if Allah ever wants to do something, He surely fulfills what He wants. So you should not see any contradiction in the Qur'an for all of it is from Allah."[73]

Furthermore, according to al-Ṭabarī, Ibn ᶜAbbās once wrote to a Jewish convert to Islam known as Abū Jallād, asking him about the tree mentioned in verse 2:35: "And We said: 'O Adam, dwell thou and thy wife in this garden, and eat freely thereof, both of you, whatever you may wish; but do not approach this one tree, lest you become wrongdoers'." Abū Jallād wrote back to Ibn ᶜAbbās claiming the tree is an ear of corn "*sunbulah*." Ibn ᶜAbbās also used to ask Kaᶜb al-Aḥbār, a Jewish convert, about some meanings of the Qur'an, for example he asked him concerning the meaning of *Umm al-Kitāb* (The Mother of the Book) and *al-Marjān* (Coral).[74]

Using the sources of the People of the Book in explaining some Islamic concepts in general and *tafsīr* in particular is allowed in Islam. Indeed, reference to Jewish and Christian sources can be made based on the following hadith: "*balligū ᶜannī wa law āyah, wa ḥaddithū ᶜan banī Isrā'īl wa la ḥaraj*"[75] (Transmit to others what you know or hear from me, even though it is only a word, and there is no harm in quoting from *banī Isrā'īl*). *Banī Isrā'īl* in the hadith refers to both Jews and Christians who are Qur'anically speaking called *Ahl al-Kitāb* (the People of Book). It is obvious that the hadith allows Muslims to quote from the People of the Book.

This permission is believed to be given for two reasons. The first is that Judaism, Christianity, and Islam share some fundamental beliefs such as belief in God, the prophets and the day of judgment Heaven as well as other things. The second is that during his lifetime, the Prophet did agree with some of what the people of the book quoted from their scriptures. For example, in *Fatḥ al-Bārī* we read that, "A Jewish Rabbi came to the Prophet of God and said: 'O, Muhammad!

We find that in (the Torah) God will put all the Heavens on one finger and the earth on one finger, and the trees on one finger, and the water and the dust on one finger, and all the other created beings on one finger. Then He will say "I am the King."' Thereupon the Prophet smiled so that his premolar teeth became visible. Then the Prophet recited the verse: (No just estimate have they made of God such as is due to Him, 39:67)."[76]

In *Sunan al-Nasā'ī*, a Jewish man is reported to have approached Prophet Muhammad accusing certain Muslims of *shirk* (polytheism) for stating "*māshā' Allāh wa shi'ta*" (How wonderful that Allah and you (Muhammad) have willed it). Upon hearing this, the Prophet instructed the Companions to say "*māshā' Allāh thumma shi'ta.*" The point being made by the Jewish man was that the letter (*wāw*) in the phrase *māshā Allāh wa shi'ta,* is a coordinating conjunction used to indicate the involvement of more than one party in an action, without necessarily determining which of the parties does the action first. Thus, to say *māshā Allāh wa shi'ta* might mean or be understood as the will of the Prophet being able to possibly come even before the will of God. This contradicts the Islamic concept of *tawḥīd* as in verse 76:30 which states: "But ye will not, except as Allah wills; for Allah is full of Knowledge and Wisdom", meaning that God wills first before anyone else. Thus, to avoid the misconception which the letter *wāw* could lead to, the Prophet commanded the Companions to replace the *wāw* with *thumma* (then), which shows the chronology of the action taking place between two parties, with the action mentioned before *thumma* occuring first, and the verb or name mentioned after *thumma* occuring later. Thus, the phrase *māshā' Allāh wa shi'ta* is rephrased as "*māshā' Allāh thumma shi'ta*" (God willed, then you willed).[77]

Differences in the Companions' Qur'anic Interpretations

Having presented the interpretation of the most prominent exegetes among the *Ṣaḥābah*, it is worth pointing out that the *Ṣaḥābah's* understanding of the Qur'an and its interpretation differed in some cases, mainly pertaining to juridical, theological, historical, and linguistic issues. Ibn Taymiyyah who viewed the Companions' differences to be those of variation rather than contradiction categorised them as broadly of two kinds: expression and illustration.

Expression means to express an idea in different words but the ultimate meaning is one. For example Ibn ʿAbbās interpreted the Qur'anic phrase "*al-Ṣirāṭ al-mustaqīm*" (the straight path) as the religion of God, whilst Ibn Masʿūd interpreted it as the Book of God. Each of these two prominent exegetes are seen to ascribe to the phrase two different meanings, but they mean or imply one thing, this is because both the religion of God and the Book of God are called the straight path.[78]

Illustration can be seen in the Companions' explaining a general term of the Qur'an, by reference to another general term to draw audience's attention to the original term instead of giving a definition in terms of its genus and difference. For example verse 35:32 states:

> Then We have given the Book for inheritance to such of Our Servants as We have chosen: but there are among them some who wrong their own souls; some who follow a middle course; and some who are, by Allah's leave, foremost [*sābiq*] in good deeds; that is the highest Grace.

According to Ibn Taymiyyah previous generations explained this verse with reference to one or more acts of obedience to God. Some stated the *sābiq* to be one who offers prayers at the earliest prescribed time, the *muqtaṣid* as the one offering prayers late but on time, and the *ẓālim* as one who deferred, for instance the evening prayer till the sun begins to set. Others referred to the *sābiq* as a generous person giving money in charity over and above meeting their obligation, the *ẓālim* as the one taking usury or failing to pay the zakah, and the *muqtaṣid* as the one who pays zakah and who refrains from taking usury, and so on.[79]

We next examine the Companions' differences in four areas: fiqh, theology, Qur'anic historical personalities, and linguistics, to see whether Ibn Taymiyyah's claim holds.

Fiqh

This refers to those verses in which the Companions differed in interpretation due to either their individual understanding of a given verse or to lack of knowledge of the Prophet's hadith on a particular issue. For instance, God states in verse 5:5:

> Today, all the good things of life have been made lawful to you. And the food of those who have been vouchsafed revelation aforetime is lawful to you, [14] and your food is lawful to them. And [lawful to you are], in wedlock, women from among those who believe [in this divine writ], and, in wedlock, women from among those who have been vouchsafed revelation before your time...

Based on this verse almost all the Companions declared the permissibility of marriage between Muslim men and Jewish or Christian women. ʿAbd Allāh ibn ʿUmar, however, held a different opinion. Quoting verse 2:221, "Do not marry unbelieving women (idolaters), until they believe" (become Muslim), he pointed out that, "God has forbidden Muslims to marry idolaters, I do not know anything greater than *shirk* and there is no sin greater than to say Jesus is my Lord."[80]

Another example concerns the prescribed waiting period of a pregnant widow or a divorcee before she is allowed to re-marry. This is known as *ʿiddah* in respect of which verse 65:4 stipulates: "and as for those who are with child, the end of their waiting-term (*ʿiddah*) [in case of divorce] shall come when they deliver their burden."

ʿAbd Allāh ibn Masʿūd understood the verse in its general sense, aware of the hadith concerning Subayʿah al-Aslamiyyah, the wife of Saʿd ibn Khawlah, who was pregnant when her husband died.

Immediately after she had given birth, the Prophet informed her that her ʿ*iddah* had been ended by the delivery. Thus, aware of this hadith, Ibn Masʿūd declared the ʿ*iddah* of a pregnant widow/divorcee as terminated with the delivery of the child. On the other hand both, ʿAlī ibn Abī Ṭālib and Ibn ʿAbbās viewed the ʿ*iddah* as being the longer of the 'two ʿ*iddah*s.' What is meant by the 'two' ʿ*iddahs*? According to Islamic Law, when a husband dies, his widow has to observe an ʿ*iddah* period of four months and ten days. Thereafter, she can marry whomever she wishes. The reference for this law is verse 2:234 which reads: "And if any of you die and leave wives behind, they shall undergo, without remarrying, a waiting-period of four months and ten days."

ʿAlī ibn Abī Ṭālib and Ibn ʿAbbās combined the above verse and verse 65:4 which enjoins:

> Now as for such of your women as are beyond, the age of monthly courses, as well as for such as do not have any courses, their waiting-period - if you have any doubt [about it] - shall be three [calendar] months; and as for those who are with child, the end of their waiting-term shall come when they deliver their burden.

ʿAlī ibn Abī Ṭālib and Ibn ʿAbbās inferred from both verses that the ʿ*iddah* of an eight-month pregnant widow is four months and ten days. If a widow is two months pregnant, the ʿ*iddah* is seven months. This is what ʿAlī and Ibn ʿAbbās referred to as *abʿad al-ajalayn* (the longest period of the ʿ*iddahs*).

Qur'anic Historical Personages and Places

The Companions also differed concerning the exact historical personages and places mentioned in certain Qur'anic verses. For example, verse 37:102 states:

> Then, when (the son) reached (the age of) (serious) work with him,

> he (prophet Abraham) said: "O my son! I see in vision that I offer thee in sacrifice: Now see what is thy view!" (The son) said: "O my father! Do as thou art commanded: thou will find me, if Allah so wills one practising Patience and Constancy!"

Which son had God commanded the prophet Abraham to sacrifice? Ismāʿīl or Isḥāq? According to Ibn Kathīr some of the Companions, including Ibn ʿAbbās, considered this to be Isḥāq, while ʿUmar ibn al-Khaṭṭāb, ʿAlī ibn Abī Ṭālib and others believed the son to be Ismāʿīl.[81]

Verse 9:108 illustrates another example of differing interpretation: "Never stand thou forth therein. There is a mosque whose foundation was laid from the first day on piety..." Which Mosque was this? Where was it located? ʿUmar ibn al-Khaṭṭāb, Zayd ibn Thābit and others believed this to be the Prophet's Mosque in Madinah, whereas Ibn ʿAbbās and others believe it to be the Qubā' Mosque,[82] which the Prophet built upon his arrival in Qubā'.

Theology

The Companions held varying theological views on certain subjects when not aware of a particular or explicit Prophetic hadith relating to it. Thus, each one would depend on his own understanding of a verse in question. For example, verse 17:1 states: "Glory to Him (Allah) Who did take His servant for a Journey by night from the Sacred Mosque to the farthest Mosque, whose precincts We did bless."

The Companions differed as to how this journey took place. Did the Prophet travel physically or was it only his soul (*rūḥ*)? Ibn ʿAbbās, Anas ibn Mālik and others, who had knowledge of the hadith in this regard, believed the Prophet to have travelled physically, whilst ʿĀ'ishah, the wife of the Prophet and Muʿāwiyah ibn Abī Sufyān believed it to be his soul.[83] Another example is shown by verse 53:7-9: "appearing in the horizon's loftiest part, and then drew near, and came close, until he was but two bow-lengths away, or even nearer."

Ibn Masʿūd and ʿĀ'ishah relate that, "the verse refers to the Angel Gabriel in the highest of the horizon and that he came closer to a distance of two bow-lengths or nearer to the Prophet. Thus, did God convey the revelation to Muhammad through the Angel Gabriel." Ibn ʿAbbās, on the other hand, was of the opinion that the verse refers to the Prophet coming closer to his Lord by a distance of two bow-lengths or nearer, and that he saw his Lord by his heart, and not with his eyes.[84]

Linguistics

Another factor that influenced the way the Companions interpreted certain Qur'anic passages was the respective dialects of their Arabic language. It is interesting to note the different interpretations ascribed. For instance, in verse 77:1, the term *al-murasalāt* (the ones sent forth) is explained by Abū Hurayrah to mean angels, while Ibn Masʿūd interprets it as referring to the winds.[85] Furthermore, in verse 85:3, the words *shāhid* and *mashhūd* (the witness and the subject of the witness), were interpreted by Abū Hurayrah to mean respectively 'Friday' and 'the day of "ʿ*Arafāt*' during Hajj,[86] whilst Ibn ʿAbbās interpreted *shāhid* to mean the Prophet Muhammad and *mashhūd* as the day of judgment. In this respect, al-Ḥasan ibn ʿAlī, the grandson of the Prophet, supported his uncle Ibn ʿAbbās's view, backing his opinion with verse 4:41 which reads: "How, then, [will the sinners fare on Judgment Day,] when We shall bring forward witnesses from within every community, and bring thee [O Prophet] as witness against them?" The point made by al-Ḥasan ibn ʿAlī was that in this verse, the Qur'an clearly describes the Prophet as a *shāhid* (a witness), thus, *shāhid* in the aforementioned verse refers to the Prophet.[87]

Again with regard to the term *al-ʿādiyāt* in verse 100:1, ʿAlī ibn Abī Ṭālib interprets it as referring to 'camels', while Ibn ʿAbbās interprets it as pertaining to 'horses.'[88] As regards the Qur'anic words "*wa al-shafʿ wa al-watr*" ("By the even and odd (contrasted)") in verse

89:3, both Abū Hurayrah and Ibn ʿAbbās interpret *al-shafʿ* as being the first day of *ʿīd al-aḍḥā* and *al-watr* as referring to the day of *ʿarafāt*. Another report by Ibn Kathīr states that Ibn ʿAbbās interpreted *al-watr* as Allah (God) and *al-shafʿ* as mankind.[89]

Some of these examples of exegetical differences amongst the Companions are irreconcilable. Thus, the argument which claims the differing interpretations of the Companions in *tafsīr* to be merely those of variation rather than contradiction cannot be sustained.

Having presented the Companions' differing interpretations of the Qur'an with supporting examples, what follows next is an overview of their sources and methodology.

Principle Characteristics of the Companions' Tafsīr, Sources, and Methodology

The sources we have consulted with regards to the exegesis of the Companions reveal that in reality they did not interpret the whole Qur'an. The Prophet himself did not explain the whole Qur'an before his death. They exercised their own judgment with regards to further interpretation on the basis that the Qur'an itself encourages Muslims to ponder over its meanings. Thus, the Companions embarked on explaining many verses that included judicial, theological, linguistic and historical considerations, making use of the following six resources in their exegesis:

1) They sometimes used Qur'anic verses to explain other verses, as noted in ʿAlī ibn Abī Ṭālib's *tafsīr*.
2) They occasionally referred to the hadith in support of their Qur'anic interpretation as in the example given in Abū Bakr's *tafsīr*.
3) They would sometimes quote the People of the Book, Jewish and Christian sources to support the meaning of some verses as noted in Ibn ʿAbbās's *tafsīr*.

4) They sometimes let the Qur'an explain itself in a process whereby verses are illustrated by other Qur'anic verses.
5) The Companions had recourse to linguistic skills, the circumstances of the revelation (*asbāb al-nuzūl*) as well as knowledge associated with pre-Islamic religious culture.
6) They occasionally resorted to poetry.

Conclusion

Scholars are divided into two groups concerning the binding authority of the Companions' interpretation. Those who consider the *Ṣaḥābah's* exegesis to be binding include Imam Mālik, Aḥmad, Ibn Ḥanbal, Ibn Taymiyyah and his student Ibn Qayyim. They based their argument mainly on the fact of the Companions' virtues and merits, for they were praised both in the Qur'an and in the hadith, and were witnesses of the Revelation. In addition, they had mastered the language of the Qur'an.

Among those who believed otherwise, that is the Companions' *tafsīr* is not binding, included al-Ghazālī, Ibn Ḥazm and Abū Ḥayyān. The focus of their argument rests on the practicality of the Companions' interpretation which contains irreconcilable contradictions in places. By this is meant that practically *speaking*, to accept as binding the *tafsīr* of the Companions, with their irreconcilable differences, would place the Muslims in a state of perplexity and confusion as such contradictions would necessarily have binding practical application in the various fields of the Muslims' life. Which binding proof should the Muslims accept? How can two binding proofs contradict one another?

See for example the issue of the *ʿiddah* of a pregnant widow discussed earlier. Consider also the example discussed of Qur'anic verse 37:102. Which son had God commanded the Prophet Abraham to sacrifice? Ismāʿīl or Isḥāq? And finally there is the example of the miraculous night journey and the ascension of the Prophet

Muhammad. Was the Prophet's body and soul involved in this journey or was it only his soul?

In sum the Companions' interpretation is without doubt important in understanding the Qur'an and has unquestioned value and intrinsic merit given their proximity to the Prophet and knowledge of the Qur'an.

CHAPTER 5

Tafsīr and Fatwas of the Successors (*Tābiᶜūn*)

SUMMARY

The Successors (the generation after the Companions) also exercised *tafsīr*. The method they employed to interpret the Qur'an involved:
a) using the Qur'an to explain the Qur'an
b) referring to the Sunnah of the Prophet
c) referring to the Hadith
d) their knowledge of Arabic (whether grammar, linguistics, poetry)
e) Personal opinion / ijtihad.

To what extent does their *tafsīr* have definitive authority, that is, is considered binding? This and their differing exegesis on Qur'anic verses and other issues is explored.

IS THE INTERPRETATION of the *Tābiᶜūn* (Successors) also considered binding or not? Our primary concern here is its legal status. A second concern is determining the characteristic and the nature of the *Tābiᶜūn's* interpretation. Unfortunately, the historical materials devoted to the discussion of this issue are not extensive as in the case of the Companions – it naturally following that scholars who did not believe the exegesis of the Prophet's Companions to be binding (i.e. al-Ghazālī, Ibn Ḥazm and others) showed no interest in discussing the authority of the *Tābiᶜūn's* interpretation. Even scholars such as Ibn Qayyim, who upheld the *Tābiᶜūn's tafsīr* as binding proof, did not elaborate much on the position of this interpretation.

Before elaborating on the nature of the *Tābiᶜūn's* exegesis we begin with a definition of the word *Tābiᶜūn*, both linguistically and Islamically.

Tābiʿūn is the plural of *Tābiʿ*. The word *tābiʿ*, an active participle, is derived from the verbal noun *tabaʿa*, meaning to follow. Thus, *tābiʿī* means a person, or a generation, that comes after another one that has gone by; someone, or a generation, that follows or succeeds a previous one – a follower, a successor. Technically, *Tābiʿ* refers to a Muslim who had no direct contact with the Prophet Muhammad (did not see him), but did have direct contact with one of his Companions (meeting him) and died as a Muslim.[1] The *Tābiʿūn*, or Successors, are considered the second generation of Islam, and the best following the Companions.

Debate on the Binding Character of the Successors' Interpretation

The majority of Sunni scholars have agreed upon the fact that the *ijmāʿ* of the Successors is a binding proof (*ḥujjah*). The question then arises as to whether the interpretation or religious fatwa of a single Successor should also be recognized as such. As usual, scholars are divided into two camps concerning this proposition.

The first group, which includes Abū Ḥanīfah, believe the interpretation of the Successors and their religious decrees to be not binding, simply because they did not have the chance of seeing the Prophet or witnessing the Revelation. Abū Ḥanīfah for instance states his position very clearly, "Whatever comes to us from God and the Prophet we accept it without any reservation, but whatever ideas come to us from *Tābiʿūn* they are men just as we are."[2]

Ibn Taymiyyah quotes Shuʿbah ibn al-ʿAjjāj (160-778)[3] to have said, "If the opinion of the *Tābiʿī* in the secondary matters (i.e. judicial issues) is not binding (*ḥujjah*), how then can it be binding in *tafsīr*?"[4] Ibn Taymiyyah supports this opinion by saying "*Wa hātha ṣaḥīḥ*" (and this is correct).[5] For Abū Ḥayyān to accept the *Tābiʿūn's* interpretation is intellectual or scholarly suicide.[6]

The second group includes – according to some reports – Aḥmad Ibn Ḥanbal and some Mālikī jurists, who believed interpretation by the immediate Successors to be binding.[7] However, according to a modern Ḥanbalī jurist, Abd Allah ibn Muhsin al-Turki, most of the Ḥanbalī jurists seemed to believe that the most authentic report to have come from Aḥmad ibn Ḥanbal indicates that the opinions of the *Tābiʿūn* are not binding.[8]

In his *Al-Ṣawāʿiq al-Mursalah*, Ibn Qayyim reasons that the Companions had learned the full meanings and text of the Qur'an from the Prophet, and that as the Successors had then learned the meanings and the words from the Companions, ergo the interpretation of both the Companions and the Successors are equally binding.[9]

Al-Zarkashī points out that although scholars like Shuʿbah ibn al-ʿAjjāj and others viewed the *tafsīr* of the *Tābiʿūn* to be non-binding, their own exegesis and that of other commentators was flawed because they nevertheless relied heavily on the opinions of the *Tābiʿūn*, who received most of their *tafsīr* from the Companions.[10]

Prominent Tābiʿūn and Tafsīr

Muslims believe that God has commanded them to seek knowledge and to teach it. Thus, in Islam, learning and teaching are equally important and inseparable. In this respect, verse 9:122 states:

> With all this, it is not desirable that all of the believers take the field [in time of war]. From within every group in their midst, some shall refrain from going forth to war, and shall devote themselves [instead] to acquiring a deeper knowledge of the Faith and [thus be able to] teach their home-coming brethren, so that these [too] might guard themselves against evil.

A popular hadith relevant to the matter under discussion is "*khayrukum man taʿallama al-Qur'ān wa ʿallamah*" (The best among you are those who have learned the Qur'an and teach it (to others)). From this perspective, the *Tābiʿūn*'s commitment is clear.

Having stated a possible reason for the involvement of the *Tābiʿūn* in interpretation, it is appropriate at this point to present examples of the *tafsīr* of some of the most prominent among them.

Mujāhid ibn Jabr (d. 104-722 AH)

Mujāhid was one of the most outstanding students of Ibn ʿAbbās, and claimed to have thoroughly gone through the whole Qur'an three times with Ibn ʿAbbās.[11] Despite this claim, one can easily observe by reading al-Ṭabarī's *Jāmiʿ al-Bayān*, Ibn Kathīr's *Tafsīr al-Qur'ān al-ʿAẓīm*, and Mujāhid's alleged *tafsīr* (recently printed), that Mujāhid made much less use of Ibn ʿAbbās's commentary than did his other students such as ʿIkrimah al-Barbarī, Saʿīd ibn Jubayr, and al-Daḥḥak ibn Muzāḥim. Mujāhid seems to be more dependent on his own opinion. Hence, he disagreed with the Companions's interpretation of some verses. One example concerns verse 2:30:

> And Lo! Thy Sustainer said unto the angels: "Behold, I am about to establish upon earth a vicegerent." They said: "Wilt Thou place on it such as will spread corruption thereon and shed blood -whereas it is we who extol Thy limitless glory, and praise Thee, and hallow Thy name?" [God] answered: "Verily, I know that which you do not know."

Mujāhid explained "we who extol Thy limitless glory, and praise Thee, and hallow Thy name?" as *nuʿaẓẓimuk wa nukabbiruk* (we aggrandize and magnify You).[12] Similar was his explanation of verses 75:22-23: "Some faces, that Day, will beam (in brightness and beauty); Looking towards their Lord." According to Ibn Kathīr, the Companions and *Tābiʿūn* were unanimously agreed that those dwelling in *Jannah* (Paradise) will see God with their own eyes, using 75:22-23 among the verses referenced to support this opinion.[13]

Mujāhid, on the other hand, interprets these verses as "Muslims will be looking forward to the reward from God." He considered the letter *ilā* (the preposition 'to') as a singular of *ālā'* ('bounties', 'favors', etc.)[14] and not as the term was read by most scholars.

Another example of Mujāhid's *tafsīr* of the Qur'an is his interpretation of verse 2:108 which reads: "Would you, perchance, ask of the Apostle who has been sent unto you what was asked aforetime of Moses?" He explains this verse using the Qur'anic verse 4:153 which states: "And an even greater thing than this did they (the Jews) demand of Moses when they said, 'Make us see God face to face'."

According to Muslim sources on Mujāhid's biography, he is said to have written a *tafsīr* of the entire Qur'an. This alleged manuscript has been published twice recently. Firstly in 1976, under the title *Tafsīr Mujāhid* by Abd al-Rahman al-Surti, a member of *Majmaᶜ al-Buḥūth al-Islāmiyyah* (The Islamic Research Institute), Pakistan, the first scholar to edit the manuscript. Secondly in 1989, by Muhammad Abd al-Salam Muhammad Ali who chose it as the subject of his Ph.D thesis, undertaken at Dār al-ᶜUlūm University, Cairo. Incidentally, Muhammad Abd al-Salam claimed his work to be more scholarly and accurate, recognizing al-Surti's efforts, but stating that he had found many mistakes.[15] Both scholars depended on the manuscript of Dār al-Kutub al-Miṣriyyah.

Western scholars such as Fred Leemhuis and Wansbrough in contrast express doubts as to the authenticity of the manuscript, even rejecting totally the authenticity of any work attributed not only to Mujāhid but to any first century Islamic scholar or *ᶜālim*. Wansbrough compared the Cairo manuscript to Mujāhid's opinion in al-Ṭabarī's *Jāmiᶜ al-Bayān*, examining in addition Mujāhid's method in the context of his own work. It was the discovery of two problems that led him to reject the authenticity of the *tafsīr* ascribed to Mujāhid. These were firstly, that it contained a defective *isnād* (chain of transmission); and secondly, the existence of a conflicting judgment based on a single authority.[16]

Leemhuis seemed to be more critical in this respect than Wansbrough. He examined the Cairo manuscript carefully together with his colleagues and their analysis led them to find that the narration of Abū Nājiḥ, the immediate narrator from Mujāhid, must have taken place around the middle of the second century AH. Lemmhuis comments, "These findings were based on the chain of transmissions as well as textual analyses of the different Mujāhid transmissions."[17]

It seems that Leemhuis undertook this serious examination of Mujāhid's work to refute or challenge Fuat Sezgin's assertion that al-Ṭabarī's work can be used as evidence of an early first century written work because of its dependency on first century literature such as that of *Tafsīr Mujāhid.* (Note, Fuat Sezgin is professor emeritus of the History of Natural Science at Johann Wolfgang Goethe University in Frankfurt, and the assertion that he made was that al-Ṭabarī's *tafsīr* can be used to prove the existence of early first century *tafsīr* because Mujāhid heavily depended on the *Ṣaḥābah's* and *Tābiʿūn's tafsīrs*).

Saʿīd ibn Jubayr (d. 95-714 AH)

Saʿīd was also one of Ibn ʿAbbās's most outstanding students, so much so in fact that Ibn ʿAbbās would even refer people to him with regards to issuing fatwas. This recognition by Ibn ʿAbbās has caused scholars to hold Saʿīd in very high esteem.

According to Ibn Khallikāns's report, Saʿīd disliked writing exegeses. On one occasion when a certain man who admired Saʿīd's knowledge of the Qur'an asked him to write a book on exegeses, he became angry remarking, "*la-an yasquṭ shiqqī Aḥabb ilayya min dhālik*" (I would rather lose a part or half of my body than do that).

Saʿīd would refer to Ibn ʿAbbās when it came to understanding the meaning of the Qur'an or knowledge of the occasions of revelation. For example, concerning verse 8:1: "They will ask thee about the spoils of war" he asks Ibn ʿAbbās as to the occasion of its revelation, with Ibn ʿAbbās responding that the verse referred to the booty gained by the Muslims following the Makkans' defeat in the battle of Badr.[18] Another example is in regard to verse 2:243:

> Art thou not aware of those who forsook their homelands in their thousands for fear of death-whereupon God said unto them, "Die," and later brought them back to life? Behold, God is indeed limitless in His bounty unto man – but most people are ungrateful.

According to Saʿīd, Ibn ʿAbbās numbered the people referred to in this verse as four thousand, stating that they had left their homes out of fear of the plague, and that when they had reached a certain place, God took their souls.[19]

Yet, despite Saʿīd's dependency on Ibn ʿAbbās's *tafsīr,* he also exercises his own opinion in exegesis an example of which can be seen in reference to verse 2:178:

> O you who have attained to faith! Just retribution is ordained for you in cases of killing: the free for the free, and the slave for the slave, and the woman for the woman.

Saʿīd states the *qiṣāṣ* 'victim retribution' is to be applied only in the case of intentional murder. He furthermore, gives an account of the background of the verse commenting that it concerned two Arab tribes who shortly before the arrival of Islam had fought with each other leaving many innocents, including women and slaves, killed. As the dispute continued despite the emergence of Islam and their conversion to it thus, God thus revealed this verse which discusses of *al-qiṣāṣ.*

ʿIkrimah al-Barbarī (d. 105-723 AH)

ʿIkrimah was one of the students of Ibn ʿAbbās who claimed that there was no verse in the Qur'an whose meaning he did not know. He transmitted a considerable portion of Ibn ʿAbbās's knowledge.[20]

Below are Qur'anic interpretations of three verses showing ʿIkrimah's relationship to Ibn ʿAbass.

The first refers to Qur'anic verse 2:198: "And when you surge downward in multitudes from Arafat, remember God at the holy place." ʿIkrimah narrates that Ibn ʿAbbās stated a specific time that Muslims should depart from ʿArafāt to Muzdalifah" (two sacred places).[21] He attributes to Ibn ʿAbbās the following statement: "During the days of *Jāhiliyyah* (pre-Islam days) the people of *al-Jāhiliyyah* used to stand at *ʿArafāt* until the sun was about to set, then they departed."[22]

He also narrates that Ibn ʿAbbās indicated the actual number of the People of the Cave mentioned in Qur'anic verse 18:22 although, the Qur'an is silent on this: "Say: 'My Sustainer knows best how many they were. None but a few have any [real] knowledge of them...'" ʿIkrimah reports Ibn ʿAbbās as stating, "I am one of those few who know the exact number of the People of the Cave, they were seven." Ibn Kathīr regards this transmission from Ibn ʿAbbās as authentic.[23]

With regards to the meaning of verse 65:1: "O Prophet! When you [intend to divorce women, divorce them with a view to the waiting period appointed for them (*ʿiddah*)," ʿIkrimah comments that *al-ḥayḍ* is *ṭuhr* "purification" (when a women finishes her monthly period). He further elaborates: "One should divorce his wife when her pregnancy is clear without doubt."[24]

Qatādah ibn Duʿāmah al-Sadūsī (d.110-728 AH)

Qatādah was one of the most outstanding exegetes among the immediate successors. Indeed, Ibn Kathīr quotes Qatādah heavily in his *tafsīr*, his name appearing in almost every page of *Tafsīr al-Qur'ān al-ʿAẓīm*. It seems that Qatādah relied more on his own opinion than those of the Prophet's Companions. His mastery of the Arabic language was reflected in his exegesis. For example, we find him using in his explanation of some Qur'anic passages the terms *taqdīm* 'preposition' and *ta'khīr* 'a subject placed in delayed position'. These are terms or concepts which have been developed by later generations, mainly by ʿAbd Al-Qāhir al-Jurjānī, al-Zamakhsharī and others and used as one of the tools to illustrate '*Iʿjāz al-Qur'ān* (the inimitability of the Qur'an).[25] An example of this can be seen in relation to verse 9:55: "Let not, then, their worldly goods or [the happiness which they may derive from] their children excite thy admiration: God but wants to chastise them by these means in this worldly life..." Qatādah explains the verse by stating that there is *taqdīm* and *ta'khīr* in the verse. He places worldly life earlier up in the *āyah* due to the principle of *taqdīm* and *ta'khīr*, thus, rephrasing the verse as: "Let not, then, their worldly goods or [the happiness which they may derive from] their children excite thy admiration in this worldly life. God wants only to punish them by means of their wealth and children."[26]

Qatādah also occasionally referred to the Arab metaphorical expression to support the meaning of a Qur'anic word he intended to explain. For example, concerning verse 74:4: "And thy garments keep free from stain!" he states, "*wa kānat al-ʿArab tusammī al-rajul idhā nakatha wa lam yafī bi ʿahd Allāh innahu ladanis al-thiyāb*" (Arabs brand a person who violates his oath and does not fulfill the covenant of God as a person with a dirty garment).[27]

Concerning Qur'anic verse 2:37: "Thereupon Adam received words [of guidance] (*kalimāt*) from his Sustainer, and He accepted his repentance: for, verily, He alone is the-Acceptor of Repentance, the Dispenser of Grace." Qatādah quotes another Qur'anic passage to explain the meaning of *kalimāt* "words." This is verse 7:23: "The two replied: 'O our Sustainer! We have sinned against ourselves - and unless Thou grant us forgiveness and bestow Thy mercy upon us, we shall most certainly be lost!'"

Qatādah and other Successors to the Prophet sometimes made a comment concerning the meaning or implication of a verse without interpreting it. For example, regarding verse 43:5: "[O you who deny the truth!] Should We, perchance, withdraw this reminder (Qur'an) from you altogether, seeing that you are people bent on wasting your own selves?" Qatādah states: "I swear, had God turned away His Book when the first few of this community rejected it, they could have been perished, but Allah, The Exalted, out of His mercy, did not do so, instead He called them to it for the period of twenty-three years."[28]

Masrūq al-Ajdaʿ (d. 63-681 AH)

Masrūq was one of the recognized scholars of the Iraqi school of *tafsīr* and fiqh. He studied under several of the Prophet's Companions and stated that he found the knowledge of the Companions to be like "a river. A river quenches one man's thirst, a river quenches two men's thirst, a river quenches ten men's thirst, a river quenches a hundred men's thirst, and a river can quench the thirst of the whole of mankind. That is ʿAbd Allāh ibn Masʿūd."[29]

After establishing his position as a student under ʿAbd Allāh ibn Masʿūd, he further went on to explain how long they would sometimes spend in learning from him, "ʿAbd Allāh used to take a whole day to explain to us a chapter of the Qur'an."[30]

Ibn ʿAbbās was one of the Companions that Masrūq learned from. One of the verses, which Ibn ʿAbbās commented on for Masrūq pertained to a verse discussed in Ibn ʿAbbās's exegesis, which mentions someone whom God had blessed with knowledge of signs [*āyāt*], but who did not use the gift of that knowledge. The verse 7:175: "And tell them what happens to him to whom We vouchsafe Our messages and who then discards them: Satan catches up with him, and he strays, like so many others, into grievous error." Masrūq quotes Ibn ʿAbbās as naming the person, although the Qur'an and hadith are silent on this. The name of the person according to Masrūq's narration is Balʿam ibn Na'tira.[31]

Masrūq also narrated from ʿĀ'ishah, the wife of the Prophet. An instance of this concerns verse 2:275 and the prohibition of selling alcohol:

> Those who gorge themselves on usury behave but as he might behave whom Satan has confounded with his touch; for they say, "Buying and selling is but a kind of usury" - the while God has made buying and selling lawful and usury unlawful..

The Prophet went to the Mosque where he read the verse to his Companions. Then, he forbade the selling of alcohol.

Al-Ḥasan al-Baṣrī (d. 110-728 AH)

Al-Ḥasan was known as an influential preacher. He was pious, trustworthy and knowledgeable in both the Qur'an and the Sunnah. Abū Jaʿfar al-Bāqir described his speech to be just like that of the Prophet's.[32] Al-Ṭabarī, Ibn Kathīr and other *mufassirūn* depended immensely on his *tafsīr*. Like his contemporaries, al-Ḥasan seemed to use much of his own opinion in his *tafsīr*. For example, in interpreting verse 25:63, "And the servants of (Allah) Most Gracious are those who walk on the earth in humility, and when the ignorant address them, they say, 'Peace!'" al-Ḥasan states:

> When Islam came to the believers (the Companions) from God, they believed in it and certainly took it into their hearts; thus, their hearts, their bodies, and their eyes became humble. I swear, when I saw them, it seemed to me that I had actually seen that the description of the verse matched them. I swear by God they were neither argumentative people nor corrupt. When the command of God came to them, they accepted it and applied it. As a result, God identified them with a beautiful description. If the ignorant people addressed them foolishly, they were very gentle. In the morning, they accompanied the servants of God. At night, they spent most of the time praying, crying out of the fear of God.

Other examples: One day al-Ḥasan was asked about the meaning of verse 78:22-23: "For the transgressors a place of destination: They will dwell therein for ages." He answered "*amma maʿnā al-aḥqāb fa laysa lahu ʿiddah illā al-khulūd fī al-nār*" (As for the meaning of *aḥqāb*, it does not have a specific period of time except dwelling in hell fire forever). In relation to the meaning of verse 2:30: "Behold, thy Lord said to the angels: 'I will create a vicegerent on earth.' They said: 'Wilt Thou place therein one who will make mischief therein and shed blood...'"?

Al-Ḥasan merely interpreted this verse using his own opinion stating: "God said to the angels I will create a vicegerent on earth, which means that he informed them about it and inspired them to predict that mankind would make mischief therein and shed blood because there had already existed on the earth the *Jinn* who had actually made mischief and shed blood." Hence, the angels' question, "Wilt Thou place therein one who will make mischief therein and shed blood...?" We also find al-Ḥasan, like many *Tābiʿūn* giving an account on the occasions of a revelation without making any reference to his source. For example, concerning the context of the revelation of verse 31:6: "But there are, among men, those who purchase idle tales, without knowledge (or meaning), to mislead (men) from the Path of Allah and throw ridicule (on the Path)," al-Ḥasan indicates that the verse was revealed concerning music and the flute.[33]

Zayd ibn Aslam (d. 136-754 AH)

Zayd was an outstanding exegete of the Madinah school of *tafsīr*. His reputation lies in the fact that he heavily relied on his independent opinion (al-*Ra'y*) in his *tafsīr*. This notion was documented in major books containing his biography.[34] But when we read major works of exegesis such as al-Ṭabarī's *Jāmiʿ al-Bayān,* Ibn Kathīr's *Tafsīr al-Qur'ān Al-ʿAẓīm,* al-Rāzī's *Mafātīḥ al-Ghayb,* al-Qurṭubī's *Al-Jāmiʿ li Aḥkām al-Qur'ān*, and others, we find comparatively fewer quotations from Zayd. I found Zayd's son, ʿAbd al-Raḥmān, mentioned more than his father in Ibn Kathīr's *tafsīr*. Does this mean Zayd's exegeses were lost? Or was it that they were very brief? Or was it that his students did not quote extensively from his *tafsīr*? Perhaps the last assumption is the most likely.

Nevertheless, Zayd was considered as one of the leading exegetes of the *Tābiʿūn*. In one of his interpretations, Zayd states in regard to the meaning of verse 2:195: "And spend of your substance in the cause of Allah, and make not your own hands contribute to (your) destruction; but do good; for Allah loveth those who do goods," that there existed a group of men in the Prophet's army who did not spend anything from their own wealth. Hence, God commanded them to spend their money for the Jihad.[35] To note is that Zayd mentions here the background of the verse, without mentioning his source. In relation to the meaning of verse 6:65: "Say: 'He hath power to send calamities on you..'." Zayd quotes the Prophet Muhammad to have explained it saying: "*lā tarjiʿū baʿdī kuffār yaḍrib baʿḍukum riqāb baʿḍ bi al-sayf*" (Do not become after my death disbelievers, some of you killing others with swords).[36]

Needless to say, Zayd never met the Prophet; therefore, he should have mentioned his source of information. This type of transmission is technically called *hadith mursal*.[37] More light on Zayd's interpretations will be shed along with those of other *Tābiʿūn* to the Prophet when their different opinions in exegeses is discussed.

Rāfiʿ ibn Maḥram Abū al-ʿĀliyah (d. 90-708 AH)

Unlike many of his contemporaries, Abū al-ʿĀliyah appeared to depend massively on the narrations of others in his exegesis,[38] especially Ubay ibn Kaʿb, who was one of his teachers. For instance Abū al-ʿĀliyah quotes from Ubay concerning the *tafsīr* of verse 7:172:

> When thy Lord drew forth from the Children of Adam - from their loins - their descendants, and made them testify concerning themselves, (saying): "Am I not your Lord (who cherishes and sustains you)?" - They said: "Yea! We do testify!"

According to Ubay, "[Before this life] God gathered all the children of Adam that will be on earth until the Day of Judgment and created them in their physical nature [and asked them the question as in the verse]."

Concerning the meaning of calamities in verse 6:65: "Say: 'He hath power to send calamities on you..'" Abū al-ʿĀliyah quotes Ubay to have said:

> There are four calamities. Two of them have already occurred after twenty-five years of the death of the Prophet and others will undoubtedly happen. The two that have not yet occurred are *al-rajm* (stoning from the heaven) and *al-khasf* (swallowing up by the earth).[39]

Despite his massive dependence on the transmission from the Companions, Abū al-ʿĀliyah utilized his own opinion in interpreting some Qur'anic passages. For example, he comments on verse 2:27: "Those who break Allah's Covenant after it is ratified, and who sunder what Allah Has ordered to be joined..." stating that, "this verse referred to the hypocrites." He further states that there exist six types of hypocritical behaviors which the hypocrites display when they are victorious: when they talk they lie; when they make a promise they do not fulfill it; when they are entrusted with something they practice betrayal; they break God's covenant; they sunder what God commands to be joined together; and they cause mischief on earth.

Having introduced some of the prominent exegetes among the *Tābiʿūn*, and their work, examined next is differences between them in five key areas: fiqh, theology, Qur'anic historical personages, linguistics, and Qur'anic phrases.

Differences in the Qur'anic Interpretations of the *Tābiʿūn*

Fiqh

Differences among the issues in the legal implications of verses may have been caused by differing understandings of the implication of those verses, a lack of knowledge of the Prophet's sayings concerning related issues, or dependence on weak hadith.

One example illustrating lack of knowledge of the Prophet's saying on a specific issue can be seen in relation to verse 2:196: "And complete the Hajj or *ʿumrah* in the service of Allah. But if ye are prevented (From completing it), send an offering for sacrifice, such as ye may find, and do not shave your heads until the offering reaches the place of sacrifice."[40]

The Prophet has specified in hadith (agreed upon by al-Bukhārī and Muslim) how many days one should fast and how many poor people one should feed when one is prevented from performing Hajj or *ʿumrah*. However, we find the *Tābiʿūn* differing concerning the number of days one should fast and the number of poor people one should feed. Mujāhid adhered to the saying of the Prophet which was to fast three days and feed six poor people, while al-Ḥasan al-Baṣrī and ʿIkrimah stated that one should fast ten days and feed ten poor people.[41] Perhaps both al-Ḥasan and ʿIkrimah did not have the knowledge of the Prophet's hadith in this regard or they were confused with the case of one who is performing the Hajj but cannot afford to offer a sacrifice. In such a situation one must fast ten days.

Another example involving lack of knowledge of certain hadith concerns Qur'anic verse 2:158: "Behold! Safa and Marwa are among the Symbols of Allah. So if those who visit the House in the Season or at other times, should compass them round, it is no sin in them."

The majority of the *Tābiʿūn* believed compassing al-Ṣafā and al-Marwah to be one of the principles of the Hajj, with failure to circumambulate them rendering the pilgrimage invalid, supporting their understanding of the verse with many hadith, including: "*isʿaw fa inna Allāh kataba ʿalaykum al-saʿy*" (Walk between al-Ṣafā and al-Marwah because the *saʿy* [special running movement] is prescribed for you by Allah).[42] Mujāhid, al-Ḥasan, and Qatādah held *al-saʿy* to be not obligatory in support of which opinion they quote verse 2:158 stressing that God did not say one must circumambulate them, but that He stated there is no blame on someone if he does so.[43]

Qur'anic Historical Personages and Places

This concerns Qur'anic references to individual personalities whose actual names are not given. The *Tābiʿūn* nevertheless tried to identify them in one way or another (probably referring to the Torah and the New Testament) and not surprisingly differed as to who they were. An example of this concerns verse 2:246:

> Hast thou not Turned thy vision to the Chiefs of the Children of Israel after (the time of) Moses? they said to a prophet (That was) among them: "Appoint for us a king,..."

The Qur'an does not mention the name of this prophet of Israel, but some of the *Tābiʿūn*, i.e. Mujāhid, Qatādah, al-Suddī and others, tried to do so, with Mujāhid stating it was Ṣāmwīl ibn Bālī, Qatadah that it was Yūshaʿ ibn Nūn, and al-Suddī naming him as Shāmʿūn.[44]

Another example is verse 27:40: "Said one who had knowledge of the Book: 'I will bring it to thee within the twinkling of an eye!'" meaning the throne of the Queen of Sheba. Who offered to bring the throne? Although the Qur'an does not mention a name Qatādah nevertheless indicates that it was Āṣif or Balkh, while according to Mujāhid it was Asṭūm.[45]

Theology

This aspect of exegetical variance refers to the *Tābiʿūns'* own understanding of a Qur'anic verse and its interpretation without depending on a hadith or statement from the *Ṣaḥābah*. An example of this interpretation can be seen in verse 4:159: "And there is none of the People of the Book (Jews and Christians) but must believe in him [Jesus] before his death (*qabla mawtihi*)." The *ḍamīr* pronoun *"hi"* meaning *his* in the phrase *qabla mawtihi* (before his death) can refer to an individual of the People of the Book or to Jesus. If the pronoun "he" refers to an individual of the People of the Book, the meaning of the verse would be that all of the People of the Book must certainly believe in Jesus as a Messenger of God before he (the individual) dies. If, however, the pronoun refers to Jesus, then the meaning would be that there are "none of the People of the Book but must believe in him before his death."

Qatādah and Mujāhid were of the former opinion. However, al-Ḥasan al-Baṣrī restricted People of the Book to refer to the Negus (king of Abyssinia) and his people, whilst ʿIkrimah interpreted the verse to mean that each member of the People of the Book had to believe in the Prophet Muhammad before his death (*lā yamūt al-Naṣrānī wa lā-al-yahūdī ḥattā yu'min bi Muḥammad*). Both al-Ṭabarī and Ibn Kathīr rejected al-Ḥasan and ʿIkrimah's interpretation whilst confirming Qatādah's.[46]

Another difference of interpretation relates to the meaning of Qur'anic verse 6:103: "No vision can grasp Him, but His grasp is over all vision: He is above all comprehension, yet is acquainted with all things." ʿIkrimah interprets this to mean that one can see God "in the hereafter," but one cannot grasp Him, similar to the way in which one sees a cloud, but cannot grasp it. According to al-Suddī and Mujāhid however nothing and no one can see God.[47]

Another example of differences in opinion concerning theological issues can be seen in relation to verse 13:39: "Allah doth blot out or confirm what He pleaseth: with Him is the Mother of the Book." Saʿīd ibn Jubayr uses another Qur'anic verse to explain the meaning of this one, namely verse 2:284: "He forgiveth whom He pleaseth, and punisheth whom He pleaseth." Qatādah on the other hand indicates that verse 13:39 is similar to verse 2:106: "None of Our revelations do We abrogate or cause to be forgotten, but We substitute something better or similar."[48]

Linguistics

This concerns individual words or terms which the *Tābiᶜūn* understood differently according to their own varying linguistic backgrounds. More interestingly, they also differed in terms of the origin of some Qur'anic words allegedly derived from foreign languages. For example, the word "*al-Ṣamad*" in verse 112:2 has been interpreted in a variety of ways: Zayd ibn Aslam sees it as *al-Sayyid* (the master), Qatādah understands it as *al-Bāqī baᶜd khalqih* (one who outlasts His creation), ᶜIkrimah explains it as *alladhī lam yakhruj minhu shay' wa lā yuṭᶜam* (one who does not expel waste or needs to be fed),[49] al-Rabīᶜ ibn Anas states it to mean *alladhī lam yalid wa lam yūlad* (He who begets not, nor has been begotten),[50] and finally according to Mujāhid, Saᶜīd ibn Jubayr, al-Suddī, and al-Dahhāk *al-Ṣamad* is *nūr yatala'la'* (a light that shines)[51]

Another example of linguistic difference in understanding is verse 36:1: "*Yāṣīn.*" What does this word mean? ᶜIkrimah, al-Daḥḥhāk and al-Ḥasan explained it as *Yā insān* (O man), with Saᶜīd ibn Jubayr (who was of Abyssinian background) confirming this meaning stating *hu wa kadhālika fī lughat al-ḥabashiyyah* (it is so in the language of Abyssinia). Zayd ibn Aslam on the other hand indicates that it is *ism min asmā' Allāh Taᶜalā* (it is one of Allah's names).[52]

Then there is the word *al-zaytūn* in Qur'anic verse 95:1. Kaᶜb al-Aḥbār and Qatadah believe it to refer to the sacred Mosque in Jerusalem, while Mujāhid and ᶜIkrimah indicate that it is the olive that is known.[53]

Finally we look at the meaning and linguistic origin of the Qur'anic phrase "*hayt lak*" in verse 12:23. According to Mujāhid and others it means seduction, whilst ᶜIkrimah, al-Ḥasan, and Qatādah state it is of the Syrian dialect or language and means *ᶜalayka* (come on). Al-Suddī mentions it is from the Coptic language and means "come on."[54] Al-Bukhārī attributes to ʿIkrimah the idea that it means "come on" in the language of the *Hurān*.[55]

Qur'anic Phrases

This category relates to terms in the Qur'an which the *Tābiʿūn* have interpreted differently due to a lack of knowledge of hadith that mentions the meaning of these phrases or because there were no hadith concerning difficult phrases, leading to each individual using his own opinion or knowledge in explaining the meaning. Thus the phrase in verse 15:87: "And, indeed, We have bestowed upon thee seven of the oft repeated [verses], and [have, thus, laid open before thee] this sublime Qur'an," has been interpreted differently. For students of Ibn ʿAbbās, mainly Mujāhid, Saʿīd ibn Jubayr and al-Daḥḥāk, along with their teacher Ibn ʿAbbās, it meant the seven longest chapters of the Qur'an. On the other hand, for al-Ḥasan al-Baṣrī and Qatādah, and eventually also Mujāhid (as he once held the former opinion), *al-sabʿ al-mathānī* meant *al-fātiḥah* (the first *sūrah* of the Qur'an) only. They quote a hadith found in *al-Bukhārī* to support this interpretation, whilst those holding the former opinion did not refer to any hadith.[56]

Ibn Kathīr supported the latter interpretation, referring also to the hadith in *al-Bukhārī*, and stating in regards to the meaning of *al-sabʿ al-mathānī* that "*hādha naṣṣ fī anna al-fātiḥah, (huwa) al-sabʿ al-mathānī wa al-Qur'ān al-ʿaẓīm*" (this is a clear statement that *al-fātiḥah* is the *al-sabʿ al-mathānī* and the sublime Qur'an).[57]

Al-Daḥḥāk explains the meaning of verse 75:29: "And one leg will be joined with another" as two things that come together for someone who has died, these two things being the people who prepare the body for burial and the angels preparing his soul. Al-Ḥasan al-Baṣrī, on the other hand, interprets it literally stating "*humā sāqāka idhā iltaffatā*" (they are your legs when they are joined). In other narrations, al-Ḥasan al-Baṣrī states: "They are your two legs when they are wrapped in the sheet." ʿIkrimah understands the meaning of verse 75:29 as *al-amr al-ʿaẓīm bi al-amr al-ʿaẓīm* ("a significant matter is joined with another significant matter"), and as for Mujāhid, the verse means calamity joined with another calamity.[58]

Having introduced some of the interpretations and exegesis of the *Tābiʿūn*, including their differences, we now turn to the characteristics, sources, and methodology of their exegesis.

Principal Characteristics of the *Tābiʿūns'* *Tafsīr*, Sources, and Methodology

Despite the claims that some *Tābiʿūn* such as Mujāhid, Saʿīd ibn Jubayr and others wrote exegeses, their texts did not cover all the verses of the Qur'an. Generally speaking, the *tafsīr* of the *Tābiʿūn* was simple and clear. It included very few quotations from poetry to support the definition of Qur'anic text, and whilst grammatical analyses are lacking, some of them, such as Qatādah did provide rhetorical and linguistic observations of some verses. They also explained a considerable number of individual words (the scope and purposes of which lie outside the purpose of this research).[59]

The *Tābiʿūn* primarily used three sources for their exegesis. One was the Qur'an. Sometimes they used Qur'anic verses to explain other Qur'anic verses, as pointed out earlier in Saʿīd ibn Jubayr's and Qatadah's interpretation of Qur'anic verses 13:39, and 2:37.

The second source was the *Ṣaḥābah,* to whom the Successors referred extensively in their exegeses. All the hadiths they employed came from the Prophet's Companions, and almost all their *tafsīr* quoted the *Ṣaḥābah.*

The third source was independent opinion. Although the *Tābiʿūn* relied heavily on the Companions for their *tafsīr*, they also employed their own independent opinion (as already illustrated), because of which they differed in their understanding of some verses.

One other source they utilized for their interpretation of the Qur'an was the *isrā'īliyyāt*, especially the students of Ibn ʿAbbās. Thus, in his *Fajr al-Islām*, Ahmed Amin states that the *tafsīr* of the *Tābiʿūn* was especially influenced by *isrā'īliyyāt*.[60] Al-Dhahabi and Adnan Nana list the most prominent sources of the *Isrā 'īliyyāt* at the time of the *Ṣaḥābah* and the *Tābiʿūn* as being Kaʿb al-Aḥbār, who was of Jewish origin, and Wahb ibn Munabih who had a Christian background.[61]

In many cases, the *Tābiʿūn* did not mention their sources when discussing *asbāb al-nuzūl*. Islamic methodology requires that sources of information be stated. This was particularly important for the generation of the *Tābiʿūn*, who were dependent on narratives and cautious about their authenticity. This caution was necessary due to the heavy fabrication in hadith which took place after the assassination of the third Caliph ʿUthmān ibn ʿAffān. The *Tābiʿūn* sometimes used Qur'anic verses to explain other Qur'anic verses and also used hadith as a support in explaining the Qur'anic verses. They also quoted their teachers and the Companions, although, they occasionally differed with their teachers' interpretations.

Conclusion

Realistically speaking, it is not easy to give a true concept or picture of the exegetical works of the *Tābiʿūn*. The existing works of some individuals, like that of the *tafsīr* of Mujāhid, are still questionable. Thus, the exegeses of the *Tābiʿūn* found in classical works of *tafsīr*, such as al-Ṭabarī's *Jāmiʿ al-Bayān* and Ibn Kathīr's *Tafsīr al-Qur'ān al-ʿAẓīm*, were never critically analyzed to determine their authenticity. Such is the case with the *tafsīr* of the *Ṣaḥābah*. This is why one finds two or sometimes more than two contradictory reports or interpretations ascribed to the same exegete.

Muslim scholars are divided into two groups in terms of the binding authority of the *Tābiʿūn* exegesis. Most believe their exegesis to be not *ḥujjah* as they did not meet the Prophet in person or witness the circumstances surrounding the revelation.

Others hold that as the exegetical works of the *Tābiʿūn* are based on the knowledge they acquired from the *Ṣaḥābah* they thus have equal standing with the work of the *Ṣaḥābah* as binding proof, because whatever knowledge the *Tābiʿūn* acquired would have been the same as that of their teachers.

Ultimately, it seems that the justifications and reasons provided by both sides hardly rest on scholastic credentials, but rather are based solely on the fact or merit of having lived at the time of the Prophet and having had contact with him.

CHAPTER 6

Tafsīr Based on Opinion

Al-Tafsīr bi al-Ra'y

SUMMARY

This is Qur'anic exegesis based on hadith and reasoning (ijtihad) and is a highly controversial area of *tafsīr*. Arguments put forward by proponents and opponents of *al-Tafsīr bi al-Ra'y* are examined as well as to what extent it is permissible, and under what conditions it is acceptable, as a form of interpretation. *Al-Tafsīr bi al-Ra'y* is divided into two categories each of which is closely analysed:

- *Al-tafsīr bi al-ra'y al-maḥmūd* (praiseworthy *tafsīr*) defined as interpretation by independent opinion which does not conflict with the Prophet's explanation of the Qur'an, or an established principle of Islam, and conforms with the Arabic language.
- *Al-tafsīr bi al-ra'y al-madhmūm* (blameworthy *tafsīr*) criticized as it does not consult properly authentic sources and defined as exegesis undertaken without proper knowledge of the sources of *tafsīr*, the Shariʿah, and sound knowledge of Arabic.

Terms and Definitions

ACCORDING TO ARABIC LEXICONS the word *ra'y* is a verbal noun. It has a variety of meanings, rendered as to see with eyes, with the mind, to reflect, to suppose.[1] According to Muslim grammarians and linguists such as Ibn Hishām al-Anṣārī and Ibn Mālik, the word *ra'ā* is derived from *ra'y*, and is a transitive verb which takes one or two direct objects. If referring to one direct object, it means to see with the eyes, i.e. *ra'aytu Zayd* meaning "I saw Zayd" (literally) with (my) eyes. If referring two direct objects it means to see with the mind or to suppose,[2] i.e. *ra'aytu Allāh Akbar min kulli shay'*, meaning literally I saw God greater than everything, or I believed that God is greater than everything, the verb *ra'ā* here meaning to believe because it takes two direct objects.

In the Qur'an, we find the term *ra'y* used in different forms (past, present, and as verbal noun) to denote the same lexical sense. For example, in verse 6:76, "When the night covered him over, he saw a star," the term *ra'ā* (he saw) is used to mean sighting with the eye.[3] Elsewhere in verse 8:48 we read, "lo! I see what ye see not," with *ra'y* used here to mean seen through the eyes. In the Prophetic hadith we find that *ra'y* is used in two senses; one as personal opinion, and two, as an equivalent to ijtihad (self exertion). With reference to the former we have a report from Ibn Isḥāq (d. 213 or 218) in which he states concerning the battle of Badr[4] that the Prophet assigned the Companions to camp at a specific place before the battle. Ḥabbāb ibn al-Mundhir asks the Prophet whether Allah inspired him to camp there or was it "just *ra'y* and a war stratagem and matter of consultation?" The Prophet replies that it was *ra'y* and a war strategem.[5]

With reference to *ra'y* used in hadith in the second sense we have the well-known narration of Muʿādh ibn Jabal. This being that when the Prophet delegated him to Yemen to invite people to Islam he asked Muʿadh, "By what would you judge people?" Muʿadh replies, "By the book of God." And if he found no answer therein questions the Prophet? "I will consult the Prophet's tradition" And if he still found no answer, then? "I will exert my mind (*ajtahid bi ra'yi*)" Muʿadh responds.[6] Using personal opinion is used here in conjunction with ijtihad.

At the time of the Companions, the term *ra'y* was also used with reference to two different meanings. First, as an independent personal opinion in the absence of a clear indication from the Qur'an or the Prophet's tradition. Second, as an equivalent to *qiyās* (analogical deduction). In his *Iʿlām al-Muwaqqiʿīn,* Ibn Qayyim reports ʿAbd Allāh ibn Masʿūd as stating: "If a legal issue is brought before you, and you do not find answers for it in the book of God, in the tradition of the Prophet, or in the statements of his Companions, then use your own personal opinion."[7]

A similar statement has been attributed to ʿUmar ibn al-Khaṭṭāb. In his letter containing instructions to Abū Mūsā al-Ashʿarī, ʿUmar advises: "When a case is presented before you and you find no clear answer to it from the Qur'an, or the tradition of the Prophet, then use your mind and analogy and weigh the case against them."[8] In this statement, *ra'y* is used as equivalent to *qiyās*.

During the era of the *Tābiʿūn*, the emergence of various politico-theological groups in Islam led to the term *ra'y* beginning to connote exegesis that was sectarian or *bidʿah*. Hence, exegesis *bi al-ra'y* eventually came to denote Qur'anic interpretation that had no basis in the tradition of the Prophet or his Companions. Thus, *ra'y* became a term of disparagement in relation to exegesis. For example, we have the case of a man once accusing Mujāhid of using *ra'y* in interpreting the Qur'an, with Mujāhid rejecting the accusation and literally crying stating: "I would not dare do that; I have learned Qur'anic exegesis from about nineteen Companions of the Prophet."[9]

ʿUbayd Allāh, a grandson of ʿUmar ibn-Khaṭṭāb, was once asked as to his opinion concerning Zayd ibn Aslam (an outstanding successor exegete of Madinah). He replies, "I do not find anything wrong with him, except that he interprets the Qur'an using his own personal opinion."[10] ʿIkrimah al-Barbarī and al-Daḥḥāk ibn Muzāḥim, were both accused by al-Naẓẓām ibn Yassār (d.450) (an outstanding Muʿtazilite) of using *ra'y*. In leveling this charge, Ibn Yassār kept warning people against their exegeses.[11] Qatādah ibn Duʿāmah and al-Ḥasan al-Baṣrī, were also both accused of using *ra'y* to support the Qadarites' perspectives (the notion that man is responsible for his bad actions, not God).[12]

During this period, the phrase *fulān min ahl al-Ra'y* "so and so belongs to the people who use *al-ra'y*," was used to depict anyone believing in the Kharijites' doctrine[13] (a sect holding that anyone who commits a grave sin is neither a Muslim nor a *kāfir*, even though his doctrine was professed only by the radical wing of the Kharijites). Despite these aforementioned meanings, generally speaking, the term *ra'y* had been used to mean ijtihad, personal opinion, *qiyās* and belief (*Iʿtiqād*). Having stated the meanings of *ra'y*, literally and rationally, we next define the term *al-tafsīr bi al-ra'y* technically.

Al-tafsīr bi al-ra'y is used to denote exegesis of the Qur'anic text which does not depend on a Hadith, but uses the intellect (exerting the mind) to understand the word of God based on sound knowledge of the Arabic language and implementation of the principles of *tafsīr*.[14] Any Qur'anic exegesis that conforms to this definition is said to be *al-tafsīr bi al-ra'y al-Maḥmūd* or *al-Mamdūḥ,* i.e., 'praiseworthy exegesis'. However, any Qur'anic exegesis that does not conform to this definition is technically called *al-tafsīr bi al-ra'y al-Madhmūm* 'blameworthy exegesis'.[15] Thus, *al-tafsīr bi al-ra'y al-Madhmūm,* is defined as exegesis undertaken without proper knowledge of the sources of *tafsīr*, the Shariʿah, and sound knowledge of Arabic. Thus, Islamically speaking, *al-tafsīr bi al-ra'y* is divided into two categories: *al-tafsīr bi al-ra'y al-Maḥmūd* and *al-tafsīr bi al-ra'y al-Madhmūm*.

Generally speaking, the former is accepted by the majority of the Sunni traditionalists, jurists, prominent theologians and Sufis, whilst the latter is rejected by all those Sunni traditionalists, jurists and theologians.[16] Before discussing the principles upon which the Sunni scholars base their rejection of *al-tafsīr bi al-ra'y al-Madhmūm*, it might be useful to examine the view of three prominent scholars who have elaborated on the issue: al-Ṭabarī, al-Ghazālī, and Ibn Taymiyyah.

Muḥammad ibn Jarīr al-Ṭabarī

In his *Jāmiʿ al-Bayān*, al-Ṭabarī states that the interpretation of the Qur'an can only be attained through four ways. First, there are some verses that can be understood only through the explanation given by the Prophet. This pertains to the ritual aspects of Islam, such as how to perform the prayer (salah), pilgrimage (hajj), etc. and other rituals. Second, the interpretation of some verses whose understanding God has preserved for Himself. This for al-Ṭabarī alludes to information concerning matters of the *ghayb* (unseen) i.e. future dates and times, such as the hour of resurrection, when Jesus will return etc. Third, understanding verses for which ignorance is not allowed or excused. This applies to very clear verses, such as for example, Qur'anic verse 2:11 which states: "When it is said to them: 'Make not mischief on the earth,' they say: 'Why, we only Want to make peace!'" For al-Ṭabarī the meaning of this verse is crystal clear, since everyone knows what making mischief means.

The fourth is interpretation of some verses which only require scholarly knowledge.[17] In the light of this it is obvious that al-Ṭabarī held that only two types of Qur'anic interpretation can be used by one who speaks or understands Arabic (that is the linguistic meaning of Qur'anic words). Another type to interpret is comprehended by scholars only. Thus, al-Ṭabarī concluded that any attempt to interpret the meaning of verses that are the sole prerogative of Allah is wrong and censurable, because such interpretation would be nothing more than guess and surmise. Hence, Allah forbade His servants to do such a thing (allege things without supporting evidence), as we see in verse 7:33:

> Say: "Verily, my Sustainer has forbidden only shameful deeds, be they open or secret, and [every kind of] sinning, and unjustified envy, and the ascribing of divinity to aught beside Him - since He has never bestowed any warrant therefor from on high and the attributing unto God of aught of which you have no knowledge."

Since there are some verses that cannot be understood without explanation of the Prophet, then any effort to interpret such verses, according to al-Ṭabarī, is blameworthy. Again, al-Ṭabarī holds that, any interpretation which disagrees with the interpretation of the Prophet Muhammad, his Companions, the Successors, or is not attained from sound Arabic language is blameworthy.[18]

Abū Ḥāmid al-Ghazālī

Being a theologian Sufi, al-Ghazālī believed the Qur'an to contain hidden meanings which could be misunderstood if one relied solely on the literal Arabic (apparent meaning "*ẓāhir*"). Yet anyone not understanding the literal Arabic would be using personal opinion in attempting to explain the hidden meanings. Hence, he argued, hadith is necessary to understand and explain the literal and actual meaning of the Qur'an. Proper and thorough interpretation of the hidden meanings can begin only when the *ẓāhir* (literal/apparent) meaning has been properly understood with the aid of hadith.[19]

This statement indicates that whilst al-Ghazālī accepted interpretation of the Qur'an by *al-ra'y* he admitted only *al-tafsīr bi al-ra'y al-maḥmūd*. As for *tafsīr bi al-ra'y al-madhmūm*, al-Ghazālī viewed it as interpretation of the Qur'an according to personal opinion in order that one may adduce an argument in favor of one's particular purpose. If this opinion did not exist in the interpreter's mind in the first place, then the meaning he sought to accredit would not appear to him from the Qur'an. More interestingly, al-Ghazālī actually explains three ways in which this can occur:

1. Sometimes it is a deliberate act despite knowledge. For instance in the case of one who derives a meaning from a certain verse for the purposes of advocating and sanctioning a *bidᶜah*, knowing very well that this is not the intended meaning of the verse.

2. Sometimes this occurs when a person is ignorant of the basic principles of the Shariᶜah. So, for example where a Qur'anic verse can be interpreted from two or more perspectives, his understanding may incline to that perspective which suits his purpose.[20] Therefore, it turns out that, he explains the verse in terms of *al-tafsīr bi al-ra'y al-Madhmūm*. If either his personal opinion or the perspective which suits his purpose did not exist, then any other perspective would not carry much weight with him.

3. Sometimes an individual might have a valid purpose for which he seeks supporting evidence in the Qur'an, using a verse to derive that proof, whilst knowing that his own purpose is not intended within it. Al-Ghazālī gives as example verse 79:17: "Go unto Pharaoh - for, verily, he has transgressed all bounds of what is right." Al-Ghazālī rejects the claim made by some that Moses was ordered to "go to the heart of the Pharaoh." Such an interpretation, he declares is sometimes used by certain religious preachers for good purpose as embellishment to their sermons and to motivate their audience, but this is forbidden. He goes on to point out that certain sects, mainly the *bāṭinis* (a sect of the Shia) employed this kind of interpretation for corrupt purposes, in order to deceive people and draw them into a false way of thought and practice; twisting the meaning of the Qur'an to support their corrupt thinking, even though they knew better.[21]

Abū al-ᶜAbbās ᶜAbd al-Ḥalīm ibn Taymiyyah

Ibn Taymiyyah was one of the leading figures of the *salafiyyah* (a group of Muslims who believe in following the Qur'an and the Sunnah in the same manner as the Companions of the Prophet and the faithful Muslims of the two succeeding generations.

Thus, he openly and emphatically declared: "Whoever adopts a different method to that of the Companions and the Successors in interpreting the Qur'an, or differs with them, even if he is a *mujtahid* (a person who qualifies to deduce a sound judgment from the Qur'an and Sunnah), is absolutely wrong in his interpretation; moreover, he is a *mubtadiᶜ*."[22] This strong statement appears to suggest that Ibn Taymiyyah rejected all types of *al-tafsīr bi al-ra'y* whether it is *al-tafsīr bi al-ra'y al-Maḥmūd* (praiseworthy personal interpretation) or *al-tafsīr bi al-ra'y al-madhmūm* (blameworthy interpretation). Reading his *Muqaddimah*, however, indicates that he in fact seems to accept *al-tafsīr bi al-ra'y al-Maḥmūd*.

Ibn Taymiyyah considered *al-tafsīr bi al-ra'y al-madhmūm* to be a flawed interpretation of the Qur'an containing two kinds of errors: error pertaining to meaning and error pertaining to words. Error in meaning (as al-Ghazālī also pointed out) concerns an interpreter having a particular dogma in mind, and then trying to find justification for it in the Qur'an by twisting the meaning of to suit his particular purpose, whilst aware that the real meaning of the verse is not applicable or suitable to the task. As for the error in words this arises through dependence on the literal meaning without considering the meaning intended by God. Thus, according to Ibn Taymiyyah, advocates of the first category approach were wrong in both word and meaning, whilst the second approach was wrong only in the focus on word-oriented interpretations.[23]

Under the first category, Ibn Taymiyyah listed the Kharijites,[24] the Rafidites,[25] the Jahmites,[26] the Muʿtazilites,[27] the Qadarites,[28] and the Murji'ites.[29] The exegeses of all these parties or sects were considered by Ibn Taymiyyah to be *bidʿah* as well as *al-tafsīr bi a-ra'y al-Madhmūm*. Under the second category, Ibn Taymiyyah mentioned the exegeses of many Sufis, preachers, and jurists.

For example the Rafidites with reference to verse 2:67: "And Lo! Moses said unto his people: 'Behold, God bids you to sacrifice a cow'" stated that the cow was none other than a human being, and in fact ʿĀ'ishah, the wife of the Prophet! Another example relates to their explanation of verse 55:19: "He has let free the two bodies of flowing water [also translated as 'seas'], meeting together." The Radifites claimed the two seas referred to ʿAlī ibn Abī Ṭālib (the Prophet's cousin) and Faṭimah (the Prophet's daughter). Such interpretation has been rejected by all Sunni traditionists, jurists, theologians and moderate Sufis.[30]

In sum, these three prominent scholars rejected *al-tafsīr bi al-ra'y al-Madhmūm* because it a) exacerbated *bidʿah*, b) disagreed with the interpretations of the Prophet, the Companions, and the Successors, and c) adhered neither to the principles of the Arabic language nor to those of the Shariʿah.

Having said this, examined next is the position of the majority of scholars in regard to the legality of *al-tafsīr bi al-ra'y al-Maḥmūd*. Are they unanimous on its legality or not?

The Question of the Legality of *Al-Tafsīr bi al-Ra'y al-Maḥmūd*

The debate as to the legality of Qur'anic exegesis based on *al-tafsīr bi al-ra'y* (independent opinion) is theological in nature, and the outcome of a political and intellectual conflict that took place early in Islamic history, following the assassination of ʿUthmān ibn ʿAffān (d. 35 AH).

The Prophet Muhammad died without appointing a successor. As a result the question of who was to succeed him boded potential division in the fledgling Muslim community, until following contentious debate the matter ended amicably with Abū Bakr ibn Abī Quḥafah (d. 13 AH) appointed as the first Caliph. Two years and a few months later, Abū Bakr died, but not before appointing, on his death bed, ʿUmar ibn al-Khaṭṭāb as the second Caliph. Following a ten year rule, ʿUmar died and ʿUthmān was chosen as the third Caliph. After twelve years of ʿUthmān's leadership, Islamic unity began to falter. Subsequently, ʿUthmān was assassinated after thirteen years of rule.

ʿAlī ibn Abī Ṭālib then became the fourth Caliph by unanimous agreement of all the Muslim governors except Muʿāwiyah ibn Abī Sufyān (d. 60 AH), the Governor of Syria. He disagreed with ʿAlī on how to deal with ʿUthmān's assassins, which led to the political struggle between them. Thenceforth Islamic unity began to fragment and the Muslim states were shaken by political unrest. As a result, Muslims became divided into four major groups. The Alids, (supporters of ʿAlī), the pro-Umayyads (supporters of Muʿāwiyah), the Kharijites, and finally the *Shukkāk* (doubters) as Ibn ʿAsākir called them[31] because they did not take any side in the politico-religious tussle. The most popular being: the Sunnis, the Shias, the Murji'ites, the Jabirites, the Qadirites, and the Muʿtazilites. Subsequently, many different sects evolved from these groups with each group strongly advocating its dogma and philosophy using the Qur'an and Hadith to prove and justify its position. Note, incidentally these trends have been relentlessly confronted for their compromising of Islamic theology and the Prophet's practice by a group of Muslim traditionists, jurists, and theologians known as the *Salafīs* (following the *salaf*, that is predecessors). The *Salafīs* are also called *ahl al-Sunnah wa al-Jamāʿah* (those who adhere to the traditions of the Prophet, the Companions, and the Successors).

To justify their positions, all the sects, including the Sunnis, have quoted both reliable and unreliable hadith sources, and presented weak arguments and far-fetched exegeses. For example, to justify their position with regard to the politico-religious conflict mentioned earlier, the Kharijites set forth the following hadith: "Carry your sword on your shoulders, and kill disbelievers;[32] and there will be a group of people who still adhere to the truth and without harm from anyone who disagrees with them."[33] Because the Kharijites considered themselves as the group adhering to the truth, they believed it their duty to kill anyone who became, according to their criteria, a disbeliever.

For their part the Shia stated the Prophet to have said: "A people will be prevented (on the Day of Judgment) from drinking from the river that God has blessed the Prophet with, and the Prophet will say: 'O God, they are my Companions.' God will say to the Prophet: 'You do not know what they did after your death.'"[34] The Shia believed these people to be the Sunnis for their betrayal of the Prophet in choosing Abū Bakr, ʿUmar, and ʿUthmān as Caliphs over ʿAlī.

On the other hand, the Sunnis quoted the Prophet reported as having said: "Follow Abū Bakr and ʿUmar after me, for God, His Prophet, and the Muslims will refuse (anyone to be a Caliph), but Abū Bakr, verily indeed, Abū Bakr is the best one of this community after the Prophet."[35]

Meanwhile, the Murji'ites cite a hadith which supposedly says: "Whoever has professed the declaration *lā ilāha illa Allāh* will enter paradise (Jannah) even if he has committed illegal sexual intercourse and stolen."[36]

Below are examples of some far-fetched Qur'anic interpretations the differing groups have mutually accused one another of using. According to the Rafidites verse 111:1: "Perish the hands of Abū Lahab! Perish he!" referred to Abū Bakr and ʿUmar.[37] Similarly, they claimed that in verse 78:1-2: "About what do they [most often] ask one another? About the Great News," ʿAlī was the Great News.[38] On the other hand, some Sunnis claimed that in verse 3:17: "Those who show patience, firmness and self-control; who are true (in word and deed); who worship devoutly; who spend (in the way of Allah; and who pray for forgiveness in the early hours of the morning" are respectively, in succession to the Prophet, Abū Bakr, ʿUmar, ʿUthmān, and ʿAlī.[39]

Certain Sunnis also claimed that concerning verse 48:29: "Muhammad is the apostle of Allah, and those who are with him are strong against Unbelievers, (but) compassionate amongst each other. Thou wilt see them bow and prostrate themselves (in prayer), seeking Grace from Allah and (His) Good Pleasure..." that the section "those who are with him" refers to Abū Bakr, "strong against Unbelievers" to ʿUmar, "compassionate amongst each other" to ʿUthmān, and "Thou wilt see them bow and prostrate themselves (in prayer)" to ʿAlī. Ibn Taymiyyah described such interpretations as nonsense (*khurāfat*).[40]

During a certain theological debate which took place between a Qadarite, a Jabarite, and a Sunni, the Qadarite quoted verse 4:79: "Whatever good, (O man!) happens to thee, is from Allah, but whatever evil happens to thee, is from thy (own) soul, and We have sent thee as an apostle to (instruct) mankind. And enough is Allah for a witness." The apparent meaning of the verse is that man is responsible for creating the evil (or calamities) that befall him. The Jabarite opposed this view arguing that the phrase "from thy (own) soul" actually referred to a hidden interrogative sentence that implied a negation of this apparent meaning, further claiming the phrase should be read as "Is that from your self?" In which case the meaning then would be that both good and evil actions are from God.[41] In other words, man was not responsible for his actions, corroborating the Jabarite belief. Upon hearing this, the Sunni declared both notions wrong, citing the previous verse (4:78): "If some good befalls them, they say, 'This is from Allah'; but if evil, they say, 'This is from thee' (O Prophet). Say: 'All things are from Allah.'"

The difference between the Jabarites and the Sunnis on this issue is that Jabarites believe that man is not responsible for his actions, and therefore God will not punish someone who does not have a choice between doing good or bad.[42] The Sunnis believe that man has been given the choice to do both good and bad, but his choice is not absolute; if his choice were absolute, that would mean that God does not have absolute power.[43] The Sunnis, at other times, attributed all good – but not evil – to God, in order to preserve the idea of the goodness of God and on the other hand to make man a responsible being, particularly for his evil deeds.

Another instance of difference lies in the question of whether we can see God. According to the Muʿtazilite doctrine, God can never been seen with physical eyes, and they base this view on verse 6:103: "No vision can grasp Him, but His grasp is over all vision: He is above all comprehension, yet is acquainted with all things." Sunnis, on the other hand, believe that God will eventually be seen, basing their view on verse 83:15 which affirms: "Verily, from (the Light of) their Lord, that Day, will they be veiled" referring to the evil doers. The Sunnis deduced from this that since evil doers will be veiled from seeing God, Muslims will not be veiled from seeing God. They further support this assumption with a hadith in which the Prophet clearly states that Muslims will see God as clearly as they see the full moon.[44]

Arguments Concerning *al-Ra'y*

These interpretations and arguments were partly the reason some Sunni scholars questioned the soundness and legality of using critical intellectual reasoning (*al-ra'y*) in *tafsīr*, whether *al-ra'y al-mamdūḥ* or *al-ra'y al-madhmūm*. This led a group of theologians and exegetes including al-Ṭabarī, al-Ghazālī, Ibn ʿAṭiyyah, al-Qurṭubī and others to come into conflict with those opponents of *al-ra'y* who differentiated between acceptable and unacceptable *ra'y* without rejecting it entirely.

Sources describing this conflict whilst advancing the arguments concerned did not mention the names of those rejecting *ra'y* in Qur'anic interpretation,[45] leaving us thus with indefinite terminology such as 'some people say', or 'those who reject *al-ra'y*, etc. This was presumably done for one of three reasons:

1. The opponents of *ra'y* were known at the time, so there was no need to mention their names
2. To avoid fermenting conflict between Sunni Muslims.
3. There were some prominent Successors who directly and indirectly rejected or expressed caution in regard to the use of *al-ra'y*. These included Sālim ibn ʿAbd Allāh, al-Qāsim ibn Muḥammad, and Saʿīd ibn al-Musayyib.

The latter is more likely the case because subsequent generations of Muslims in general gave weight to the opinion and attitude of the first and second generations because of the praise which the first received in the Qur'an and in hadith. Hence, given this omission in names, in examining the arguments put forward by opponents of *al-ra'y* in literature I will do so in general terms, except where reference is made to a specific individual, or where an individual is known for rejecting *ra'y* in his works, such as Ibn Ḥazm.

Arguments of the Opponents of al-Ra'y

Arguments by those opposing *al-ra'y* is discussed under the following four categories: Qur'an, Hadith, sayings of the *Ṣaḥābah*, and statements of the *Tābiᶜūn*.

Qur'an

Reference is mainly made to three Qur'anic verses. The first is verse 4:59: "and if you are at variance over any matter, refer it unto God and the Apostle." Extrapolating from this to *al-Ra'y*, the implication is as there is difference of opinion the final judgment should be referred to God and His Prophet, which action, if not carried through, constitutes disobedience of a divine command. Thus, anyone else's opinion is rejected.[46]

The second is verse 16:44: "and We have sent down unto you (Muhammad) (also) the Message; that you may explain clearly to men what is sent for them..." The point being that God has stated clearly that He has entrusted the Prophet only with the mission of explaining the Qur'anic text to mankind; thus, any attempt by anyone else to elucidate the Qur'an using his own opinion is unnecessary at best.

The third is verse 7:33 which addresses the Prophet: "Say: 'Verily, my Sustainer has forbidden only shameful deeds, be they open or secret, and [every kind of] sinning, and unjustified envy, and the ascribing of divinity to aught beside Him - since He has never bestowed any warrant therefor from on high and the attributing unto God of aught of which you have no knowledge." The verse makes clear that the stating of things concerning Allah without correct and necessary knowledge is a great a sin as the sins mentioned at the beginning of the verse. Any interpretation, therefore, without information from the Prophet is prohibited.[47]

Hadith

Three main hadiths are quoted. The first is the well-known hadith narrated by Ibn ʿAbbās, which reports that the Prophet said: "Whoever explains the Qur'an according to his personal opinion, shall take his place in Hell." As the hadith does not differentiate between *al-ra'y al-Maḥmūd* and *al-ra'y al-madhmūm,* it is concluded by opponents of *al-Ra'y* that indulging in both (*al-ra'y al-Maḥmūd* and *al-ra'y al-madhmūm*) is a wrong practice.

The second hadith is on the authority of Jandub ibn ʿAbd Allāh, and indicates the Prophet to have said: "Whoever says anything about the Qur'an, by his own opinion, becomes a disbeliever." Al-Tirmidhī and others have declared the hadith unsound because of the lack of reliability of one of its narrators, Suhayl ibn Ḥazm. Both Imam Aḥmed and al-Bukhārī have also disregarded Suhayl's hadith report.[48]

The third hadith is from the wife of the Prophet who is quoted as having said that the Prophet did not use to comment on anything in the Qur'an except for a few verses, which the Angel Jibrīl (Gabriel) taught him.[49] The point being made that as the Prophet himself did not interpret the Qur'an using his own opinion and that it was rather the Angel Jibrīl who inspired him, who are we to then exercise *al-ra'y*?

Sayings of the Ṣaḥābah

When Abū Bakr al-Ṣiddīq was asked to explain the meaning of a specific word or words of the Qur'an, he expressed his fear to do so by saying: "What earth shall bear me, and what heaven shall shelter me if I speak what I do not know not concerning the Qur'an?"[50]

It is reported that ʿUmar ibn al-Khaṭṭāb cited verse 80:31 ("and fruits and herbage (*abban*)") stating that: "We know what the term 'fruits' is, but what does '*abban*' mean?" adding: "It is unnecessary to know this, for otherwise it would become a constraint (*takalluf*)." Both statements illustrate the fact that Abū Bakr and ʿUmar refrained from exercising *ra'y* (their own opinion) because they knew this was prohibited.

Another example is that of Ibn ʿAbbās. He was once asked concerning the meaning of a Qur'anic verse but declined to comment on it. Now, as Muslims knew, or believed, that he had been given a special gift from God with regards to Qur'anic knowledge in answer to a prayer made for him by the Prophet, it was then assumed that his refusal to answer was due to him knowing that recourse to *ra'y* was prohibited.[51]

Statements of the Successors

ʿUbayd Allah ibn ʿUmar (d. 140 AH) stated that he found learned men in Madinah, including Sālim ibn ʿAbd Allāh, al-Qāsim ibn Muḥammad and others, abstaining from making comments on the Qur'an using their own opinion.[52] Saʿīd ibn al-Musayyib, was the most knowledgeable figure of his time, yet whenever his students asked him anything about the Qur'an he kept silent, as if he had not heard them and (sometimes) reply "we do not say anything about the Qur'an."[53]

Responses of the Proponents of al-Ra'y

Among the verses the proponents of *ra'y* have quoted in support of their argument is verse 4:59: "and if you are at variance over any matter, refer it unto God and the Apostle." Note, this is the same verse the opponents of *al-ra'y* cite in defense of their position. Al-Qurṭubī and others however did not accept it as a statement of proof against the prohibition of exegesis by *al-ra'y*. In their view, the verse actually limits Qur'anic interpretation, making exegesis subject to two conditions only: firstly interpretation is to be confined to the transmitted tradition (*al-naql*), and secondly interpretation is to take into account the principle of 'that which is heard' (*al-masmūʿ*) from the authority of "the Prophet Muhammad" and his Companions. They believed, therefore, that one must refrain from deducing or eliciting meanings from the Qur'an unless these two elements are observed lest the meaning of the verse(s) be something other than what was heard from the authoritative sources. From this perspective other types of interpretation seem to be forbidden. Hence, al-Qurṭubī concluded that it is sufficient to use only the *tafsīr* from the tradition of the Prophet.

Furthermore, he argued that the Companions themselves used their own opinions in interpreting the Qur'anic text. Had that not been the case, the Prophet's prayer in favor of Ibn ʿAbbās "O God, grant him the knowledge of Islam and teach him the meaning of the Qur'an" would have served no purpose.[54]

On the other hand, al-Ghazālī seems to take a more critical stand vis-à-vis the notion of using *al-naql* and *al-masmūʿ* as the exclusive basis for interpretation. He states "...these were intended to confine the understanding of the Qur'an to the transmission of hadith and to that which is heard from the authorities. It is wrong however, to accept that the purpose was to limit our understanding of the Qur'an to the words of authorities."[55]

In respect to the second argument, the proponents of *ra'y*, including Ibn ʿAṭiyyah, al-Zarkashī, and others, argued that no one disputed the fact that the Prophet had been given the responsibility of explaining the Qur'an to mankind, but they point out his interpretation was made according to the necessities of his time, and for the people of that particular time. They contend that after the death of the Prophet, the need for more explanation of the Qur'an arose, simply because the Prophet's interpretations, though possibly clear to his Companions, would not necessarily be clear to subsequent generations. Thus, *ra'y* is permissible, provided the basic rules of *tafsīr* are applied.[56]

For his part, al-Ṭabarī warned that the verses the supporters of *ra'y* set forth for their arguments needed careful explanation. He agreed that there were some verses whose meanings could not be understood without the explanation of the Prophet, going on to remark that verse 7:33; "the attributing unto God of aught of which you have no knowledge," refers to the interpretation that can only be attained based on the Prophet's explanations, as opposed to what can be obtained through sound Arabic usage.[57]

Concerning hadith, al-Ṭabarī and al-Qurṭubī responded to the hadith of Ibn ʿAbbās "Whoever explains the Qur'an according to his personal opinion, shall take his place in Hell" by stating that the *ra'y* which the hadith prohibited is that which pertains to the *mutashābihāt* (verses whose meanings are known only to God), such as those mentioning the time Jesus will return to the world, or difficult passages of the Qur'an which require explanation from the Prophet. Using *ra'y* in such situations, they maintained, was prohibited.[58] Al-Qurṭubī further adds that this prohibition does not pertain to the interpretation of grammarians, linguists and jurists, because their interpretation is based on knowledge.[59]

With respect to the Companions's statements and attitudes, Ibn ʿAṭiyyah, responded to Abū Bakr's statement by presenting some probable answers. He states that Abū Bakr might have said this at the very beginning of his Caliphate to prevent Muslims from engaging in interpretation haphazardly, or perhaps because at the beginning of his Caliphate he was of the opinion that interpretation should not be made by mere personal opinion. Ibn ʿAṭiyyah explains that as time passed Abū Bakr realized that independent opinion in interpretation was inevitable. Thus, when asked about the meaning of the Qur'anic word *kalālah* (in verse 4:12), Abū Bakr replied: "(What) I say (regarding the meaning of *kalālah*) is my opinion. If it is correct, thanks be to God. If it is wrong, it is from Satan, and God is innocent of it." Then he adds, "*kalālah* is a deceased (person) who does not leave behind him a father or a son."

A similar case concerned the issue of compiling and codifying the Qur'an into one book. Abū Bakr initially hesitated and refused, later finding that codification was unavoidable. Thus, he submitted to opinion.[60]

Concerning ʿUmar's attitude toward the meaning of verse 80:31, "and fruits and herbage," this has been interpreted as a kind of discipline. ʿUmar wanted Muslims to avoid using unnecessary opinion in regard to unnecessary things. With regard to Ibn ʿAbbās's behavior, it was thought that he refused to interpret one of the verses that was left to him alone to interpret. And with regard to the refraining of both the Companions and the Successors from engaging in Qur'anic interpretation, al-Ṭabarī states:

> The attitudes or actions of those who did not abstain from interpretation was similar to the actions of those of them who refrained from giving legal opinions concerning particular events and occurrences, that is to say, they [all] believed that God did not cause His Prophet to die until after he had perfected His religion to His servants, and they knew that God had a judgment in a text or through an indication for every event, but [the former believed] perhaps, that they had to search it out, otherwise, they would be denying that God's judgment on these events existed among them. Finally, [regarding those who refrained from engaging in interpretation,] they could have feared that by their own effort (ijtihad) they were not able to carry out the charge God had entrusted to the learned among His servants. It was the same with the learned among the pious predecessors who refrained from speaking about the interpretation and exegesis of the Qur'an. They did so out of caution, lest they should fail to accomplish the objective of speaking correctly, – not because the interpretation of (this verse) was veiled from the men of knowledge in the community and that it did not exist among them.[61]

Ibn ʿAṭiyyah seems displeased with al-Ṭabarī's conclusion that the main reason those learned Companions and the Successors refrained from interpretation was piety, stating simply: "too many of the prominent predecessors (*salaf*) who were merely concerned or sympathetic with Muslims interpreted the Qur'an."[62] After the proponents of *al-ra'y* had refuted the arguments of the opponents they set forth the following evidence in support of their view. Firstly verse 38:29:

> (Here is) a Book which We have sent down unto thee, full of blessings, that they may mediate (ponder) on its Signs, and that men of understanding may receive admonition.

Ibn ᶜAṭiyyah comments that the significance of the verse in terms of *ra'y* lay in the word "*li yatadabbarū*" (to reflect, to ponder). He states that it originally meant the final end of something. Thus, one who ponders over the meanings of verses is the one who can arrive at an understanding of their actual meanings. Ibn ᶜAṭiyyah thus concludes that to ponder over something is nothing other than an exercise in *ra'y*, and therefore were resort to *ra'y* not permissible, this verse would serve no purpose.[63]

Another popular verse referred to in this regard by the exponents of *ra'y* is verse 4:83 which points out:

> If they would but refer it unto the Apostle and unto those from among the believers who have been entrusted with authority, such of them as are engaged in obtaining intelligence would indeed know [what to do with] it.

According to al-Ghazālī this verse endorsed the use of *ra'y* because God affirms the validity of *istinbāṭ* (inference) by men of learning. And it is unquestionable that, *instinbāṭ* is something 'beyond *al-masmūᶜ*.'[64]

Al-Ṭabarī elaborated further on both verses arguing that God's encouragement to believers to ponder over the Qur'an's verses is an indication that the exercise of *ra'y* in understanding Qur'anic verses is possible and must be further pursued to present a logical argument: "It is impossible to say to someone who does not comprehend that which is being said to him, '*iʿtabir*,' ('take admonition'), unless he understands and reasons what is being said to him. Otherwise, it would be useless to do so. It is likewise impossible to say to some non-Arabs who do not understand Arabic to take advice from Arabic poems, proverbs and wise speeches. Similarly, God would not command people to ponder over the Qur'an's verses, unless there were some indications which would lead to the meanings of its verses. Thus, to interpret the verses which are not the sole prerogative of God is permissible."[65]

Concerning the hadith evidence presented by the proponents of *ra'y*, namely Ibn ʿAbbās' narration whereby the Prophet said: "O God, grant him the knowledge of Islam and teach him the meaning of the Qur'an" (*wa ʿallimhu al-ta'wīl*), the point al-Ghazālī and al-Qurṭubī make is that if interpretation of the Qur'an is confined to Prophetic hadith only, then the Prophet's prayer for Ibn ʿAbbās to bestow him with understanding of Qur'anic interpretation would have no raison d'être.

Another well-known hadith is that reported by Muʿādh ibn Jabal, in which he indicates that the Prophet approved the exercise of ijtihad by saying: "*idha ijtahad al-ḥākim fa akhṭa' falahū ajr, wa in ijtihada fa-aṣāba falahū ajrān* ("When a judge makes ijtihad and errs, therein he shall have one reward. And whosoever performs ijtihad and if he is correct, he shall have a double reward").

Concerning the Companions' sayings supporting the use of *al-ra'y*, the following is quoted concerning a question once asked of ʿAlī ibn Abī Ṭālib: "Did the Prophet single you out [to be endowed] with special comprehension and understanding concerning knowledge of the Qur'an?" ʿAlī replies: "No, except that God bestows upon a servant understanding of the Qur'an."[66] In this respect al-Ghāzalī asks: "If there is no meaning other than [that which is based on] the transmission of the interpretation of the authority, what is the meaning of the understanding [of the Qur'an] that God bestows upon a servant?"[67]

Al-Ṭabarī reports that both Ibn Masʿūd and Ibn ʿAbbās used to give comprehensive interpretations of the Qur'an with Ibn Masʿūd's exegesis of one surah alone taking an entire day to explain.[68] Worth noting here is that the Prophet never gave such a long interpretation of any surah, thus, it can only be concluded that detailed interpretation of this nature could have only come from opinions or commentaries. As for the respect given to the Successors' statements, again al-Ṭabarī quotes Saʿīd ibn Jubayr who was reported to have said: "Whoever reads the Qur'an and cannot explain it, (that is to say, did not understand it), is just like a blind person or a bedouin"[69] (the latter generally speaking considered not intelligent).

Nonetheless, Abū Muḥammad ibn Ḥazm rejects the use of all kinds of personal opinion in Islam in general and in the Qur'an in particular. To him, no one, including the Companions, has any right or authority to utilize his own opinion in this regard, and whoever does use his opinion in either deducing the law, or the meaning of the Qur'an, and assumes that such is the meaning meant by God of a particular verse, or ascribes that to God, is a liar.[70] Ibn Ḥazm based his rejection of personal opinion on the following Qur'anic verses: "We have neglected nothing in the book" (6:38), and "Follow what has been sent down unto you by your Sustainer" (7:3). Ibn Ḥazm reasons that as God has stated clearly in verse 6:38 that He did not leave anything out the Qur'an thus contains all that needs to be known in Islam and there is no need therefore for anyone to add his opinion. Further, the second verse commands mankind to follow the revelation, not someone else's opinion.[71]

As already mentioned, the first of the two strongest arguments of the proponents of *ra'y* is verse 4:83 and the other is the popular hadith of Muʿādh ibn Jabal in which the Prophet approved of using ijtihad.

As regards the hadith reported by Muʿādh, Ibn Ḥazm considered it invalid because of al-Ḥārith ibn ʿUmar who is historically considered to be *majhūl* (unknown narrator). Furthermore, according to Ibn Ḥazm, al-Bukhārī also reportedly rejected this hadith.[72]

It appears that as a result of all these theological or exegetical debates on Qur'anic interpretation objections were raised concerning both *al-tafsīr bi al-ra'y al-maḥmūd*, and *al-tafsīr bi al-ra'y al-madhmūm*. Consequently, a new principle known as the "prerequisites of the *mufassir* (exegete)" was developed and added to the sciences of Qur'anic exegesis. In relation to these prerequisites some guidelines had already been given by certain Companions and Successors, before scholars such as al-Zarkashī and al-Suyūṭī codified them in their works. For example, in his work *Al-Itqān*, al-Suyūṭī reports that ʿAlī ibn Abī Ṭālib witnessed a story teller speaking about Qur'anic interpretation. ʿAlī asks him, "Do you know about abrogating and abrogated (verses)"? He (the story teller) replies, "No" to which ʿAlī responds, "You destroyed (your self) and destroyed others."[73] Another codified guideline is that of Ibn ʿAbbās according to whom one part of Qur'anic exegesis can be obtained through mere knowledge of the Arabic language, a part can be understood by scholars through their ijtihad, and a portion can only be known through the Prophet's explanation. All these aspects have been incorporated into the prerequisites of interpretation.

Al-Bayhaqī, quotes Imam Mālik ibn Anas as having said "No man who interprets the Qur'an without knowledge of Arabic would be brought before me without my inflicting punishment on him."[74] Al-Suyuṭī lists fifteen prerequisites of *tafsīr* in his work, and here we have categorized them under six headings as follows:

1. Hadith of the Prophet: one must be well versed in this science.
2. Arabic Language: one must master all aspects of the Arabic language
3. Islamic Jurisprudence: one must be highly knowledgeable of, and/or exposed to the different opinions of the various legal scholars in all aspects of Islamic Law.
4. One must have pure belief (opposite of heresy) and a clear perspective of theological issues, understanding them in the way the Companions, Successors and Sunnis scholars did.

5. One must have knowledge of the abrogating and abrogated verses, and the occasions of revelations.
6. One must be gifted with a specialized knowledge (*ʿilm al-Mawhibah*).

In discussion of *al-tafsīr bi al-ra'y al-maḥmūd*, and *al-tafsīr bi al-ra'y al-madhmūm*, the work of Muqātil ibn Sulaymān is also worthy of consideration and this is examined next.

Muqātil Ibn Sulaymān's al-Wujūh wa al-Naẓā'ir

This work is generally believed to be the first complete book of *al-tafsīr bi al-ra'y*.[75] The book and the author were controversial. Some scholars, like Imam al-Shāfiʿī, highly praised Muqātil's knowledge of interpretation, with al-Shāfiʿī stating: "All people are indebted to Muqātil in *al-tafsīr*," and ʿUbadah ibn Kathīr claiming that there was noone living (in his era at any rate) who was more knowledgeable of the Qur'an than Muqātil.[76] While these scholars praised Muqātil we find in contrast some prominent critics of Hadith literature such as al-Bukhārī, Yaḥyā ibn Maʿīn (d. 274 AH), al-Dhahabī and others, portraying Muqātil as a liar, and a *mujassim* (anthropomorphist).[77] However Muqātil was considered to be the first exegete who resorted to *ra'y*, simply because despite living in an era in which interpretation was being taught by narration with full accounts of the chains of transmission (*isnād*) given, he took the liberty of deleting these chains (*asānīd*) throughout his work depending rather on his own personal opinion alone.

Muqātil's work *Al-Wujūh wa al-Naẓā'ir* goes under a variety of names or titles, with the following two titles being the most popular: *Kitāb al-Wujūh wa al-Naẓā'ir* and *Al-Ashbāh wa al-Naẓā'ir*. *Al-Wujūh wa al-Naẓā'ir* deals basically with *mushtarak*, or homonyms, that is to say words written and pronounced in the same manner, but having different or opposite meanings. The category of *Mushtarak* corresponds to semantic lexicology.[78]

The methodology that Muqātil adopted in his *tafsīr* was of two kinds, the conceptual and the general method that Sunnis employed in their interpretations of the text, which was to explain the text by referring to its background, or to interpret the *ṣifāt* verses (verses pertaining to God's attributes) without negating or twisting their obvious meaning. Consider the following Qur'anic verse 48:10: "Behold, all who pledge their allegiance (*yubāyiᶜūnaka*) to thee pledge their allegiance to God: the hand of God is over their hands." Muqātil, in accordance with his approach, thus gives a few details on that meeting with regards to explaining the text in terms of its background:

> Those who gave the loyalty pledge under the tree in the sacred territory of Makkah, were the embodiment of *bayᶜah al-Riḍwān* and the number of the Muslims that day was one thousand and four hundred.

To illustrate the conceptual aspect of Muqātil's methodology we examine the word *kafara* (to disbelieve) and its substantive *kufr* mentioned several times in the Qur'an. The word's meaning differs in each of the passages in which it is mentioned. Muqātil compiled the occurrences of *kufr* and then explained the word's meanings in each verse. He goes on to state that one aspect of *kufr* is to reject the oneness of Allah, as in verse 2:6 which states: "As to those who reject Faith, it is the same to them whether thou warn them or do not warn them; they will not believe." A second aspect of *kufr* is to be ungrateful to Allah, as in verse 27:40: "...and if any is grateful, truly his gratitude is (a gain) for his own soul; but if any is ungrateful, truly my Lord is Free of all Needs, Supreme in Honour!"

The third aspect, states Muqātil, is to declare oneself free, separate, and different as in verse 29:25; "on the Day of Judgment ye shall disown each other..."[79]

Summary and Comments

In the light of these discussions we can conclude that *al-tafsīr bi al-ra'y al-maḥmūd* (praiseworthy *tafsīr*) can be defined as interpretation by independent opinion which does not conflict with the Prophet's explanation of the Qur'an, or an established principle of Islam, and conforms with the Arabic language, that is with sound Arabic usage and grammar.

At the time of the Prophet and during the tenure of the first two Caliphs, Abū Bakr and ʿUmar, the term *ra'y* held no negative connotations, being understood as personal opinion and analogy. Following the assassination of ʿUthmān, the third Caliph, Muslims suffered internal division, with generally speaking, each group, including the supporters of Abū Bakr and ʿUmar, using the Qur'an to support their own perspective.

The Sunni and the Shia in particular distorted the meanings of certain verses with far-fetched exegeses using fabricated hadith to support their own particular point of view. As a result, some prominent scholars such as Saʿīd ibn al-Musayyib, Sālim ibn ʿAbd Allāh, al-Qāsim ibn Muḥammad and others abstained from *tafsīr*. Subsequently, the term *ra'y* became identified with sectarianism. These theological political schools continued to spread across the Muslim world and are with us today. Their exegeses became polemical in nature, leading eventually to the grouping and division of *al-tafsīr bi al-ra'y* into kinds: *al-tafsīr bi al-ra'y al-maḥmūd* (praiseworthy) and *al-tafsīr bi al-ra'y al-madhmūm* (blameworthy). There also evolved qualifications for a *mufassir* to save the integrity of *al-tafsīr* (Qur'anic exegesis).

Nonetheless, historically as the different schools of thought evolved as a result of various theological or political differences, *al-tafsīr* became unfortunately embroiled in polemics, leading to an inevitable loss of objectivity. For instance, Mujāhid's interpretation of verse 75:22–3: "Some faces, that Day, will beam (in brightness and beauty); looking towards their Lord", differs not only from that of the explanation given by the Prophet and that of his Companions, but also in such a way that it actually contradicts them. Worth noting also is that whilst Mujāhid's *tafsīr* is not labeled as *bid^{c}ah*, that of the Mu^{c}tazilites, who interpreted in the same way as Mujāhid, is labeled as such, meaning they were accused of *bid^{c}ah* whilst Mujāhid was not.

A critical look at the arguments of both the opponents and the proponents of *al-ra'y* in defense of their position reveals that some arguments needed more support while others are deemed irrelevant. For example, the opponents of *ra'y* would quote verse 16:44 ("and We have sent down unto you (Muhammad) (also) the Message; that you may explain clearly to men what is sent for them") to back their prohibition of *ra'y*. In my opinion this argument is a weak one, practically speaking, for the Prophet did not explain the whole Qur'an, not even most of it, and his Companions consequently used their own opinion in explaining some of its verses.

But whatever the case, the majority position of scholars is that *al-tafsīr bi al-ra'y* (under the grouping *al-tafsīr bi al-ra'y al-maḥmūd*) is permissible subject to certain conditions, for men endowed with sound knowledge and based on sound sources.

CHAPTER 7

Trends in Modern Qur'anic Interpretation

FROM 1750 UNTIL the middle of the 20th century, the occupation and decline of the Muslim world became increasingly pronounced, with the civilisation eroding under the cultural and political influence of the West penetrating ever deeper all aspects of Muslim life, socially, politically, educationally, culturally, and economically.

In an effort to stem the tide, various revivalist ideas and reform movements emerged seeking to re-establish and strengthen Islamic identity, India and Egypt being a case in point. Some of these movements sought to achieve their goals by adopting rational, intellectual and scientific approaches to interpreting Islam as a way of life. Thus new trends appeared in Islamic literature in general and *tafsīr* in particular. Examined next are aspects relating to six of these trends:

1. Intellectual
2. Scientific
3. Rhetorical
4. Philological
5. Traditional
6. Natural History

Note, J. J. G. Jansen accurately observed that no modern exegete has produced a work devoted exclusively to one particular aspect. He, however, divided the modern exegetical field into three – not six – categories: scientific, traditional, and day-today Muslim affairs.[1]

1. Intellectual and Social Interpretation

Advocates of this approach aimed at waking Muslims up to the realization that the Qur'an was revealed first and foremost to guide mankind, and that it educates man on how to achieve success in this life and the Hereafter. Thus, the Qur'an is presented as the answer to all of mankind's problems and man's spiritual and worldly needs. Muslims must seek, in the Qur'an alone, the solutions to all their problems, in every sphere of their life: be it the social, economic, political, day-to-day affairs, or other areas, etc. According to this approach, Muslims must understand the Qur'an as a book of guidance to be used according to how Muslims perceive their problems within the modern world. This is contrary to relying on classical Qur'anic interpretation at all times. This perspective holds that classical interpretations, although correct for their own particular time and point in history, are not necessarily applicable to present day Muslims.[2]

Tafsīr al-Qur'ān al-Ḥakīm

The most popular exponent of this trend is represented by the voluminous work *Tafsīr al-Qur'ān al-Ḥakīm*, popularly known as *Tafsīr al-Manār.* The work is actually a combination of the works of Shaykh Muhammad Abduh and his student, Muhammad Rashid Rida. Abduh delivered a series of lectures on *tafsīr* at al-Azhar University for a period of six years. He began lecturing from 1317 AH up to 1323 AH, the year he died, and only gave the interpretation of the first four surahs of the Qur'an.

Muhammad Rashid Rida, who was Muhammad Abduh's most outstanding student, published his own notes and his teacher's lectures in *Al-Manār Journal.* Subsequently, he compiled all of Abduh's lecture notes with some of his own comments and interpretations, which covered twelve surahs. Abduh approved surahs one to four before he died. Rashid Rida continued this effort alone after the death of his teacher from surah 4:125 to 12:107. Rida faithfully indicated the parts for which he and his teacher were jointly responsible, marking where Abduh's words ended and his own additions began.[3] The work was published in Beirut by Dār al-Fikr, in twelve volumes.[4]

Shaykh Abduh's purpose for producing the interpretation was to impress on the Muslims that the Qur'an was a religious book that essentially was revealed to guide mankind to that which would lead to success in this life and the hereafter.[5]

Furthermore, Rashid Rida explained in detail the wishes that his teacher desired to accomplish through his teaching and exegesis. He stated that there is nothing in our religion that is in conflict with present modernization – except some issues concerning usury.

Rashid Rida quotes Abduh to have stated: "I am ready to establish harmony between true Islam and whatever the Ottoman Empire might need to reach the standard of civilization achieved by the West, through the process followed by the West. I will do this through the instruction of the Qur'an and the authentic tradition of the Prophet, not through a particular school of thought in Islam."[6]

The Characteristics and Methodology of Abduh's Exegesis

In his *Islam and Modernism in Egypt*, Charles Adams has excellently described the character of Abduh's commentary as follows.

> He places the primary emphasis upon the guidance of the Qur'an, in a manner which agrees with the verse which describes it, and the warnings and good tidings and guidance and correction for which it was sent down, at the same time giving care to the requirements of the present day conditions with respect to acceptability of phrasing, and having regard for the capacity of different classes of readers and understanding.[7]

The following statement from Abduh provides a clear image of his exegesis: "Today, *tafsīr* is in the eyes of our people (Muslims), but before today, it was nothing more than imitation of the classical [works of] scholars, although these works may have deviated from the main purpose of the Qur'an. [However,] God will not ask [anybody] on the Day of Judgment about what was previously understood [by others]. Rather, He will ask, what did you understand about His Book? Did you ponder over the meaning of the Book that was given to you?"[8]

This is clear indication that Abduh based his exegesis on his own personal opinion in understanding the Qur'an. As a result, he rejected some established principles, or interpreted them differently from the way the majority of Muslim scholars had understood them. Abduh's new approach concerns, for example, his interpretation of Angels, Satan, and the Qur'anic account of the flight of birds.[9]

Finally, *Tafsīr al-Manār* contains a variety of interpretations and propositions ranging from the Prophet's interpretation, that of his Companions, to that of the immediate Successors and to linguistic considerations such as rhetoric, quotations from Jewish and Christian sources, and judicial issues.

The work, generally speaking, has been well received by the Muslim world. However, some scholars, such as Subhi al-Salih, Fahd Abd al-Rahman al-Rumi and others, have been critical of *Tafsīr al-Manār*,[10] and these criticisms have focused mainly on those ideas that reject established Islamic principles as mentioned.

Muhammad Rashid Rida's contribution to Qur'anic exegesis consists of opinions which differ in small measure from those of his teacher, with the exception of a few concepts concerning the application of hadith, an area where Rashid Rida seemed to adhere more to classical thinking than did his teacher.

2. The Scientific Approach

Because of the scientific advances of the modern world, this approach strongly advocates that the Qur'an must be understood in the light of modern science, rather than in terms of a jurisprudential approach. One of the representative key works of this trend is *Al-Jawāhir fī Tafsīr al-Qur'ān al-Karīm* (Pearls from the *Tafsīr* of the Noble Qur'an) by Shaykh Jawhar Tantawi (d. 1940). Tantawi was a lecturer at Dār al-ʿUlūm in Cairo, and whilst there he taught Qur'anic interpretation and also published *tafsīr* articles in a magazine called *Majallat al-Malāji' al-ʿAbbāsiyyah*. Subsequently, he compiled these lectures into twenty-five volumes which were then published in Cairo.[11]

In his introductory statement, Tantawi states the reason for writing his work: "When I examined the Muslim community, I found that most of the Muslim intellectuals ignored the importance of physical science. Only a very few of them thought about it. Thus, I intended to write a Qur'anic interpretation, in the hope that it would inspire Muslims to study the physical sciences, medicine, mathematics, engineering, astronomy and other sciences." Clearly he meant to inspire Muslim scholars through his interpretation of Qur'anic verses relating to scientific propositions, so that they would follow his new approach of scientific exegesis.

Tantawi was strongly convinced that in the twentieth century Qur'anic exegesis utilising a scientific approach methodology was more important than classical interpretation. He declared that the scientific approach to Qur'anic interpretation was incumbent upon individuals whereas jurisprudence was not. Thus, he openly attacked the jurists when he stated: "The knowledge that we incorporated in Qur'anic exegesis is the knowledge that the insignificant jurists of Islam ignored. This is the time of revolution. This is the time in which realities come out"[12] (that is this is a time where we should reject classical *tafsīr* and base *tafsīr* on modern science).

He would begin each of his explanations by elucidating a particular passage of the Qur'an word by word. He would then follow this with various forms of elaboration. For example, when a verse related to a branch of modern science, he would give a detailed scientific explanation on the subject, quoting modern sciences. He also used pictures, plants and other things in *Al-Jawāhir fī Tafsīr al-Qur'ān al-Karīm* for purposes of illustration. Tantawi also used Jewish and Christian sources, such as the Gospel of Barnabas.[13]

Contemporary scholars did not warmly embrace Tantawi's methodology. Subhi al-Salih, Jansen, and others criticized it for, in their opinion, its excessive attention to scientific considerations and other ideas, so much so that the work was not considered a true exegesis.[14]

3. Rhetorical – Literary Rhetoric

The style of this approach is rhetorical, with much attention given to literary sociological considerations, and the objectives of the trend are the same as those of Muhammad Abduh's work. *Fī Ẓilāl al-Qur'ān* by Sayyid Qutb, published in Cairo in eight volumes, is a famous example of this approach. Sayyid Qutb's educational background was Arabic literature and sociology, and he was an active member of the Muslim Brotherhood, the most powerful Islamic movement in Egypt. In his introductory statement, Sayyid Qutb states that the solution to the Muslim community and mankind's problems lies in the teaching and practicing of the Qur'an only, simply because the Qur'an was a book revealed primarily to guide mankind to achieve peace and happiness.[15]

In *Fī Zilāl al-Qur'ān* Qutb first gives a general overview of the whole surah, outlining its objectives and ultimate goal. He then discusses the text phrase by phrase or verse by verse. He does not explain word by word as many classical works have done. If any hadith of the Prophet concerning the meaning of a particular verse existed Qutb would mention it, as well as the occasions of the revelation. At the end a brief summary of the surah would usually be provided, pointing out the relationship between that surah and the next.

Although the dominant style of *Fī Ẓilāl al-Qur'ān* is rhetorical, Qutb invariably refers his readers to Islamic legal literature, stating that juristic matters are not the purpose of his *tafsīr*. Interestingly enough, he gives theological arguments very little attention.

Fī Ẓilāl al-Qur'ān has been overwhelmingly acclaimed by Muslims worldwide simply because it focuses on the social problems experienced by Muslims of his time, and as Muhammad Ayyub has rightly pointed out the work has had a wide reception in both Sunni and Shia communities.[16]

4. Philological Interpretation and Historical Commentary

This approach advocates that the Qur'an must be understood through the Arabic language simply because it has been revealed in Arabic. According to this approach, one must know the chronological order of the Qur'an and the circumstances of time and place surrounding the revelation of the text. Whilst no complete work of *tafsīr* exists which represents this trend, there is however, one incomplete work which serves this purpose. Entitled, *Tafsīr al-Bayān li al-Qur'ān al-Karīm* it was written by Aishah bint Abd al-Rahman al-Shati, best known best as Bint al-Shati.

The concept of this trend was initiated by Amin al-Khuli (d. 1967), who never published a Qur'anic commentary, although he taught Qur'anic interpretation at *Al-Jāmiʿah al-Miṣriyyah* (the Egyptian University) in Giza. For Amin al-Khuli, the ideal *tafsīr* commentary should be divided in two parts. The first providing a study of the background of the Qur'an, the history of its genesis, Arab society at the time of the revelation, Arabic language, etc among other topics. The second providing commentary and exegesis on the verses of the Qur'an in the light of preliminary studies.[17]

Bint al-Shati, a student of Amin al-Khuli who became his wife later, was exposed to this method by her husband and became very enthusiastic concerning it. She began to advocate it in 1964 giving many lectures on the subject matter.[18] More interestingly, she summarized the principles of the trends as she expanded or articulated her husband's work *Manhaj Tajdīd* under the following four headings:

1) Thematic: The basis of the method is the collection of all surahs and verses of the topics to be studied.
2) Contextual understanding: To understand a particular Qur'anic notion, in context, verses on it are placed in the chronological order of their revelation so that the circumstances of time and place may be known. Traditional reports on the "occasions of revelations" are taken into consideration only as far as those occasions are contextual circumstances and associated with the revelation of a particular verse. They are not its purpose or its cause sine qua non. From this perspective, the significance lies in the generality of words, not the specificity of the occasion.
3) Linguistic understanding: To understand the meanings of words – since Arabic is the language of the Qur'an – the original linguistic meaning is sought which gives the sense of feeling for the Arabic word in its various material and figurative uses. The Qur'anic meaning is then noted by collecting all forms of the word in the Qur'an and studying their particular context in specific verses and surahs and their general context in the Qur'an as a whole.
4) Understanding subtleties of expression: To do this both the letter and the spirit of a particular text in its Qur'anic setting are considered. Then statements of exegetes are examined in relation to the text studied, and only what agrees with the text is accepted. To be avoided are all sectarian interpretations and all instructive *Iisrā'īliyyā*t (Jewish-Christian materials) forced on *tafsīr* literature. In like manner, grammatical and rhetorical usage in the Qur'an is to be considered the criterion by which the rules of grammarians

and rhetoricians are judged, not vice versa, since most of these were people for whom Arabic was not their mother tongue.[19]

As far as Bint al-Shati's methodology and some of her important findings and details are concerned, see Muhammad Sharif and Boullata.[20] Bint al-Shati's *tafsīr* has been described by Manna al-Qattan as an acceptable effort. However, he expresses some concern over the deficiency of this method with regard to certain aspects of the Qur'anic sciences, including the miracles associated with the Qur'anic laws and basic principles. Muhammad Sharif also held reservations similar to those of al-Qattan.[21]

5. The Traditional Approach

This approach relies heavily on classical *tafsīr* and literature, but it also addresses some issues of modern times. Representatives of the trend include Shaykh Muhammad Jamal al-Din al-Qasimi (1866–1914) and his work *Maḥāsin al-Ta'wīl* and Muhammad al-Tahir ibn Ashur, author of the famous *Al-Taḥrīr wa al-Tanwīr.* Discussion focuses on the latter.

Al-Sheikh Muhammad al-Tahir ibn Ashur was a contemporary Tunisian scholar (d. 1960), and one of the most outstanding Muslim scholars of the 20th century. He was a competent *uṣūlī* (legal theorist), a *mufassir*, a judge and the *Muftī* of Tunisia. *Al-Taḥrīr wa al-Tanwīr*, his famous *tafsīr* commentary, was originally published under the title *Taḥrīr al-Maʿnā al-Sadīd wa Tanwīr al-ʿAql al-Jadīd min al-Tafsīr al-Majīd* but later shortened by him to *Al-Taḥrīr wa al-Tanwīr min al-Tafsīr.*

The work is highly comprehensive in nature and typically classical in approach. It can be fairly described as an "encyclopedia." Ibn Ashur claimed his *tafsīr* to contain the best found in *tafsīr* literature, as well as the best found in *tafsīr* books, "*Fa fīh aḥsan māfī al-tafāsīr wa fīh aḥsan min māfī al-tafāsīr,*" (that is in his book one finds the best explanation of *tafsīr*, and also in his book one finds the best information among all other books of *tafsīr*).

Ibn Ashur in his words had long dreamt of producing a *tafsīr* of the Qur'an with a view to elucidating its subtlety and general legislation (*al-Tashrī*ᶜ), but given the enormous difficulty of the task at hand hesitated, remaining undecided, until one day when given the position of a judge, and its attendant responsibilities, he gave up all hope. After serving the court for a while, he became *muftī* of Tunisia which meant that he now had the authority to issue fatwas (Islamic legal opinion). This meant that at long last he could actually start working on his own Qur'anic commentary and realize the dream he had cherished for so long. In the now famous *tafsīr* which resulted Ibn Ashur claims to have included subtleties which no one before him had mentioned. In this respect, he further indicates that he conducted ground-breaking research, on the basis of new sources, resulting in the recording of new findings, which Allah had blessed him with, and which no exegete prior to him had ever mentioned, based that is on the sources available to him. By this he means that others may also have discovered them but not according to the sources available.

In regard to the *tafsīr* itself, according to Ibn Ashur he focused on aspects of Qur'anic miracles, rhetorical subtlety, and *Asālīb al-Isti*ᶜ*māl* (literally, 'usage styles'), an Arabic phrase used to refer to the various Qur'anic styles, the coherence or relationship between Qur'anic verses, and elaboration on the meaning of Qur'anic terms and their exact dialectical usage not mentioned by many Arabic lexicons.

In terms of the *tafsīr's* methodology before discussing any surah Ibn Ashur begins by mentioning its name. If the Prophet named the surah, he mentions the corresponding hadith. If a Companion, then he mentions both the corresponding hadith and the names of the *Ṣahābī*, or *Ṣaḥābah*. If the surah has other names, he mentions these and explains why this particular name was chosen. Secondly, he states to which of the two phases (Makkan or Madinan) the surah belongs. Thirdly, he indicates the position of the surah in terms of the chronological order of the revelation. Fourthly, he mentions the total number of verses which the surah contains. Lastly, he explains the purpose and objectives of the surah.

The work in addition cites numerous hadith, references to *asbāb al-nuzūl* (occasions the circumstances of revelation), *tafsīr* statements by the Companions and the Successors, names of various exegetes as well as *mufassirūn*, and an intensive and sustained discussion on *balāghah* (rhetoric), philological analysis, grammar, *munāsabāt bayn al-āyāt* (relationships between the verses), fiqh (Islamic jurisprudence) etc.

6. Natural History

This trend is described by Muhammad al-Dhahabi (1915-1977) as one that is preferred or used by renegades, while Jansen terms it a natural history approach. Al-Dhahabi, as a Muslim, was concerned with the contents of *tafsīr* works, while Jansen rather looked at them from a Western scholar's viewpoint.[22] The trend contends that all *tafsīr* literature is useless. It even rejects some of the established principles of the Qur'an and Hadith as well as the miracles of the prophets Abraham, Moses, Jesus, Solomon and so on, claiming to be a new method of understanding the Qur'an. One of its outstanding exponents is Muhammad Abu Zayd, who penned the controversial *Al-Hidāyah wa al-ʿIrfān*, a work confiscated by al-Azhar University who declared its author an apostate and issued a fatwa rejecting its contents.[23]

Conclusion

QUR'ANIC EXEGESIS has a long history. It aims to make clear the true meaning of the Qur'an. Each generation of exegetes has approached *tafsīr* from perspectives unique to the time, place and circumstances of the era in which they lived. Qur'anic interpretation began with the Prophet Muhammad, the supreme exegete, who gave precise and clear explanations. After his death, the Companions believed they had a divine obligation to disseminate and teach the Qur'an and its interpretation to the next generations of Muslims. During their time, four major schools of Qur'anic interpretation emerged named after the areas in which they became prominent: the Makkan School (led by ʿAbd Allāh ibn ʿAbbās), the Madinah School (led by Ubay ibn Kaʿb), the Iraq School (led by ʿAbd Allāh ibn Masʿud), and the Shām School (Greater Syria or Levant).

Each of these schools produced a number of highly regarded authorities on interpretation. During the era of the *Tābiʿūn*, the method and nature of interpretation was not much different from that of the Companions. It consisted of a combination of rote (or near rote) transmission and personal, but well founded intellectual opinion.

Later the *tafsīr* of the Companions and that of the Successors became the subject of heated debate among scholars centered on whether or not their *tafsīr* was a binding proof (a *ḥujjah* or *ḥujjiyyah*), an issue which would have future consequences at the Shariʿah level. Among the proponents of the Companions' Qur'an interpretation as being binding on future generations, were Imam Mālik, Imam

Aḥmad ibn Ḥanbal, Ibn Taymiyyah and Ibn Qayyim. Among its opponents were Imam Abū Ḥanīfah, Imam al-Shāfiʿī, al-Ghazālī, Abū Ḥayyān and ibn ʿAṭiyyah. The arguments of those who held that the Companions' *tafsīr* was a binding proof, were mostly based on the merits of the Companions, whereas the arguments of those who believed otherwise were based on textual evidence and intellectual analysis.

As for the authoritative nature of the *tafsīr* of the *Tābiʿūn*, little concern was given to it. Ibn Qayyim was one of, if not the strongest, believers in the binding character of their *tafsīr*.

During the first century of Islam no exhaustive *tafsīr* work existed that covered the entire text of the Qur'an. The only known extant commentary of this type is al-Ṭabarī's *Jāmiʿ al-Bayān ʿan Ta'wīl Āy al-Qur'ān*. This work covers the whole Qur'an, surah by surah and verse by verse. Yet, both Ibn Ḥazm and al-Tahar ibn Ashur make two claims: first, that a comprehensive *tafsīr* did exist prior to al-Ṭabarī's, written by Abu ʿAbd al-Raḥman Baqīʿ ibn Makhlad ibn Yazīd (d. 273/889), but that it was subsequently lost; secondly, that this commentary was more comprehensive than al-Ṭabarī's. This view is supported by Tahir ibn Ashur who simply stated that he found some volumes of this work in Tunisia without giving further details, and by Ibn Ḥazm who commented that there was no *tafsīr* commentary comparable to Baqīʿ's interpretation.

After the fourth century AH three main developments occurred in the field of Qur'anic exegesis, these being: the use of unverified statements, the age of specialization, and the emergence of reprehensible interpretation or *tafsīr al-bidʿah*. Al-Suyūṭī described the new trend as the age of the shortening of the chains of narration (*ikhtiṣār al-asānīd*).

The emergence of these three developments subsequently led to two further important developments in the field of Qur'anic interpretation. These were: *al-tafsīr bi al-ma'thūr* and its natural counterpart *al-tafsīr bi al-ra'y* as two distinctive fields. Various scholars further divided the latter into two categories: *al-tafsīr bi al-ra'y al-maḥmūd* and *al-tafsīr bi al-ra'y al-madhmūm*. The second *al-tafsīr bi al-ra'y al-maḥmūd* involved the formation or recognition of scholarly and intellectual prerequisites for sound ijtihad to ensure proper participation in the sciences of Qur'anic interpretation.

The age of specialization is characterized by an expansion of *tafsīr* into specialties with descriptions such as juristic, grammatical, intellectual as well as other forms of *tafsīr*. The emergence of *bidᶜah al-tafsīr* – as termed by Ibn Taymiyyah, al-Suyūṭī and al-Dhahabī – is actually sectarian *tafsīr* produced by Mu ᶜtazili, Shia or Sufi commentators.

Nonetheless, Muslim scholars have remained prolific in their production of Qur'anic commentary. New exegesis trends continued to appear, creating new *tafsīr* categories such as scientific, literary, natural history and philological interpretation. As noted previously, it was common for classical scholars to write *tafsīr* works with the main purpose of educating their generation. May Allah reward them for their laudable intentions.

In the twentieth century and in our own time, following in the footsteps of earlier *mufassir*, many contemporary scholars have striven hard to bring a proper understanding of the Qur'an to Muslims, and indeed to the world at large, as fully as possible, in an attempt to widen knowledge of the guidance contained therein, and how to live our lives in accordance with its principles. Generating precise comprehension of the Qur'an and the true meaning of its verses is in my opinion the essence of perhaps the most important of the Islamic sciences, Qur'anic exegesis or *tafsīr*.

The message, for Muslims at least, is clear, success both in this life and the hereafter cannot be achieved except by Allah's will and as a result of a life lived in accordance with the tenets laid down in His message to mankind – the Qur'an. It is therefore imperative that the text is given the study, attention, focus, priority, and the *respect* that it deserves.

GLOSSARY

Ab*ʿ*ad al-ajalayn the longest period of the(ʿ*iddahs*)
ʿ***Adālah*** justice
ʿ***Ādil*** a just person
Ahl al-ḥaqīqhah the people of truth, reality
Ahl al-Sunnah wa al-Jamā*ʿ*ah people who adhere to the tradition of the Prophet, Companions, and Successors
Asālīb al-isti*ʿ*māl a literary style, stylistic peculiarity, rhetorical subtlety
Athar trace
Athar khuffa al-ba*ʿ*īr incision made in the foot of the camel in order to determine and trace the foot print
Awwala to return, to arrive at the final end, to interpret
Āyāt (plur. of *āyah*) verses of the Qur'an
Balāgah Arabic rehtoric
Bayān explanation
Bid*ʿ*ah innovation
Bismi Allāh In the name of Allah
Bushrā good tiding
Faqad kafar indeed, he has disblieved
Fassar explanation
Fatāwā (sing. fatwa) legal verdicts, legal opinion
al-Fātiḥah lit. the opening, the first chapter of the Qur'an
Fulān min ahl al-ra'y so and so is of the people of opinion
Fuqahā' (sing. faqīh) Muslim jurists, those who are learned in fiqh
Gharīb strange words
Ḥabr hādhihi al-ummah scholar of the Muslim community
Hadith the Prophet Muhammad's sayings, actions and his tacit approval
Ḥasanah good
Hijrah immigration of the Prophet Muhammad and his Companions from Makkah to Madinah
al-Ḥurūf al-muqaṭa*ʿ*ah the abbreviated letter of the Qur'an
ʿ***Iddah*** prohibited period for a widow or a divorcee to get married; four months and ten days for a widow and three cycles for a woman who experiences monthly periods and three months for a woman who does not have a monthly period
Iḥrām to profess intention, and wear the statutory clothing, for performing pilgrimage
Ijtihād lit. exertion, and technically is excessive effort a jurist makes to deduce the law
Ikhtāranī he chose me
Ikhtiṣār shortening, abreviating
Isrā'iliyyāt hadith reports originating from Jewish and Christian sources
Isṭifā' choosing, selection
Istinbāṭ inference
Istishhādāt citation of a verse to prove and support a claim or an opinion
I*ʿ*tiqād belief
Ittaqū al-tafsīr refrain from Qur'anic exgesis
Iyāla arrangement, regency

Jāhiliyyah lit. ignorance and technically, Arab traditional practice which Islam condemned when the Prophet Muhammad became a Messenger; also, unIslamic behavior
Kalālah a person dies without leaving behind neither descendants nor ascendants as heirs
al-Karīm lit. the Generous, the Honorable – one of Allah's names
al-Khasf baseness, ignomity, swallowing up by earth
Khilāfah a ruler of the Islamic State
Khurāfāt fairly tale, fable, nonsense
Kufr disbelief
al-Kursiy the chair, also God's Throne
al-Kutub al-Ṣittah the six books of Hadith considered to be the most authentic ones
La ᶜamrī upon my life. This phrase does not mean you are swearing by your life. It is a cultural expression which Arabs use
al-Madhdmūm blameworthy
Madhhab a school of fiqh or thought
al-Maḥmūd praiseworthy
al-Mamdūḥ praisworthy
Maqṣūduhā its meaning, objective
al-Marwah a Hill in Makkah considered as symbol of God
Mashhūd that which is witnessed, the Day of judgment
al-Masmūᶜ that which is heard
al-Ma'thūr lit. 'the traced', the transmitted information traced back to the Prophet, his Companions and the second generation of Muslims
Mubtadiᶜah innovators in Islam
Mufassirūn exegetes, commentators of the Qur'an
Muḥaddithūn scholars of Hadith
Mujassim anthropomorphist
Mujtahid a qualified scholar who exercises ijtihad
Mulḥid renegade, heritic, unbelieving
Munāsabāt proportional relations among the verses of the Qur'an, proportions
Muqtaṣid one who takes the middle course, a moderate
al-Mushāhadāt witnesses (of the truth)
Mutashābihāt verses which are open to different interpretations, verses which are not entirely clear
Naḥw Arabic grammar
al-Naql transmission
Niᶜmah blessing
Qāla he said
Qawl saying, statement
Qirā'ah recitation
Qiṣāṣ just retaliation
Qiyās analogy
Quṣṣāṣ story tellers
al-Raḥīm The Beneficent – one of Allah's names
al-Raḥmān The Merciful – one of Allah's names
Ra's al-mufassirīn head, leader of the exegetes, outstanding exegate
al-Ra'y opinion
Ribā usury
Ṣaḥābah Companions of the Prophet Muhammad
Ṣaḥābī a Companion
Salaf predecessors, *Ṣaḥabah* and *Tābiᶜīn*
Shāhid a witness
Sharīᶜah Islamic Law
Ṣifāt attributes,
Silsilat al-kadhib chain of lie, rejected chain of narration
al-Sirāṭ al-mustaqīm the straight path
Ṣūfīs group of people who practice Sufism (mysticism)
Sūrah a chapter of the Qur'an
Tābiᶜīn a person who met one of the Companions of the Prophet Muhammad but did not meet the Prophet
Tabyīn illustration

Tafsīr Qur'anic exegesis
al-Tafsirah a physician's examination of urine to determine a patient's illness
al-Tafsīr al-mawḍūʿī thematic exegesis of the Qur'an
Ta'khīr a subject placed in delayed position grammatically
Tarjumān al-Qur'ān interpretator of Qur'an, a title given to Ibn ʿAbbās
Tawḥīd Believing in One God, unity of God
Ta'wīl interpretation
Uḥud a mountain in Madinah
Ulī al-amr those who are in charge of people, leaders of the community
ʿUrf usage
Uṣūl al-fiqh principles of fiqh
Ẓāhir Manifest
Zakah obligatory charity
Zuhd asceticism

NOTES

CHAPTER 1

1 Al-Suyūṭī, Jalāl-Dīn ʿAbd al-Raḥmān ibn Abū Bakr, *Al-Itqān fī ʿUlūm al-Qur'ān*, 1st edn., (Beirut: Dār al-Kutub al-ʿImiyyah, 1987/1407).

2 Ibn Ashur, Muhammad, al-Tahir, *Al-Tahrīr wa al-Tanwīr* (Tunis: Al-Dār al-Tunisiyyah li al-Ṭibāʿah wa al-Nashr, n.d.), vol. 1, p. 5.

3 Al-Suyūṭī, *Al-Itqān,* vol. 2, p. 382.

4 Ibid., vol. 2, p. 381.

5 Ibid., vol. 2, p. 439.

6 Ibn Kathīr, al-Imām al-Hāfiẓ al-Qurashī, al-Dimashqī, *Mukhtaṣar Tafsīr Ibn Kathīr*, ed., Muhammad Ali al-Sabuni, new edn., (Dār al-Maʿrifah, 1994), vol. 2, p. 438.

7 Abū Jaʿfar Muḥammad ibn Jarīr al-Ṭabarī, *Jāmiʿ al-Bayān ʿan Ta'wīl Āy al-Qur'ān*, eds., Mahmud Muhammad Shakir and Ahmed Muhammad Shakir, (Cairo: Dār al-Maʿārif, n.d), vol. 1, p. 204.

8 Al-Suyūṭī, *Al-Itqān*, vol. 2, p. 413.

9 Ibn Ḥajar al-ʿAsqalānī, *Fatḥ al-Bārī fī Sharḥ Ṣaḥīḥ al-Bukhārī* (Cairo: al-Maṭbaʿah al-Salafiyyah, n.d.), vol. 8, p. 265.

10 Al-Tirmidhī, Abū ʿĪsā Muḥammad ibn Sūrah, *Sunan al-Tirmidhī*, ed., Abd al-Rahman Muhammad Uthman, 1st edn., (Cairo: Dār al-Fikr, 1964/1384,), vol. 2, p. 397.

11 Aḥmad ibn Ḥanbal , *Al-Fatḥ al-Rabbānī li Tartīb Musnad al-Imām Aḥmad ibn Ḥanbal Al-Shaybānī*, ed., Abd al-Rahman al-Banna (Cairo: Dār al-Shihāb), vol. 18, pp. 175-176.

12 Al-Ṭabarī, *Jāmiʿ al-Bayān*, vol. 1, p. 204.

13 Muṣʿab ibn ʿUmayr was the first ambassador in Islam. He was sent by the Prophet to Madinah to teach the people of Madinah the Qur'an. He died in the battle of Uhud.

14 ʿAlī ibn Abī Ṭālib was a cousin and a son-in law to the Prophet Muhammad. He was also the fourth Caliph.

15 Ibn Saʿd, Muḥammad ibn Saʿd ibn Manīʿ al-Zuhrī, *Al-Ṭabaqāt al-Kubrā* (Beirut: Dār Ṣādir, 1957), vol. 2, pp. 107-110.

16 Ibid., vol. 2, pp. 98-99.

17 Ibn Taymiyyah, Taqiy al-Dīn Aḥmad ibn ʿAbd al-Ḥalīm, *Muqaddimah fī Uṣūl al-Tafsīr,* ed., Adnan Zorzo, (Beirut: Dār al-Qur'ān al-Karīm, 1979/1399), p. 61.

18 Al-Suyūṭī, *Al-Itqān*, vol. 2, p. 413.

19 Ibn Taymiyyah, *Muqaddimah fī Uṣūl al-Tafsīr*, p. 61.

20 Ibn Saʿd, *Al-Ṭabaqāt al-Kubrā*, vol.2, p. 164.

21 Al-Suyūṭī, *Al-Itqān*, vol. 2, p. 413.

22 Ibn Sa^cd, *Al-Ṭabaqāt al-Kubrā*, vol. 2, p. 164.

23 Zaglul, Shahatah al-Sayyid, *Ubay ibn Ka^cb: Al-Rajul wa al-Muṣḥaf.* 1st edn., (Cairo: Al-Haya'ah al-Miṣriyyah al-^cĀmmah li al-Kitāb, 1978), pp. 33-6.

24 Ibid., p. 28.

25 Ibn ^cAsākir, *Tārīkh Dimashq*, vol. 1, p. 102.

26 Ibn Sa^cd, *Al-Ṭabaqāt al-Kubrā*, vol. 2, p. 125.

27 Khayr al-Dīn al-Zirikli, *Al-A^clām: Qāmūs Tarajim li Ashhar al-Rijāl wa al-Nisā' min al-^cArab wa al-Musta^cribīn wa al-Mustashriqīn* (Beirut: Dār al-^cIlm li al-Malayīn, 1980), vol. 3, p. 322. Ibn Ḥajar al-^cAsqalānī, *Tahdhīb al-Tahdhīb,* vol. 3, p. 265.

28 Ibn Sa^cd, *Al-Ṭabaqāt al-Kubrā*, vol. 2, p. 161.

29 Al-Zirikli, *Al-A^clām*, vol. 4, p. 96; Abū ^cAbd Allāh Shams al-Dīn Muḥammad ibn Aḥmad ibn ^cUthmān al-Dhahabī, *Tadhkirat al-Ḥuffāẓ*, vol. 1, p. 48.

30 Mujāhid ibn Jabr was a famous student of Ibn ^cAbbās. He narrated *tafsīr* and hadith from more than 12 *Ṣaḥābah* and was the source of narration for more than 28 immediate *Tābi^cūn* (followers) and later narrators of *tafsīr*, hadith and fiqh jurisprudence. He claimed to have studied the whole Qur'an with Ibn ^cAbbās three times. During each session, he would stop at the end of each verse and ask Ibn ^cAbbās about the place and context of its revelation. Mujāhid was described as the head of *mufassirūn* and was known as a *thiqah* (trustworthy). See Al-Dhahabī, *Siyar A^clām al-Nubalā'* (Cairo: Ma^chad al-Makhṭūṭāt al-^cArabiyyah, 1952-1956), vol. 4, p. 449.

31 Sa^cīd ibn Jubayr is one of Ibn ^cAbbās' students. He narrated *tafsīr* and hadith from about 110 *Ṣaḥābah*, and was the source of narration for more than 86 students of him. Ibn ^cAbbās appreciated greatly his knowledge. When the people of Iraq came to Ibn ^cAbbās asking religious questions, he told them: "Why are you asking me when you have someone among you in Iraq like Sa^cīd ibn Jubayr?" Sa^cīd ibn Jubayr was recognized as *thiqah.* See Al-Dhahabī, *Siyar a^clām al-Nubalā'*, vol. 4, p. 328 and Ibn Sa^cd, *Al-Ṭabaqāt*, vol. 6, p. 179.

32 ^cIkrimah al-Barbarī was an outstanding student of Ibn ^cAbbās and lived with him at his home. ^cIkrimah learnt and narrated from more than 10 *Ṣaḥābah* and was the source of narration for more than 20 Successors and later narrators. Ibn ^cAbbās recognized publically his knowledge and encouraged him to give fatwas in his presence. ^cIkrimah claimed that there was no verse in the Qur'an about which he had not heard some information. Some of his contemporaries described him as *al-Baḥr* (the ocean) and as *thiqah.* See Al-Dhahabī, *Tadhkirat al-Ḥuffāẓ*, vol. 1, p. 96.

33 ^cAlqamah is one of the outstanding students of Ibn Mas^cūd. Ibn Ḥajar, *Tahdhīb al-Tahdhīb*, vol. 7, pp. 276-279.

34 Also one of the outstanding students of Ibn Mas^cūd. Ibid., vol. 7, p. 149.

35 One of the students of Ubay ibn Ka^cab. Ibid., vol. 9, p. 421.

36 Abū al-^cĀliyah was one of the students of the Madinah School. Al-Dhahabī, *Siyar A^clām al-Nubalā'*, vol. 4, pp. 207-212.

37 Outstanding exegete of the Madinan school of *tafsīr*. Al-Dhahabī, *Tadhkirat al-Ḥuffāẓ*, vol. 1, p. 132.

38 One of the students of the Shām School of *Tafsīr*. Ibn Saᶜd, *Al-Ṭabaqāt al-Kubrā*, vol. 2, p. 161.

39 One of the students of the Shām School of *Tafsīr*. Ibn Ḥajar, *Tahdhīb al-Tahdhīb*, vol. 3, p. 265.

40 Al-Shawkānī, Muḥammad ibn ᶜAlī, *Fatḥ al-Qadīr al-Jāmiᶜ bayn fannay al-Riwāyah wa al-Dirāyah min ᶜIlm al-Tafsīr* (Beirut: Maḥfūẓ al-ᶜAlī, n.d.), vol. 5, p. 338.

41 Ibn Ḥajar, *Tahdhīb al-Tahdhīb*, vol. 1, p. 263.

42 Ibn Saᶜd, *Al-Ṭabaqāt al-Kubrā*, vol. 5, p. 467. See Al-Dhahabī, *Siyar Aᶜlām al-Nubalā'*, vol. 4, p. 45.

43 Goldziher, Ignaz, *Muslim Studies*. Translated from German by C.R. Berber and S.M. Stern, 2nd edn., (Chicago: Aldine, New York, Altherton, n.d.), vol. 2.

44 Nabia Abbott, *Studies in Arabic Literary Papyri II: Qur'anic Commentary and Tradition* (Chicago: The University of Chicago Press, 1967), p. 112.

45 Shuᶜbah ibn al-ᶜAjjāj was given the title "Amīr al-Mu'minīn fī al-Ḥadīth" (the Commander of the Faithful in Hadith). He was the first scholar to do a critical study of Hadith. He was described as a *thiqah*. Al-Dhahabī, *Tadhkirat al-Ḥuffāẓ*, vol. 1, p. 19. Ibn Taymiyyah, *Muqaddimah fī Uṣūl al-Tafsīr*, p.105.

46 Wakīᶜ ibn al-Jarrāḥ was known for his extraordinary memory. One of his contemporaries said he heard him narrating 700 hadith by heart. He is considered as one of the outstanding scholars of Hadith. See. ᶜAbd al-Raḥman ibn Muḥammad ibn Abū Ḥatim al-Tamīmī al-Rāzī, *Kitāb al-Jarḥ wa al-Taᶜdīl* (India: Mabṭaᶜah al-Majlis Dā'irat al-Maᶜarifah al-ᶜUthmāniyyah, 1952/1371), vol. 1, pp. 219-20.

47 Sufyān ibn ᶜUyaynah held the reputation of being the most knowledgeable and expert in Hadith in the Hijaz (Makkah and Madinah). He was one of the outstanding scholars of Hadith. He has been described as a *thiqah*. See, Al-Rāzī, *Kitāb al-Jarḥ wa al-Taᶜdīl*, vol. 1, pp. 32-5

48 Abū ᶜUbaydah al-Muthannā al-Taymī was a notable linguistic and man of literacy. Al-Dhahabī, *Siyar Aᶜlām al-Nubalā'*, vol. 1, p. 369.

49 Published in three volumes by Ahmad Yusuf Najati and Ali Najjar in 1955.

50 Aḥmad ibn Muḥammad ibn Abī Bakr ibn Khallikān, *Wafayāt al-Aᶜyān wa Anbā' abnā' al-Zamān* (Cairo: Maktabah al-Nahḍah al-Miṣriyyah, 1948-1950), vol. 1, p. 139. See also, Nasr Hamid Abu Zayd, *Al-Ittijāh al-ᶜAqlī fī al-Tafsīr: Dirasah fī Qaḍiyyat al-Majāz fī al-Qur'ān ᶜInda al-Muᶜtazilah* (Beirut: Dār al-Tanwīr li al-Ṭibāᶜah wa al-Nashr, 1982), p.100.

CHAPTER 2

1 Muḥammad ibn Yazīd ibn Mājah was one of the authors of the famous six books known as *Al-Kutub al-Sittah* in the science of Hadith. He is considered as an "Imam in

Hadith" (leading master in Hadith). See Al-Dhahabī, *Siyar Aʿlām al-Nubalā'*, vol. 13, pp. 277-9.

2 ʿAbd al-Raḥman ibn Muḥammad ibn Abū Ḥatim al-Tamīmī al-Rāzī was a famous critic of Hadith. Among his works are *Kitāb al-Jarḥ wa al-Taʿdīl*, *ʿIlal al-Ḥadīth*. Al-Dhahabī, *Siyar Aʿlām al-Nubalā'*, vol. 1, p. 468.

3 Al-Ḥusayn ibn Dāwūd al-Masīsī known as Sunayd. He was described as *al-ḥāfiẓ*, a man with a strong memory, that is to say he memorized a great number of hadiths. See Ibn Taymiyyah, *Muqaddimah fī Uṣūl al-Tafsīr*, pp. 78-80.

4 Goldziher remarked "Were this book to have reached us we would have not needed to read any later generation's work in *tafsīr*" (translation mine), *Goldziher, Die Richtungen der Islamischen Koranauslegung* (Leiden, Brill. 1920), pp. 85-86.

5 Ibn Ḥazm holds that the *tafsīr* of Baqīʿ ibn Makhlad ibn Yazīd (d. 273/889) exceeded al-Ṭabarī's work. He further stated that no *tafsīr* work can be compared with Baqīʿ's. See Ibn Bashkuwāl, *Kitāb al-Ṣilah* (Cairo: Al-Dār al-Miṣriyyah li al-Tarjamah, 1996), p. 116. Also, Ibn Ashur stated that al-Ṭabarī is indebted in his methology to Yaḥyā ibn Sallām's work, the methodology combines *athar* and *ʿaql* (narration and *ijtihād*). See Ibn Ashur, *Al-Tafsīr wa al-Rijāluh*, p. 37.

6 Al-Suyūṭī, *Al-Itqān*, vol. 2, p. 419. See also, Muhammad Abd al-Adhim Al-Zarqani, *Manāhil al-ʿIrfān fī ʿUlūm al-Qur'ān*, vol. 2, pp. 32-3.

7 Al-Suyūṭī, *Al-Itqān*, vol. 2, p. 419.

8 Muhammad Husayn al-Dhahabi, *Al-Tafsīr wa al- Muffasirūn*, 1st edn., (Cairo: Dār al-Kutub al-Hadīthah, 1961/1381). p. 29.

9 Ibn Taymiyyah, *Muqaddimah fī Uṣūl al-Tafsīr*, p. 76; Al-Suyūṭī, *Al-Itqān*, vol. 2, p. 419.

10 *The Encyclopedia of Islam*, vol.II, E-K (Leiden: E.J. Brill, and London: Luzac and CO, 1927), vol. 7, pp. 735-6; Muhammad Husayn al-Dhahabi, *Al-Tafsīr wa al- Muffasirūn*, vol. 1, p. 228.

11 Abū Isḥāq Ibrāhīm ibn al-Sarī ibn Sahl known as Al-Zajjāj. See Ibn Kathīr, *Al-Bidayah wa al-Nihāyah*, ed., Muhammad Abd al-Aziz al-Najdi (Riyadh: Mu'assasah al-Kutub, n.d.), vol. 12, p. 147.

12 Muhammad Husayn al-Dhahabi, *Al-Tafsīr wa al- Muffasirūn*, vol. 1, pp. 138-9.

13 The book was published in eight volumes by Dār al-Kutb in Egypt. The work was considered the first grammatical *tafsīr* in the sense of covering the whole Qur'an. See Muhammad Husayn al-Dhahabi, *Al-Tafsīr wa al-Muffasirūn*, vol. 1, pp. 138-9.

14 Abū Ḥayyān, Muḥammad ibn Yūsuf ibn ʿAlī al-Andalusī, *Al-Baḥr al-Muḥīṭ*, vol. 1, p. 5.

15 Muhammad Hussayn al-Dhahabi, *Al-Tafsīr wa al-Muffasirūn*, vol. 2, pp. 416-29.

16 Ibid., vol. 2, pp. 430-5.

17 Muḥammad ibn ʿAlī Shams al-Dīn al-Dāwūdī, *Ṭabaqāt al-Muffasirīn*, vol. 2, p. 66.

18 Abū ʿAbd Allāh Muḥammad ibn Aḥmad al Anṣārī Al-Qurṭubī, *Al-Jāmiʿ li Aḥkām al-Qur'ān* (Cairo: Dār al-Kutub al-ʿArabiyyah li al-Ṭibāʿah wa al-Nashr, 1967-1387), vol. 1, pp. 2-3.

19 Hasan Diya al-Din Atr, *Al-Aḥruf al-Sab*ᶜ *wa Manzilat al-Qirā'āt Minhā.* 1st edn., (Beirut: Dār al-Bashā'ir al-Islāmiyyah, 1988/1409), pp. 317-20.

20 Al-Suyūṭī, *Al-Itqān*, vol. 2, p. 249. Abū Ḥayyān Muḥammad ibn Yūsif al-Andalusī, *Al-Baḥr al-Muḥīṭ*, vol. 1, p. 5.

21 Ahmed Ali al-Salus, *Bayn al-Shī*ᶜ*ah wa al-Sunnah: Dirāsah Muqāranah fī al-Tafsīr wa Uṣūlih* (Cairo: Dār al-Iᶜtiṣām, 1989), p. 178.

22 Ayoub, Muhammad M., *The Qur'an and Its Interpreters* (Albany State University of New York, 1984), p. 1369.

23 Ibid., p. 178.

24 Al-Salus, *Bayn al-Shī*ᶜ*ah wa al-Sunnah*, p. 178.

25 Abū ᶜAlī al-Faḍl ibn al-Ḥasan al-Ṭabarsī, *Majma*ᶜ *al-Bayān fī Tafsīr al-Qur'ān,* 2nd edn., (Cairo: Dār al-Fikr, 1954-1957), vol. 1, pp. 112-3.

26 Ibid., vol. 1, pp. 75-7.

27 Ibn Taymiyyah, *Majmū*ᶜ *Fatāwā Shaykh al-Islām Aḥmed ibn Taymiyyah,* ed., Ahmed Abd al-Rahman ibn Muhammad ibn Qasim al-Najdi al-Hanbali, (Makkah: Maṭbaᶜah al-Nahḍah al-Hadīthah 1404/1983), vol. 3, pp. 384-386.

28 Al-Qāḍī ᶜAbd al-Jabbār ibn Aḥmed Hamadānī was known as one of the champion scholars of the Muᶜtazilites. Among his famous works are: *Tanzīh al-Qur'ān* ᶜ*an al-Maṭā*ᶜ*in, Tathbīt Dalā'il Nubuwwat Sayyidina Muḥammad, Mutashābah al-Qur'ān*; Al-Suyūṭī, *Ṭabaqāt al-Mufassirīn*, p.234.

29 Al-Zamakhsharī, Abū al-Qāsim Mahmūd ibn ᶜUmar al-Khawarizmī was a recognized scholar of the Arabic language and *tafsīr.* Of his well known works are: *Asās al-Balāghah, Al-Fā'iq fī Gharīb al-Ḥadīth*; Ibn Khallikān, *Wafayāt al-A*ᶜ*yān*, vol. 4, p. 255.

30 Al-Zamakhsharī, *Al-Kashshāf* ᶜ*an Ḥaqā'iq Ghawāmiḍ al-Tanzīl wa* ᶜ*Uyūn al-Aqāwīl fī Wujūh al-Ta'wīl* (Cairo: Muṣṭafā al-Bābī al-Ḥalabī wa Awladuh, 1966), vol. 1, p. 3.

31 Abū Ḥayyān, *Al-Baḥr al-Muḥīṭ,* vol. 1, p. 4.

32 Ibn Khaldūn, ᶜAbd al-Raḥmān, *Muqaddimat Ibn Khaldūn*, 4th edn., (Beirut: Iḥyā' al-Turāth al-ᶜArabī, n.d.), vol. 3, p. 998.

33 Al-Ṭabarī, *Jāmi*ᶜ *al-Bayān,* vol. 30, p. 345.

34 Al-Zamakhsharī, *Al-Kashshāf*, vol. 4, p. 192.

35 Musaid ibn Sulayman al-Tayyar, *Al-Athar al-Lughawī fī Ikhtilāf al-Mufassirīn*, p. 149; Goldziher, *Kitāb Madhāhib al-Tafsīr al-Islāmī*, p. 89.

36 Muhammad Hussayn al-Dhahabi, *Al-Tafsīr wa al-Muffasirūn*, vol. 2, p. 240.

37 Ibid., vol. 2, p. 240.

38 Al-Dhahabī, *Tadhkirat al-Ḥuffāẓ*, vol. 3, p. 249. Al-Suyūṭī, *Ṭabaqāt al-Mufassirīn*, p. 31.

39 Al-Sulamī was the Shaykh of the Sufis in Khurasan. He was described as a man of knowledge. Al-Suyūṭī, *Ṭabaqāt al-Mufassirīn*, p. 31.

40 Al-Dāwaūdī, Muḥammad ibn ᶜAlī ibn Aḥmad, *Ṭabaqāt Muffasirīn* (Cairo: Maktabah Wahbah, 1972), vol. 2, pp. 138-9.

41 Al-Suyūṭī, *Al-Itqān*, vol. 2, p. 249.

42 Muhammad Rashid Rida, *Tafsīr al-Qur'ān al-Ḥakīm* known as *Tafsīr al-Mannār* (Beirut: Dār al-Fikr, n.d.), vol. 2, pp. 400-1.

43 Ibn ʿArabī, Muḥy al-Dīn, *Al-Futūḥāt al-Makkiyah* (Beirut: Mu'assasah al-Iʿlāmī li al-Maṭbūʿāt, 1973), vol. 2, p. 432.

44 Al-Ṭabarī, *Jāmiʿ al-Bayān*, vol. 4, p. 104. Ibn Kathīr, *Tafsīr Ibn Kathīr*, vol. 1, p. 347.

45 Al-Ālūsī, Shihāb al-Dīn Maḥmūd ibn ʿAbd Allāh al-Ḥusaynī, *Rūḥ al-Maʿānī fī Tafsīr al-Qur'ān al-ʿAẓīm wa al-Sabʿ al-Mathānī* (Beirut: Dār al-Turāth al-ʿArabī, n.d.), vol. 12, p. 168.

46 Al-Zarkashī, Abū ʿAbd Allāh Badr al-Dīn Muḥammad ibn ʿAbd Allāh, *Al-Burhān fī ʿUlūm al-Qur'ān*, ed., Muhammad Abu Fadl Ibrahim, (Cairo: Dār Iḥyā' al-Kutub al-ʿArabiyyah, 1957), vol. 1, p. 7.

47 Al-Suyūṭī, *Ṭabaqāt al-Mufassirīn*, p.31.

48 Muhammad Abd al-Azim Al-Zurqani, *Manāhil al-ʿIrfān fī ʿUlūm al-Qur'ān* (Cairo: Dār Iḥyā' al-Kutub al-ʿArabiyyah, ʿĪsā al-Bābī al-Ḥalabī, n.d.), vol. 2, p. 18. See Ahmad Von Denffer, *ʿUlūm al-Qurān*, p. 134.

49 Al-Qushayri, Abd al-Karim ibn Hawazin ibn Abd al-Malik, *Laṭā'if al-Ishārāt: Tafsīr Ṣūfī Kāzmil li al-Qur'ān* (Dār al-Kutub al-ʿArabiyyah, 1968), vol. 1, p. 57.

50 Judah Muhammad Muhammad Mahdi, *Al-Wāḥidī wa Manhajuhu fī al-Tafsīr* (Cairo: Al-Majlis al-Aʿlā li al-Shu'ūn al-Islāmiyyah, 1979), p. 152.

51 Al-Suyṭī, *Al-Itqān*, vol. 2, p. 395; Ibn Taymiyyah, *Muqaddimah fī Uṣūl al-Tafsīr*, p. 105.

52 Shihāb al-Dīn al-Ālūsī, *Rūḥ al-Maʿānī fī Tafsīr al-Qur'ān wa al-Sabʿ al-Mathānī*, vol. 1, p. 1.

53 Ibn Taymiyyah, *Muqaddimah fī Uṣūl al-Tafsīr*, pp. 90-1. Al-Suyūṭī, *Ṭabaqāt al-Mufassirīn*, p. 30.

54 Saʿīd ibn al-Musayyib was known as the jurist of Madinah. He was one of the most knowledgable *Tābiʿī*. See al-Dhahabī, *Tadhkirat al-Ḥuffāẓ*, vol.1, p.54-7.

55 Muhammad Ali al-Saboony, *Mukhtaṣar Tafsīr Ibn Kathīr Ikhtiṣār wa Taḥqīq*, vol. 1, p. 7.

56 Jawdah Muhammad Muhammad al-Mahdi, *Al-Wāḥidī wa Mahajahu fī al-Tafsīr*, p. 153; Al-Zarkashī, *Al-Burhān*, vol. 2, p. 162.

57 Al-Zarkashī, *Al-Burhān*, vol. 2, p. 162.

58 Abū Ḥāmid al-Ghazālī, *Iḥyā' ʿUlūm al-Dīn* (Cairo: Dār Ihyā' al-Kutb al-ʿArabiyyah, n.d.), vol. 1, p. 29.

59 Ibn ʿAṭiyyah, ʿAbd al-Ḥaqq ibn Ghālib, *Muqaddimatān fī ʿUlūm al-Qur'ān* (Cairo:Maṭbaʿah al-Khanijī, 1972), pp.186-7.

60 Al-Zarkashī, *Al-Burhān*, vol. 2, p. 162.

61 Ibn Taymiyyah, *Muqaddimah fī Uṣūl al-Tafsīr*, p. 52.

62 Al-Ghazālī, *Iḥyā' ʿUlūm al-Dīn*, vol. 1, p. 292. Al-Zurqani, *Manāhil al-ʿIrfān*, vol. 2, p. 49.

Notes

CHAPTER 3

1 Lane, *Arabic-English Lexicon,* vol. 1, p. 232; Ibn Manẓūr, Muḥammad ibn Mukram, *Lisān al-ʿArab* (Beirut: Dār Ṣādir, n.d.), vol. 1, p. 6.

2 Muhammad Muhsin Khan, *Sahih Al-Bukhari*, Arabic-English, (Riyadh: Dār al-Salām, 1994), p. 110.

3 Ibn Ḥazm, Abū Muḥammad ʿAlī ibn Aḥmad ibn Saʿīd al-Andalusī, *Al-Iḥkām fī Uṣūl al-Aḥkām,* ed., Ahmad Shakir, 2nd edn., (Beirut: Dār al-Āfāq al-Ḥadīthah, 1983/1403), vol. 6, p. 47.

4 Ibn Qayyim al-Jawziyyah, *Iʿlām al-Muaqqiʿīn ʿan Rabb al-ʿAlamīn,* 2nd edn., ed., Muhammad Muhyiddin Abd al-Alamin, (Beirut: Dār al-Fikr, 1977/1397), vol. 1, p. 55.

5 Al-Suyūṭī, *Tadrīb al-Rāwī fī Sharḥ Taqrīb al-Nawawī*, ed. Abd al-Wahhab Abd al-Latif, (Cairo: Dār al-Kutb al-Ḥadīthah, 1966). See also, Al-Shawkānī, *Fatḥ al-Qadīr* (Madinah: al-Maṭbaʿah al-Salafiyyah, n.d.), vol. 1, p. 103.

6 Al-Zarkashī, *Al-Burhān,* vol. 2, p. 157. See Goldziher, *Die Richtungen*, p. 63.

7 Ibn al-Ṣalāḥ, ʿUthmān ibn ʿAbd al-Raḥmān Taqī al-Dīn, *Muqaddimah Ibn al-Ṣalāḥ*, p. 128.

8 Al-Zurqani, *Manāhil al-ʿIrfān*, vol. 2, p. 12.

9 Muhammad Husayn al-Dhahabi, *Al-Tafsīr wa al-Muffasirūn*, vol. 1, p. 153.

10 Abd al-Ghani Abd al-Khaliq, *Ḥujiyyah al-Sunnah*, 1st edn., (Beirut: Dār al-Qur'an, 1986), p. 413.

11 Ibn Taymiyyah, *Muqaddimah fī Uṣūl al-Tafsīr,* p. 105; Ibn Qayyim, *Iʿlām al-Muaqqiʿīn,* vol. 4, p. 153.

12 Ibn al-Ṣalāḥ, *Muqaddimah Ibn al-Ṣalāḥ,* ed., Aisha Bint al-Shati, (Cairo: Dār al-Kutub, n.d.), p. 128.

13 Abd Allah ibn Abd al-Muhsin al-Turki, *Uṣūl Madhhab al-Imām Aḥmad: Dirāsah Uṣūliyyah Muqāranah* (Riyadh: Maṭbaʿah al-Riyāḍ, 1397/1977), pp. 179–80.

14 Al-ʿAsqalānī, *Fatḥ al-Bārī* (Cairo: al-Maṭbaʿah al-Salafiyyah, n.d), vol. 1, p. 45 and vol. 1, p. 70.

15 Ibn Qayyim, *Iʿlām al-Muaqqiʿīn,* vol. 1, p. 55.

16 Muhammad Husayn al-Dhahabi, *Al-Tafsīr wa al- Muffasirūn,* vol. 1, p. 149.

17 Ibn Taymiyyah, *Muqaddimah fī Uṣūl al-Tafsīr,* p. 37.

18 Al-Ṭabarī, *Jāmiʿ al-Bayān,* vol. 1, p. 38.

19 Al-Suyūṭī, *Al-Itqān,* vol. 2, pp. 430–453.

20 Al-Zarkashī, *Al-Burhān,* vol. 1, p. 16.

21 Al-Nawawī, Abū Zakariyyā Yaḥyā ibn Sharaf ibn Ḥussayn, *Matn al-Arbaʿīn al-Nawawiyyah,* Arabic and English, trans., Ezzeddin Ibrahim and Denys Johnson-Davies, (Damascas, 1977), p. 45.

22 Al-Nasā'ī, Abū ʿAbd al-Raḥmān Aḥmed ibn Shuʿayb ibn ʿAlī, *Tafsīr al-Nasā'ī*, eds., Abd al-Khaliq al-Sharif and Said ibn Abbas al-Julayni, (Cairo: Maṭbaʿah al-Sunnah, 1990), pp. 422–3.

23 Ibn Ḥajar, *Fatḥ al-Bārī*, vol. 8, p. 743.
24 That is to say a hadith in which the first of the chain of narrators, or all them, are not mentioned.
25 R. Marston Speight, *The Function of Hadith*, pp. 72–9.

CHAPTER 4

1 Ibn Manẓūr, *Lisān al-ʿArab*, vol. 1, p. 520.
2 Ibid., vol. 1, p. 520.
3 Ibn Ḥajar, *Al-Iṣābah fī Tamyīz al-Ṣaḥabah*, vol. 2, p. 83.
4 Ibid., vol. 2, p. 83.
5 Al-Āmidī, Sayf al-Dīn, *Al-Iḥkām fī Uṣūl al-Aḥkām*, ed., Abd Al-Razzaq Afifi, 2nd edn., (Beirut: Al-Maktab al-Islamī, 1402 AH), vol. 4, pp. 140–145.
6 Muhammad Hashim Kamali, *Principle of Islamic Jurisprudence* (Cambridge: Islamic Text Society, 1991), p. 249. The scholars also unanimously agreed that the opinion of a *ṣahābī* is not binding on the other *ṣaḥābī*.
7 Badran Abu al-Aynayn, *Uṣūl al-Fiqh*, 1st edn., (Cairo: Dār al-Fikr, 1976), p. 149.
8 Al-Sarkhasī, Imām Abū Bakr Muḥammad ibn Aḥmad ibn abī Sahl, *Uṣūl al-Sarkhasī*, ed., Abu al-Wafa al-Afghani, (Beirut: Dār al-Maʿrifah .n.d.)., vol. 1, p. 110.
9 Al-Ghazālī, *Al-Mustaṣfā min ʿIlm Uṣūl al-Fiqh*, vol. 1, p. 616.
10 Ibn Qayyim, *Iʿlām al-Muaqqiʿīn*, vol. 4, pp. 126–31.
11 Al-Āmidī, *Al-Iḥkām*, vol. 4, p. 152.
12 Ibn Qayyim, *Iʿlām al-Muaqqiʿīn*, vol. 4, p. 151.
13 Ibn Taymiyyah, *Majmūʿ Fatāwā*, vol. 13, p. 364. See Umar Faruq Abd Allah, *Malik's Concept of Amal in the Light of Maliki Legal Theory* (Chicago: The University of Chicago, 1978–1398), vol. 1, p. 162.
14 Ibn Qayyim, *Iʿlām al-Muaqqiʿīn*, vol. 4, p. 137.
15 Ibid., vol. 4, p. 131.
16 Ibid., vol. 4, p. 132.
17 Ibid., vol. 4, p. 138.
18 Ibid.
19 Ibid.
20 Ibid.
21 Ibid., vol. 4, p. 139–148.
22 Al-Ansārī, Niẓām al-Dīn, *Kitāb Fawātiḥ al-Raḥmūt bi Sharḥ Musallam al-Thubūt wa maʿahū Al-Mustaṣfā min ʿIlm Uṣūl al-Fiqh* (Beirut: Dār al-Arqam ibn Abī al-Arqam li al-Ṭibāʿah wa al-Nashr, 1944–1414), vol. 2, pp. 187–8.
23 Al-Shawkānī, *Irshād al-Fuḥūl ilā Taḥqīq al-Ḥaq min ʿIlm al-Uṣūl*, p. 83.
24 Al-Āmidī, *Al-Iḥkām*, vol. 4, p. 149.
25 Ibid., vol. 4, p. 150.
26 Al-Ghazālī, *Al-Mustaṣfā min ʿIlm Uṣūl al-Fiqh*, vol. 1, p. 261.

27 Al- Āmidī, *Al-Iḥkām*, vol. 4, p. 151; Al-Ghazālī, *Al-Mustaṣfā min ʿIlm Uṣūl al-Fiqh*, vol. 1, p. 261.

28 Al-Āmidī, *Al-Iḥkām*, vol. 4, p. 150.

29 Al-Ghazālī, *Al-Mustaṣfā min ʿIlm Uṣūl al-Fiqh*, vol. 1, p. 621

30 Al-Turki, *Uṣūl Madhhab al-Imām Aḥmad*, p. 401.

31 Al-Ghazālī, *Al-Mustaṣfā min ʿIlm Uṣūl al-Fiqh*, vol. 1, p. 285. See Al-Āmidī, *Al-Iḥkām*, vol. 4, p. 154.

32 Abū Ḥayyān, *Al-Baḥr al-Muḥīṭ*, vol. 1, p. 5.

33 Ibn Ḥazm, *Al-Iḥkām*, vol. 5, p. 92.

34 Al-Zurqani, *Manāhil al-ʿIrfān*, vol. 2, p.16.

35 Al-Suyūṭī , *Al-Itqān*, vol2, p. 412.

36 Al-Saboony, Muhammad Ali, *Mukhtaṣar Tafsīr Ibn Kathīr*, vol. 1, p. 557.

37 Ibid., vol. 3, p. 262.

38 Al-Ṭabarī, *Jāmiʿ al-Bayān*, vol. 27, p. 457.

39 Al-Saboony, *Mukhtaṣar Tafsīr Ibn Kathīr*, vol. 1, p. 482.

40 Ibid., vol. 1, p. 557.

41 Ibid., vol. 3, p. 735.

42 Ibid., vol. 3, p. 262.

43 Al-Suyūṭī, *Al-Itqān* , vol.2, p. 412.

44 Abū Muḥammad al-Ḥusayn ibn Masʿūd al-Baghawī, *Maʿālim al-Tanzīl* (Multan: Idarat Talifat Ishrafiyya, 1988), vol. 1, p. 373.

45 Al-Wāḥidī, ʿAlī ibn Aḥmad, *Al-Basīṭ fī Tafsīr al-Qur'ān al-Majīd*, eds., a group of *ʿUlamā'*, 1st edn., (Cairo: Dār al-Kutub al-ʿIlmiyyah, 1992), vol. 1, p. 240.

46 Muhammad Ibrahim Sharif, *Buḥūth fī Tafsīr al-Qur'ān: Tārīkhuhu, Ittijāhātuhu, wa Manāhijuhu* (Cairo: Jāmiʿat al-Qāhirah, n.d.), p. 163.

47 Al-Saboony, *Mukhtaṣar Tafsīr Ibn Kathīr*, vol. 2, p. 343.

48 Al-Suyūṭī, *Al-Durr al-Manthūr fī al-Tafsīr bi al-Ma'thūr*, vol. 1, p. 347.

49 Al- Shawkānī, *Fatḥ al-Qadīr*, vol. 1, p. 213.

50 Al-Wāḥidī, *Al-Basīṭ*, vol. 1, p. 129.

51 Muhammad Ibrahim Sharif, *Buḥūth fī Tafsīr al-Qur'ān*, p. 110.

52 Ibid.

53 Ibn Ḥajar, *Fatḥ al-Bārī*, vol. 8, p. 175. See Khan, *Sahih Al-Bukhari*, Arabic-English, vol. VI, pp. 19-20.

54 Ibn Ḥajar, *Fatḥ al-Bārī*, vol. 8, pp. 367-8; Khan, *Sahih Al-Bukhari*, vol. VI, pp.179-80.

55 Ibn Ḥajar, *Fatḥ al-Bārī*, vol. 8, p. 265; Khan, *Sahih Al-Bukhari*, vol. VI, p. 99.

56 Ibn Taymiyyahh, *Muqaddimah fī Uṣūl al-Tafsīr*, p. 89; Al-Suyūṭī, *Al-Itqān*, vol. 2, p. 413.

57 Al-Suyūtī, *Al-Itqān*, vol. 2, pp. 414-417.

58 The only exception is surah 9, *al-Tawbah* where the *Bismillah* is not mentioned. There are two different opinions given for this. The first concerns the surah being a separate one, that is when the *Ṣahābah* were compiling the Qur'an into book form, they were not certain whether the previous surah, *al-Anfāl*, and *al-Tawbah* were one surah as the

Bismillah was not there. Thus, they separated between the two by drawing a line. The second reason is that the surah was revealed in connection with dissolving a peace treaty, and expresses God's anger with the polytheists. The *Bismillah* being about peace and mercy, it was in this instance not revealed. According to Arab custom, when someone wants to express his anger or seriousness by speech, he does not follow the formal procedure of speech by beginning with *Bismik Allahumma*, "In/With Your Name Our Lord". See: Ibn Ashur, *Al-Tanwīr wa al-Taḥrīr*, vol. 6, p. 101.

59 Abū Ṭāhir Muḥammad ibn Yaʿqūb Fayrūz Ābādī, *Tanwīr al-Miqbās* (*Tafsīr ibn ʿAbbās*), (Pakistan: Al-Maktaba al-Furūqiyya Malkan, n.d.), p.2.

60 Al-Shawkānī, *Fatḥ al-Qadīr*, vol. 1, p. 18; Ibn Kathīr, *Tafsīr Ibn Kathīr*, vol. 1, p. 17.

61 Al-Ṭabarī, *Jāmiʿ al-Bayān*, vol. 1, p. 79; Al-Shawkānī, *Fatḥ Al-Qadīr*, vol. 1, p. 29.

62 Muḥammad ibn Marwān al-Suddī al-Ṣaghīr was described by Hadith critics, such as Yaḥyā ibn Maʿīn, Ibn Ḥibbān, as a liar. Ibn Ḥajar, *Tahdhīb al-Tahdhīb*, vol. 9, p. 436.

63 Muḥammad ibn al-Sā'ib al-Kalbī was criticized by Imam Aḥmed ibn Ḥanbal and others. Imam Aḥmed stated al-Kalbī's *tafsīr* was worthless. See Ibn Khallikān, *Wafayāt al-Aʿyān*, vol. 4, p. 309.

64 Abū Sāliḥ was criticized by scholars of Hadith as unworthy. Ibn Khallikān, *Wafayāt*, vol. 4, p. 309.

65 Al-Suyūtī, *Al-Itqān*, vol.2, p. 435.

66 Nāfiʿ ibn Al-Azraq was one of the head of the Kharijites who terrified the Umayyad Dynasty. See Al-Dhahabī, *Lisān al-Mizān*, vol. 6, pp. 114-5

67 Aishah Abd al-Rahman Bint al-Shati, *Al-Iʿjāz al-Bayānī li al-Qur'ān wa Masā'il ibn al-Azraq: Dirāsah Muqāranah Lughawiyyah wa Bayāniyyah*, 2nd edn, (Cairo: Dār al-Maʿrifah, 1987), pp. 289-305.

68 Goldziher, *Die Richtungen*, p. 372.

69 John Wansbrough, *Qur'anic Studies: Sources and Methods of Scriptual Interpretation* (Oxford: Oxford University Press, 1977), pp. 216-17.

70 Andrew Rippin, "Bulletin of the School of Oriental and African Studies," vol. XLV, part. 1184, pp. 24-5.

71 Abū al-ʿAbbās Muḥammad ibn Yazīd al-Mubarrid, *Al-Kāmil fī al-Lughah wa al-Adab,* 1st edn., (Beirut: Mu 'assat Al-Risālah, 1986), vol. 3, pp. 1144-55. Al-Suyūṭī, *Al-Itqān*, vol. 1, p. 225. Sezgin, Fuat, *Tārīkh al-Turāth al-ʿArabī*: *Fī ʿUlūm al-Qur'ān wa al-Ḥadīth*, trans., Mahmud Fahmi Hijazi, (Riyadh: Jāmiʿat Muḥammad ibn Suʿūd al-Islāmiyyah, 1981), vol. 1, part 1, p. 65.

72 Ibn Ḥajar stated that Nāfiʿ had written his questions on two pages and read the questions from the two pages. Ibn Ḥajar, *Fatḥ al-Bārī*, vol. 8, p. 557.

73 Khan, *Sahih Al-Bukhari*, vol. VI, pp. 321-324.

74 Ibn ʿAbbas was not the only *ṣaḥābī* who used the sources of the People of the Book in explaining some Qur'anic verse, among the few names to be mentioned in this regard, ʿAbd Allāh ibn ʿUmar, and ʿAbd Allāh ibn ʿUmrū ibn al-ʿĀṣ. See, Nana, Ramzi, *Al-Isrā'īliyyāt wa Āthāruhā fī Kutub al-Tafsīr*, 1st edn., (Damascus: Dār al-Qalam, 1970-1390), pp. 78-89.

75 Al-Bukhārī, Abū ʿAbd Allāh Muḥammad ibn Ismāʿīl, *Al-Jāmiʿ al-Ṣaḥīḥ*, vol. 1, p. 331.
76 Ibn Ḥajar, *Fatḥ al-Bārī*, vol. 8, pp. 550–1.
77 Al-Shaykh Abd Al-Rahman ibn al-Hasan al-Shaykh, *Fatḥ Al-Majīd* (Riyadh, Dār al-Iftā'), pp. 379–80.
78 Ibn Taymiyyah, *Muqaddimah*, pp. 41–3; Ibn Kathīr, *Tafsīr Ibn Kathīr*, vol. 1, p. 23; Al-Shawkānī, *Fatḥ al-Qadīr*, vol. 1, p. 24.
79 Ibn Taymiyyah, *Introduction to the Principles of Tafseer*, (UK: Al-Hidaayah Publishing & Distribution, 1993), pp. 20–1.
80 Al-Jaṣṣāṣ, Abū Bakar Aḥmad ʿAlī, *Aḥkām al-Qur'ān* (Istanbul: Maktabah al-Awqaf al-Islamiyyah, 1916 CE/1335 AH), vol. 1, p. 332.
81 Ibn Kathīr, *Tafsīr Ibn Kathīr*, vol. 3, p. 186.
82 Ibid., vol. 2, p. 170.
83 Ibn Qayyim, *Zād al-Maʿād*, vol. 2, p. 48; Al-Ṭabarī, *Jāmiʿ al-Bayān*, vol. 27, p. 289; Ibn Kathīr, *Tafsīr Ibn Kathīr*, vol. 2, pp. 363–4
84 Ibn Kathīr, *Tafsīr*, vol. 3, p. 398. Al-Shawkānī, *Fatḥ al-Qadīr*, vol. 5, p. 110.
85 Al-Saboony, *Mukhtaṣar Tafsīr Ibn Kathīr*, vol. 3, pp. 623–4.
86 Day of ʿArafāt is the 9th day of Dhul Hijjah, the 12th month of the Islamic calendar. It is the greatest day of the Hajj (Muslim Pilgrimage).
87 Al-Saboony, *Mukhtaṣar Tafsīr Ibn Kathīr*, vol. 3, pp. 623–4.
88 Ibn Kathīr, *Tafsīr Ibn Kathīr*, vol. 4, p. 579.
89 Ibid., vol. 4, pp. 540–41.

CHAPTER 5

1 Ibn Kathīr, *Al-Bāʿith al-Ḥathīth fī Ikhtiṣār ʿUlūm al-Ḥadīth* (Beirut, Dār al-Fikr, 1967), p. 78.
2 Al-Sarkhasī, *Uṣūl al-Sarkhasī*, vol. 1, p. 114.
3 Shuʿbah ibn al-ʿAjjāj ibn al-Ward is considered as trustworthy with a strong memory. He was described as *Amīr al-Muḥaddithīn*. He was the first scholar to scrutinize the *isnād* (chain) of hadith in Iraq. See Ibn Ḥajar al-ʿAsqalānī, *Tahdhīb al-Tahdhīb*, vol. 1, p. 351.
4 Ibn Taymiyyah, *Muqaddimah fī Uṣūl al-Tafsīr*, p. 105.
5 Ibid.
6 Abū Ḥayyān, *Al-Baḥr al-Muḥīṭ*, vol. 1, p. 4.
7 Abu Zahrah, Muhammad, *Al-Muʿjizhah al-Kubrā: Al-Qur'ān*, p. 513.
8 Al-Turki, *Uṣūl Madhhab al-Imām Aḥmad*, p. 180.
9 Ibn Qayyim, *Al-Ṣawāʿiq al-Mursalah* (Riyadh: Dār Al-Hijrah, n.d.), vol. 2, pp. 345–6.
10 Al-Zarkashī, *Al-Burhān*, vol. 1, p. 24.
11 Al-Suyūṭī, *Al-Itqān*, vol. 2, p. 418.
12 Al-Ṭabarī, *Jāmiʿ al-Bayān*, vol. 2, p. 490; Ibn Kathīr, *Tafsīr Ibn Kathīr*, vol. 1, p. 124.
13 Also the popular hadith in both al-Bukhārī and Muslim, "You will see your Lord as you see this moon." Al- Bukhārī, *Al-Jāmiʿ al-Ṣaḥīḥ*, vol. 4, p. 146.

14 Al-Ṭabarī, *Jāmi*[c] *al-Bayān*, vol. 28, p. 320; Ibn Kathīr, *Tafsīr Ibn Kathīr*, vol. 7, p. 171.

15 Muhammad Abd al-Salam Abu al-Nil, *Tafsīr al-Imām Mujāhid ibn Jubayr*, 1st edn., (Cairo: Dār al-Fikr-al-Ḥadīthah, 1989), pp. 2-15.

16 Wansbrough, *Qur'anic Studies*, pp. 120-139.

17 Fred Leemhuis "Origins and Early Development of the *Tafsīr* Tradition" in A. Rippin, ed., *Approaches to the History of the Interpretation of the Qur'an*, pp. 19-21.

18 Ibn Kathīr, *Tafsīr Ibn Kathīr*, vol. 3, p. 273.

19 Ibid., vol. 1, p. 242.

20 Ibn Ḥajar, *Tahdhīb al-Tahdhīb*, vol. 1, pp. 42-4; Muhammad Husayn al-Dhahabi, *Al-Tafsīr wa al-Mufassirūn*, vol. 1, p. 111.

21 A sacred place for Muslims in Makkah where they spend the whole day in [c]Arafāt and a night in Muzdalifah during the annual pilgrimage (Hajj).

22 Ibn Kathīr, *Tafsīr Ibn Kathīr*, vol. 1, p. 427.

23 Ibid., vol. 4, p. 378.

24 Al-Suyūṭī, *Al-Durr al-Manthūr fī al-Tafsīr bi al-Ma'thūr* (Beruit: Dār al-M[c]ārif, n.d).

25 See for example Abd al-Qahir al-Jurjani, *Dalā'il al-I*[c]*jāz* (Cairo: Muṣṭafā al-Bābī al-Ḥalabī, 1967), pp. 42-8.

26 Ibn Kathīr, *Tafsīr Ibn Kathīr*, vol. 3, p. 267.

27 Al-Ṭabarī, *Jāmi*[c] *al-Bayān*, vol. 1, p. 546; Ibn Kathīr, *Tafsīr Ibn Kathīr*, vol. 7, p. 154.

28 Ibn Kathīr, *Tafsīr Ibn Kathīr*, vol. 1, p. 141.

29 Ibn Ḥajar, *Tahdhīb*, vol. 10, pp. 109-111.

30 Ibn Kathīr, *Tafsīr Ibn Kathīr*, vol. 3, pp. 109-111; Al-Suyūṭī, *Al-Durr al-Manthūr fī al-Tafsīr bi al-Ma'thūr*, vol. 1, p. 345.

31 Ibn Kathīr, *Tafsīr Ibn Kathīr*, vol. 3, p. 258. Bal[c]am was one of the Prophet Moses's disciples.

32 Ibn Ḥajar, *Tahdhīb al-Tahdhīb*, vol. 2, pp. 263-270.

33 Ibn Kathīr, *Tafsīr Ibn Kathīr*, vol. 7, p. 199.

34 See for example, Ibn Sa[c]d, *Ṭabaqāt Ibn Sa*[c]*d*, vol. 4, p. 412; Al-Dhahabī, *Mīzān al-I*[c]*tidāl fī Naqd al-Rijāl*, vol. 1, p. 313; Ibn Ḥajar, *Tahdhīb al-Tahdhīb*, vol. 3, pp. 397-95.

35 Al-Shawkānī, *Fatḥ al-Qadīr*, vol. 1, p. 193.

36 Ibn Kathīr, *Tafsīr Ibn Kathīr*, vol. 3, p. 42.

37 *Hadith Mursal* is a hadith that one of the *Tābi*[c] ascribed directly to the Prophet without mentioning any of the Companions's names. Such hadith is generally classified as weak hadith. See al-Nawawī, *Sharḥ Ṣaḥīḥ Muslim* (Beirut: Dār al-Fikr, n.d.), vol. 1, pp. 131-2.

38 Abū al-[c]Āliyah is one of the outstanding exegetes of the Madinah school of *tafsīr*. He has been described by scholars of Hadith as *thiqah* (trustworthy). See Ibn Ḥajar, *Tahdhīb al-Tahdhīb*, vol. 3, pp. 284-5; Al-Dhahabī, *Mizān*, p. 249.

39 Ibn Kathīr, *Tafsīr Ibn Kathīr*, vol. 3, p. 40.

40 Ibid., vol. 1, pp. 412-413.

41 Ibid.

42 Ibid., vol. 1, p. 350.

43 See for detailed discussion on this matter, Muhammad al-Amin ibn Muhammad ibn Muhammad al-Mukhtar al-Jakani al-Shinghiti, *Aḍwā' al-Bayān fī Īḍāḥ al-Qur'ān bi al-Qur'ān* (Beirut: Aᶜlām Al-Kutab, n.d.), vol. 5, pp. 231-247.

44 Ibn Kathīr, *Tafsīr Ibn Kathīr*, vol. 1, p. 533.

45 Ibid., vol. 4, p. 237.

46 Ibid., vol. 4, p. 249.

47 Ibid., vol. 7, pp. 74-5.

48 Ibid., vol. 4, p. 304.

49 Ibid., vol. 7, p. 412.

50 Ibid.

51 Ibid.

52 Ibid., vol. 5, p. 600.

53 Ibid., vol. 7, p. 476.

54 Ibid., vol. 8, p. 432.

55 Ibn Ḥajar, *Fatḥ al-Bārī*, vol. 8, p. 463.

56 Al- Bukhārī, *Ṣaḥīḥ al-Bukhārī*, vol. 4, p. 356.

57 Ibn Kathīr, *Tafsīr Ibn Kathīr*, vol. 4, pp. 173-2. Having realized the contradiction between the two interpretations, Ibn Kathīr stated: "But this does not mean that other Qur'anic verses cannot be described as *al-sabᶜ al-mathānī*." He further stated that the whole chapters of the Qur'an can be qualified as *al-sabᶜ al-mathānī*.

58 Ibn Kathīr, *Tafsīr Ibn Kathīr*, vol. 7, p. 173.

59 *Ṣaḥīḥ al-Bukhārī*, vol. 4, pp. 123-170.

60 Amin, Ahmad *Fajr al-Islām*, p. 205.

61 Muhammad Husayn al-Dhahabi, *Al-Isrā'iliyyāt fī al-Tafsīr wa al-Ḥadīth* (Cairo: Majmaᶜ al-Buḥūth al-Islāmiyyah, 1963), pp. 76-85, and Ramzi Nana, *Al-Isrā'īliyyāt wa Āthāruhā fī Kutub al-Tafsīr*, pp. 78-92.

CHAPTER 6

1 Ibn Manẓūr, *Lisān al-ᶜArab* (Beirut: Dār Ṣādir, n.d.), vol. 14, pp. 299-300.

2 Jamāl al-Dīn Abū Muḥammad ibn ᶜAbd Allāh ibn Yūsuf ibn Hishām al-Anṣārī, *Al-Taṣrīḥ ᶜalā al-Tawḍīḥ*, eds., Majmūᶜah min al-ᶜUlamā, (Beirut: Dār al-Fikr, n.d.), vol. 1, p. 26.

3 Abū Hayyān, *Al-Baḥr al-Muḥīṭ*, vol. 3, p. 178.

4 Badr was the first war that took place in Islam between Muslims and non-Muslims in the third year of hijrah.

5 Abū Muḥammad ᶜAbd al-Malik ibn Hishām, *Sirat al-Nabī*, ed., Muhammad Muhyi al-Din Abd al-Hamid (Beirut: Dār al-Fikr, n.d.), vol. 2, p. 259. See Safiyyu al-Rahman al-Mubarakpuri, *Al-Raḥīq al-Makhtūm*, 1st edn., (Saudi Arabia: Maktabah Dār al-Salām, 1915), vol. 1, p. 435.

6 Ibn Ḥazm, *Al-Iḥkām*, vol. 6, p. 26.
7 Ibn Qayyim, *Iʿlām al-Muaqqiʿīn*, vol. 1, p. 63.
8 Ibn Ḥajar, *Tahdhīb al-Tahdhīb*, vol. 3, p. 395.
9 Ibid., vol. 8, pp. 351-356.
10 Ibid., vol. 3, p. 397.
11 Al-Jāhiz, ʿAmrū ibn Baḥr ibn Maḥbūb, *Kitāb al-Ḥayawān*, ed., Abd al-Salam Harun, (Cairo: Maṭabaʿah al-Khaniji, n.d.), vol. 1, pp. 168-7. The use of the term *ra'y* with a negative connotation was not limited only to the circle of theologians, it was also extended to include different scholars of jurisprudence. Genereally speaking, the Ḥanafī school was described as a school of *ra'y* while the Mālikī school was believed to be a school of *athar* 'tradition'.
12 Muhammad Husayn al-Dhahbi, *Al-Tafsīr wa al-Muffasirūn*, vol. 1, pp. 347-9; Al-Ghazālī, *Iḥyā' ʿUlūm al-Dīn*, vol. 1, p. 292. See Al-Qurṭubī, *Al-Jāmiʿ li Aḥkām al-Qur'ān*, vol. 1, p. 32.
13 Ibn Manẓūr, *Lisān al-ʿArab*, vol. 14, p. 300.
14 Al-Ghazālī, *Iḥyā' ʿUlūm al-Dīn*, vol. 1, p. 292.
15 Ibid.
16 Muhammad ibn Abd al-Rahman ibn Abd al-Rahim al-Mubarakpuri, *Tuḥfat al-Ahwadhī bi Sharḥ Jāmiʿ al-Tirmidhī*, ed., Abd al-Rahman Uthman, (Beirut: Dār al-Fikr, n.d.), vol. 1, pp. 270-80.
17 Ibn Taymiyyah, *Majmūʿ Fatāwā*, vol. 13, p. 471.
18 Al-Ṭabarī, *Jāmiʿ al-Bayān*, vol. 1, p. 79.
19 Al-Ghazālī, *Iḥyā' ʿUlūm al-Dīn*, vol. 1, pp. 292-5.
20 Ibid., vol. 1, p. 292.
21 Ibid.
22 Ibn Taymiyyah, *Muqaddimah fī Uṣūl al-Tafsīr*, p. 89.
23 Ibid., p. 91.
24 Kharijites are followers of ʿAlī ibn Abī Ṭālib who turned against him following the battle of Ṣiffīn when he was forced to agree to arbitration with Muʿāwiyah, which concession angered them. Ibn Taymiyyah, *Muqaddimah fī Uṣūl al-Tafsīr*, p. 81.
25 Rafidites are an extremist sect of Shia. They believe that Abū Bakr and ʿUmar have deprived ʿAlī from being *khalīfah* (caliph) just after the death of the Prophet. The title *Rawāfiḍah* was given to them by Zayd ibn ʿAlī Zayn al-ʿĀbidīn (d. 122 AH/740 CE) when he approved the caliphate of Abū Bakr and ʿUmar though he believed in his grandfather's right ʿAlī ibn Abī Ṭālib to the caliphate – and his followers rejected that. Hence he labeled them *Rawāfiḍah* (rejecters), Muhammad Abu Zahrah, *Tārīkh al-Madhāhib al-Islāmiyyah (fī al-Siyāsah wa al-ʿAqā'id)* (Beirut: Dār al-Fikr, n.d.), p. 245.
26 Jahmites are the followers of Jahm ibn Ṣafwān. Jahm was a faithful student of Jaʿd ibn Dirham. Jaʿd was executed in 736 CE, by the Umayyad governor Khālid ibn ʿAbd Allāh, because he preached that people have no free will. Jahmites believed that man has no free will and is absolutely determined. They interpreted *īmān* (faith) as being

knowledge of God only, and involved no action. Abu Zahrah, *Tārīkh al-Madhāhib al-Islāmiyyah (fī al-Siyāsah wa al-ʿAqā'id)*. See Abu Aminah, Bilal Philips, *The Fundamentals of Tawhid* (Riyadh: Islamic Monotheism: Tawheed Publication, 1990), p. 4.

27 Muʿtazilites believed in six principles, and one can never be considered a *muʿtazilī* (sing of Muʿtazilites) without believing in them. They are: *tawḥīd* (indivisible oneness of God), *ʿadl* (justice), *waʿd* (promise of paradise for those who are truly believers), *waʿīd* (warning against disobeying God), *manzilah bayn manzilatayn* (intermediate state), and *al-amr bi al-maʿrūf wa al-nahyi ʿan al-munkar*, (enjoining what is right and forbidding what is wrong). The alleged founder of the Muʿtazilites was Wāṣil ibn ʿAṭā' (d.131 AH). The reason for branding them Muʿtazilites goes as follows. One day Wāṣil was sitting in al-Ḥasan al-Baṣrī's learning circle when the issue of the position of a Muslim who commits a major sin was raised, Wāṣil said that he was neither a Muslim nor a non-Muslim but between belief and disbelief. Al-Ḥasan the teacher, however, did not welcome Wāṣil's answer and stated that he was a sinner. Thus, Wāṣil *iʿtazal* (stayed away) from al-Ḥasan's class. See Abū al-Ḥasan al-Ashʿarī, *Maqālāt al-Islāmiyyīn wa Ikhtilāf al-Muṣallīn*, 1st edn., (Cairo: Maṭbaʿat al-Nahḍah al-Misriyyah, 1969-1389), pp. 235-45.

28 The Qadarites are a sect that believe that man created his own evil but that good comes from Allah only.

29 The Murji'ites are the extreme opponents of the Kharijites. They believe that *īmān* is nothing but knowledge and that one does not lose his *īmān* regardless of how grave a sin he might commit. Furthermore, they believed that the questions of punishing a sinner in hell is left to the will and mercy of God. The extremists among them believed that given faith, sin will cause no harm in the hereafter. The issue of the evolution of the theological schools of thought in Islam is not clear cut. A person might have a combination of tenets from various sects of belief. For example, one might be a *shīʿī* (sing of Shia) at the same time that he is a Muʿtazilī, or one might be a Sunni and a Murji'ī at the same time, etc. For detailed accounts on the sects, one can refer to Abū al-Fatḥ Tāj al-Dīn al-Shahrastānī's *Kitāb al-Milal wa al-Niḥal*; Ṭāhir al-Baghdādī's, *Al-Farq bayn al-Firaq*; Abū al-Ḥasan al-Ashʿarī's, *Maqālāt al-Islāmiyyīn*; M. Geijbel, *An Introduction to Islam: Muslim Beliefs and Practices*, part 3; Goldziher's *Introduction to Islamic Theology and Law*, trans., Andras and Ruth Hamori, (Princeton: Princeton University Press, 1981).

30 Ibn Taymiyyah, *Muqaddimah fī Uṣūl al-Tafsīr*, pp. 82-84.

31 Abu Zahrah, *Tārīkh al-Madhāhib al-Islāmiyyah (fī al-Siyāsah wa al-ʿAqā'id)*, p. 67.

32 This hadith has no *isnād*, thus, is rejected. See Muhammad Abd Al-Rahman al-Sakhawi, *Al-Maqāṣid al-Ḥasanah* (Cairo: Maktabat Al-Khanijī, 1956), p. 85.

33 Ibn Qutaybah, Abū Muḥammad ʿAbd Allāh ibn Muslim, *Ta'wīl Mukhtalaf al-Ḥadīth* (Beirut: Dār al-Kutb al-ʿArabiyyah, n.d.), p. 4.

34 Ibid., p. 5.

35 Muhammad Ajjaj al-Khatib, *Al-Sunnah Qabl al-Tadwīn*, 2nd edn., (Cairo: Dār al-Fikr, 1971), p. 236.

36 Ibid., p. 5.
37 Abū Lahab is one of the Prophet Muhammad's uncle who became one of his greatest enemies.
38 Ibn Taymiyyah, *Muqaddimah fī Uṣūl al-Tafsīr*, p. 76.
39 Ibid., p. 79
40 Ibid., p. 81
41 Ibn Qutaybah, *Ta'wīl Mukhtalaf al-Ḥadīth*, vol. 1, p. 159.
42 Ibid., p. 137.
43 Ibid.; Ibn Ḥazm, *Al-Fiṣal fī al-Milal wa al-Niḥal* (Cairo: Maktabah wa Maṭbaᶜah Muhammad Ali Sabihah, n.d.), vol. 1, p. 56.
44 Muhammad ibn Salih al-Uthaymin, *Sharḥ al-ᶜAqīdah al-Wāsiṭiyyah li Shaykh al-Islām ibn Taymiyyah*, ed., Muhammad Khalil Harras, 3rd edn., (Riyadh: Dār al-Hijrah li al-Nashr wa al-Tawzīᶜ, 1955), pp. 107-9; Ibn Qutaybah, *Ta'wīl Mukhtalaf al-Ḥadīth*, pp. 13-8.
45 This attitude is against Islamic scholarship. Traditionally speaking, reference should be given when you quote someone.
46 Al-Āmidī, *Al-Iḥkām*, vol. 4, p. 149.
47 Ibn Taymiyyah, *Muqaddimah fī Uṣūl al-Tafsīr*, pp. 112-113.
48 Al-Qurṭubī, *Al-Jāmiᶜ li Aḥkām al-Qur'ān*, vol. 1, p. 32; Al-Tirmidhī, *Sunan al-Tirmidhī*, 1st edn., (Cairo: Dār Al-Fikr, 1964-1384), vol. 4, p. 386.
49 Al-Qurṭubī, *Al-Jāmiᶜ li Aḥkām al-Qur'ān*, vol. 1, p. 111.
50 Al-Ṭabarī, *Jāmiᶜ al-Bayān*, vol. 1, p. 183.
51 Al-Qurṭubī, *Al-Jāmiᶜ li Aḥkām al-Qur'ān*, vol. 1, p. 33.
52 Abul Quasem, Muhammad, *The Recitation and Interpretation of the Qur'an: Al-Ghazali's Theory* (London, Boston, and Melbourne: Kegan Paul International, 1982), pp. 90-92.
53 Ibn ᶜAṭiyyah, *Muqaddimatān fī ᶜUlūm al-Qur'ān*, p. 187; Al-Zarkashī, *Al-Burhān*, vol. 2, p. 12.
54 Al-Ṭabarī, *Jāmiᶜ al-Bayān*, vol. 1, p. 88.
55 Al-Ghazālī, *Iḥyā' ᶜUlūm al-Dīn*, vol. 1, p. 292.
56 Ibn ᶜAṭiyyah, *Muqaddimatān fī ᶜUlūm al-Qur'ān*, p. 186.
57 Al-Ṭabarī, *Jāmiᶜ al-Bayānᶜ*, vol. 1, p. 93.
58 Ibid., vol. 1, p. 190.
59 Al-Qurṭubī, *Al-Jāmiᶜ li Aḥkām al-Qur'ān*, vol. 1, p. 32.
60 Ibn ᶜAṭiyyah, *Muqaddimatān fī ᶜUlūm al-Qur'ān*, p. 185.
61 Al-Ṭabarī, *Jāmiᶜ al-Bayānᶜ*, vol. 1, p. 290.
62 Ibid.
63 Ibn ᶜAṭiyyah, *Muqaddimatān fī ᶜUlūm al-Qur'ān*, p. 185.
64 Al-Ṭabarī, *Jāmiᶜ al-Bayānᶜ*, vol. 1, p. 83.
65 Ibid., vol. 1, p. 290.
66 Ibn Ḥazm, *Al-Iḥkām*, vol. 6, p. 35.
67 Ibid., vol. 1, p. 81.

68 For many verses presented by Ibn Ḥazm to support his position, see Ibn Ḥazm, *Al-Iḥkām*, vol. 5, pp. 36–100.

69 Ibn Ḥazm, *Al-Iḥkām*, vol. 5, p. 36.

70 Ibid., pp. 21-22.

71 Ibid., p. 35.

72 Ibid., vol. 2, pp. 400–1.

73 Al-Zarkashī, *Al-Burhān*, vol. 1, p. 18.

74 Ibid., vol. 1, p. 129.

75 Al-Dhahabī, *Tadhkirat al-Ḥuffāẓ*, vol. 1, p. 174.

76 A. Rippin, *Approaches to the History of the Interpretation of the Qur'an*, ed., (Oxford: Oxford University Press, 1988), p. 17.

77 Rippin, *Approaches to the History of the Interpretation of the Qur'an*, p. 168.

78 Abbott, *Studies*, pp. 92–3.

79 Ibid.

CHAPTER 7

1 J.G. Jansen, *The Interpretation of the Koran in Modern Egypt* (Leiden: E.J. Brill, 1974), pp. 7-8.

2 Muhammad Rashid Rida, *Tafsīr Al-Manār*, vol. 1, p. 17, vol. 4, p. 43.

3 Rida, *Tafsīr Al-Manār*, vol. 1, pp. 15–16. See *Islamic Studies Presented to Charles J. Adams*, eds., Wael, B. Hallaq and Donald, P. Little, (Leiden; New York: Brill, 1990), p. 22.

4 Muhammad Husayn al-Dhahabi, *Al-Tafsīr wa al-Mufassirūn*, vol. 2, p. 528.

5 Muhammad Rashid Rida, *Tafsīr Al-Manār*, vol. 1, p. 17.

6 Ibid., vol. 1, p. 239; See Goldziher, *Madhāhib al-Tafsīr al-Islāmī*, p. 353.

7 Charles Adam, *Islam and Modernism in Egypt* (Oxford: Oxford University Press, 1933), p. 111.

8 Muhammad Rashid Rida, *Tafsīr Al-Manār*, vol. 2, pp. 25–6.

9 Abd al-Majid Abd al-Salam al-Muhtasibi, *Ittijahāt al-Tafsīr fī al-ᶜAṣr al-Rāhin*, 2nd edn., (Jordan: Jamᶜiyyah ᶜUmmāl al-Maṭābiᶜ al-Taᶜāwuniyyah, 1982 CE/1402 AH), pp. 157, pp. 183–5. See Muhammad Husayn al-Dhahbi, *Al-Tafsīr wa al-Muffasirūn*, vol. 2, p. 543.

10 Fahd Abd al-Rahman al-Rumi, *Manhaj al-Madrasah al-ᶜAqliyyah al-Hadīthah fī al-Tafsīr* (Beirut: Mu'assasah al-Risālah, 1981), vol. 1, pp. 149–54; Subhi al-Salih, *Mabāḥith fī ᶜUlūm al-Qūr'ān*, 2nd edn., (Beirut: Dār al-Malāyīn, 1986), p. 297.

11 Al-Shaykh Tantawi Jawhari, *Al-Jawāhir fī Tafsīr al-Qur'ān* (Cairo: Matbaᶜah Muṣtafā al-Babī al-Ḥalabī wa Awlāldih, 1951), vol. 1, p. 2.

12 Ibid., vol. 1, p. 116.

13 Muhammad Husayn al-Dhahabi, *Al-Tafsīr wa al-Mufassirūn*, vol. 2, p. 487.

14 Subhi al-Salih, *Mabāhith fī ᶜUlūm al-Qur'ān*, p. 297.

15 Sayyid Qutb, *Fī- Ẓilāl al-Qur'ān*, 10th edn., (Beirut: Dār al-Shurūq, 1982/1400), vol. 1, pp. 11-16.

16 Ayoub, *The Qur'ān and its Interpreters*, vol. 1, p. 39.

17 Jansen, *The Interpretation of the Koran in Modern Egypt*, p. 65.

18 Muhammad Ibrahim Sharif, *Ittijahāt al-Tajdīd fī Tafsīr al-Qur'ān fī Miṣr* (Cairo; Dār al-Turath, 1982), p. 597. See also Issa, J. Boullata, "Modern Qur'an Exegesis: A Study of Bint al-Shati's Method", *The Muslim World*, no. 64, 1979, p.104.

19 Boullata, "Modern Qur'an Exegesis", *The Muslim World*, no.64, pp.104-105.

20 Muhammad Ibrahim Sharif, *Ittijahāt al-Tajdīd fī Tafsīr al-Qur'ān*, pp. 595-610; See also Boullata, "Modern Qur'an Exegesis", pp. 104-112.

21 Al-Qattan, Manna ibn Khalil, *Mabāḥith fī ʿUlūm al-Qur'ān* (Cairo: Maktabat Wahba, 1981), p. 375.

22 Muhammad Husayn al-Dhahabi, *Al-Tafsīr wa al-Mufassirūn*, vol. 1, p. 500; *The Interpretation of the Koran in Modern Egypt*, p. 35.

23 Muhammad Husayn al-Dhahabi, *Al-Tafsīr wa al-Mufassirūn*, vol. 2, pp. 500-9.

BIBLIOGRAPHY

Abd Allah ibn Abd al-Muhsin al-Turki, *Uṣūl Madhhab al-Imām Aḥmad: Dirāsah Uṣūliyyah Muqāranah* (Riyadh: Maṭbaʿah al-Riyāḍ, 1397/1977).

ʿAbd al-Ḥaqq ibn Ghālib ibn ʿAṭiyyah, *Muqaddimatān fī ʿUlūm al-Qur'ān* (Cairo:Maṭbaʿah al-Khaniji, 1972).

Abd al-Majid Abd al-Salam al-Muhtasibi, *Ittijahāt al-Tafsīr fī al-ʿAṣr al-Rāhin* (Jordan: Jamʿiyyah ʿUmmāl al-Maṭābiʿ al-Taʿāwuniyyah, 1982-1402).

Abd al-Qahir Al-Jurjani, *Dalā'il al-Iʿjāz* (Cairo: Muṣṭafā al-Bābī al-Ḥalabī, 1967).

ʿAbd al-Raḥmān ibn Khaldūn, *Muqaddimat ibn Khaldūn*, 4th edn., (Beirut: Iḥyā al-Turāth al-ʿArabī, n.d.).

Abū al-ʿAbbās Muḥammad ibn Yazīd al-Mubarrid, *Al-Kāmil fī al-Lughah wa al-Adab,* 1st edn., (Beirut: Mu 'assat Al-Risālah, 1986).

Abū ʿAbd al-Raḥmān Aḥmed ibn Shuʿayb ibn ʿAlī al-Nasā'ī, *Tafsīr al-Nasā'ī*, eds., Abd al-Kaliq al-Sharif and Said ibn Abbas al-Julayni, (Cairo: Maṭbaʿah al-Sunnah, 1990).

Abū ʿAlī al-Faḍl ibn al-Ḥasan Al-Ṭabarsī, *Majmaʿ al-Bayān fī Tafsīr al-Qur'ān*, 2nd edn., (Cairo: Dār al-Fikr, 1954-1957).

Abū Ḥayyān, Muḥammad ibn Yūsuf ibn ʿAlī al-Andalusī, *Al-Baḥr al-Muḥit* (Riyadh: Maktabah wa Maṭbaʿah al-Ḥashr al-Ḥadīth, 1969).

Abū Jaʿfar Muḥammad ibn Jarīr al-Ṭabarī, *Jamiʿ al-Bayān ʿan Ta'wīl Āy al-Qur'ān,* eds., Mahmud Muhammad Shakir and Ahmed Muhammad Shakir, (Cairo: Dar al-Maʿārif, n.d.)

Abū Muḥammad ʿAbd Allāh ibn Muslim ibn Qutaybah, *Ta'wīl Mukhtalaf al-Ḥadīth* (Beirut: Dār al-Kutb al-ʿArabiyyah, n.d.).

Abū Muḥammad ʿAbd al-Malik ibn Hishām, *Sirat al-Nabī*, ed., Muhammad Muhyi al-Din Abd al-Hamid (Beirut: Dār al-Fikr, n.d.).

Abū Muḥammad al-Ḥusayn ibn Masʿūd al-Baghawī, *Maʿālim al-Tanzīl* (Multan: Idarat Talifat Ishrafiyya, 1988).

Abū al-Qāsim al-Aṣfahynī, Al-Ḥusayn ibn Muḥammad ibn al-Mufaḍḍil 'Known as' al-Rāghib al-Aṣfahānī, *Mufradāt Alfāẓ al-Qur'ān* (Lahore: Ahl al-Ḥadīth Ikadami,1971).

Abū Ṭāhir Muḥammad ibn Yaʿqūb Fayrūz Ābādī, *Tanwīr al-Miqbās* (*Tafsīr Ibn ʿAbbās*), (Pakistan: Al-Maktabah al-Furūqiyya Malkan, n.d.)

Abu Zahrah, Muhammad, *Ibn Ḥazm: Ḥayātuh wa ʿAṣruh Āra'ahu wa Fiqhuh* (Beirut: Dār al-Fikr al-ʿArabī, n.d.).

______, *Al-Muʿjizhah al-Kubrā: Al-Qur'ān*

Ahmad Ali, *Aḥkām al-Qur'ān* (Istanbul: Maktabah al-Awqaf al-Islamiyyah, 1916 CE/ 1335 AH).

Bibliography

Ahmad Umar Abd Allah Al-Ghani, "Al-Tafsīr bi al-Ma'thūr", (MA thesis, al-Jāmiᶜah al-Islāmiyyah, Madinah, Suadi Arabia, 1980).

Ahmed Ali al-Salus, *Bayn al-Shīᶜah wa al-Sunnah: Dirāsah Muqāranah fī al-Tafsīr wa Usūlih* (Cairo: Dār al-Iᶜtiṣām,1989).

Aishah Abd al-Rahman Bint al-Shati, *Iᶜjāz al-Bayānī li al-Qur'ān wa Masā'il ibn al-Azraq: Dirāsah Muqāranah Lughawiyyah wa Bayāniyyah*. 2nd edn., (Cairo: Dār al-Maᶜrifah, 1987).

Al-Ālūsī, Shihāb al-Dīn Maḥmūd ibn ᶜAbd Allāh al-Ḥusaynī, *Rūḥ al-Maᶜānī fī Tafsīr al-Qur'ān al-ᶜAẓīm wa al-Sabᶜ al-Mathānī* (Beirut: Dār al-Turāth al-ᶜArabī, n.d.).

Al-Āmidī, ᶜAli ibn Muḥammad Sayf al-Dīn, *Al-Iḥkām fī Uṣūl al-Aḥkām*, ed., Abd Al-Razzaq Afifi, 2nd edn., (Beirut: Almaktab al-Islamī, 1402 AH).

Andrew Rippin, "Tafsir Studies", *The Muslim World*, vol. LXII, 1979/1982.

______, *Approaches to the History of the Interpretation of the Qur'an*, ed., (Oxford: Clarendon press, N.Y. Oxford University Press, 1988).

______, "Bulletin of the School of Oriental and African Studies".

Al-Anṣārī, Niẓām al-Dīn, *Kitāb Fawātiḥ al-Raḥmūt bi Sharḥ Musallam al-Thubūt, wa maᶜahū al-Mustaṣfā min ᶜIlm Uṣūl al-Fiqh* (Beirut: Dār al-Arqam ibn Abī al-Arqam li al-Ṭibāᶜh wa al-Nashr, 1944-1414).

Atr Hasan Diya al-Din, *Al-Aḥruf al-Sabᶜ wa Manzilat al-Qirā'at Minhā*, 1st edn., (Beirut: Dār al-Bashā'ir al-Islāmiyyah, 1988/1409).

Badran Abu al-Aynayn, *Uṣūl al-Fiqh,* 1st edn., (Cairo: Dār al-Fikr, 1976).

Boullata, Issa J., "Modern Qur'an Exegesis: A Study of Bint al-Shati's Method", *The Muslim World*, 1974.

Al-Bukhārī, Abū ᶜAbd Allāh Muḥammad ibn Ismāᶜīl *Al-Jāmiᶜ al-Ṣaḥīḥ* (al-Maktab al-Islāmī, n.d.).

Charles Adam, *Islam and Modernism In Egypt* (Oxford: Oxford University Press, 1933).

Al-Dāwaūdī, Muḥammad ibn ᶜAlī ibn Aḥmad, *Ṭabaqāt al-Mufassirīn* (Cairo: Maktabah Wahbah, 1972).

Al-Dhahabī, Abū ᶜAbd Allāh Shams al-Dīn Muḥammad ibn Aḥmad ibn ᶜUthmān, *Siyar Aᶜlām al-Nubalā'* (Cairo: Maᶜhad al-Makhṭūṭāt al-ᶜArabiyyah, 1952-1956).

______, *Tadhkirat al-Ḥuffāẓ*.

Al-Dhahabi, Muhammad Husayn. *Al-Tafsīr wa al-Mufassirūn*, 1st edn., (Cairo: Dār al-Kutub al-Hadīthah, 1961/1381).

______, *Al-Isrā'iliyyāt fī al-Tafsīr wa al-Ḥadīth* (Cairo: Majmaᶜ al-Buḥūth al-Islāmiyyah, 1963).

Fahd Abd al-Rahman al-Rumi, *Manhaj al-Madrasah al-ᶜAqliyyah al-Ḥadīthah fī al-Tafsīr* (Beirut: Mu'assasah al-Risālah, 1981).

Fred Leemhuis, "Origins and Early Development of the *Tafsīr* Tradition" in A. Rippin, ed., *Approaches to the History of the Interpretation of the Qur'an*.

Al-Ghazālī, Abū Ḥāmid, *Iḥyā' ᶜUlūm al-Dīn* (Cairo: Dār Ihyā' al-Kutb al-ᶜArabiyyah, n.d.).

Goldziher, Ignaz, Muslim Studies. Translated from German by C.R. Berber and S.M Stern. 2nd edn., (Chicago: Aldine, New York, Altherton, n.d.).

______, *Die Richtungen Der Islamischen Karanauslegung* (Leiden, Brill. 1920).

______, *Madhāhib al-Tafsīr al-Islāmī*.

Ibn ʿArabī, Muḥy al-Dīn, *Al-Futūḥāt al-Makkiyah* (Beirut: Mu'assasah al-Iʿlāmī li al-Maṭbūʿāt, 1973).

Ibn Ashur, Muhammad al-Tahir, *Al-Taḥrīr wa al-Tanwīr* (Tunis: al-Dār al-Tunisiyyah li Ṭibāʿah wa al-Nashr, n.d.).

Ibn ʿAṭiyyah, ʿAbd al-Ḥaqq ibn Ghālib. *Muqaddimatān fī ʿUlūm al-Qur'ān*. (Cairo: Maṭbaʿah al-Khanijī, 1972).

______, *Al-Muḥarrir al-Wajīz fī Tafsīr al-ʿAzīz*, 1st edn., ed., Abd al-Salam al-Shafi Muhammad, (Beirut: Al-Dār al-ʿIllmiyyah, 1993).

Ibn Ḥajar al-ʿAsqalānī, *Al-Durar al-Kāminah fī Aʿyān al-Ma'ah al-Thāminah*, ed., Muhammad sayyed Jad al-Haqq, (Cairo: Maṭbaʿah al-Madanī, n.d.).

______, *Al-Isābah fī Tamyīz al-Ṣaḥābah* (Cairo:Maktabat al-Kulliyah, 1969).

______, *Fatḥ al-Bārī fī Sharḥ Ṣaḥīḥ al-Bukhārī* (Cairo: al-Maṭbaʿah al-Salafiyyah, n.d).

______, *Tahdhīb al-Tahdhīb*.

Ibn Ḥazm, Abū Muḥammad ʿAlī ibn Aḥmad ibn Saʿīd al-Andalusī. *Al-Iḥkām fī Uṣūl al-Aḥkām*, ed., Ahmad Shakir, 2nd edn., (Beirut: Dār al-Āfāq al-Ḥadīthah, 1983/1403).

______, *Al-Muḥallā bi al-Athar*, ed., Abd al-Ghaffar Sulayman al-Bandari, (Beirut: Dār al-Kutub al-ʿIlmiyyah, 1988/1408).

______, *Al-Fiṣal fī al-Milal wa al-Niḥal* (Cairo: Maktabah wa Maṭbaʿah Muhammad Ali Sabihah, n.d).

Ibn Kathīr, al-Imām al-Ḥāfiẓ Abū al-Fidā' Ismāʿīl.

______, *Tafsīr al-Qur'ān al-ʿAẓīm*. New edn. Ed by a group of *ʿUlamā'*, (Beirut: Dār al-Andalus, n.d.)

______, *Al-Bidāyah wa al-Nihāyay*, ed., Muhammad Abd al-Aziz al-Najdi, (Riyadh: Mu'assasah al-Kutub, n.d.).

______, *Al-Baʿith al-Ḥathīth Sharḥ Ikhtiṣār ʿUlūm al-Ḥadīth* (Cairo: Dār al-Kutub, 1982).

Ibn Khaldūn, ʿAbd al-Raḥmān. *Muqaddimat Ibn Khaldūn*, 4th edn., (Beirut: Iḥyā' al-Turāth al-ʿArabī, n.d.)

Ibn Manẓūr, Muḥammad ibn Mukarram, *Lisān al-ʿArab* (Beirut: Dār Ṣādir, n.d.).

Ibn Qayyim al-Jawziyyah, *Iʿlām al-Muaqqiʿīn ʿan Rabb al-ʿAlamīn*, 2nd edn., ed., Muhammad Muhyiddin Abd al-Alamin, (Beirut: Dār al-Fikr, 1977/1397).

______, *Kitāb Shifā' al-ʿAlīl fī Masā'il al-Qaḍā' wa al-Qadar wa al-Ḥikmah wa al-Taʿlīl*, ed., al-Sayyid Muhammad Badr al-Din Abu Firas al-Nasani al-Halabi, (Riyadh: Maktabat al-Riyadh al-Hadīth, 1323 AH).

Ibn Qutaybah, Abū Muḥammad ʿAbd Allāh ibn Muslim, *Ta'wīl Mukhtalaf al-Ḥadīth* (Beirut: Dār al-Kutb al-ʿArabiyyah, n.d.).

Ibn Sa'd, Muḥammad ibn Sa'd ibn Manī' al-Zuhrī, *Al-Ṭabaqāt al-Kubrā* (Beirut: Dār Ṣādir, 1957).

Ibn al-Ṣalāḥ, 'Uthmān ibn 'Abd al-Raḥmān Taqī al-Dīn, *Muqaddimah Ibn al-Ṣalāḥ*, ed., Aisha Bint al-Shati, (Cairo: Dār al-Kutub, n.d.).

Ibn Taymiyyah, *Majmū' Fatāwā Shaykh al-Islām Aḥmed ibn Taymiyyahh,* ed., Ahmed Abd al-Rahman ibn Muhammad ibn Qasim al-Najdi al-Hanbali, (Makkah: Maṭba'ah al-Nahḍah al-Hadīthah, 1404/1983).

______, *Muqaddimah fī Uṣūl al-Tafsīr,* ed., Adnan Zorzo, (Beirut: Dār al-Qur'ān al-Karīm, 1979/1399).

______, *Sharḥ al-'Aqīdah al-Wāsiṭiyyah,* ed., Muhammad Khalil Harras, 3rd edn., (Riyadh: Dār al-Hijrah li al-Nashr wa al-Tawzī', 1955).

______, *Majmū' Fatāwā Shaykh al-Islām Aḥmed ibn Taymiyyah,* ed., Ahmed Abd al-Rahman ibn Muhammad ibn Qasim al-Najdi al-Hanbali, (Makkah: Maṭba'ah al-Nahḍah al-Hadīthah 1404/1983).

Al-Jāhiz, 'Amrū ibn Baḥr ibn Maḥbūb, *Kitāb al-Ḥayawān*, ed., Abd al-Salam Harun, (Cairo: Maṭaba'ah al-Khanijī, n.d.).

J.J.G. Jansen, *The Interpretation of the Koran in Modern Egypt* (Leiden: E.J. Brill, 1974).

Jawhari Shaykh Tantawi, *Al-Jawāhir fī Tafsīr al-Qur'ān* (Cairo: Matba'ah Muṣtafā al-Babī al-Ḥalabī wa Awlāldih, 1951).

John Wansbrough, *Qur'anic Studies: Sources and Methods of Scriptual Interpretation* (Oxford: Oxford University Press, 1977).

Juda, Mohammad Mohammad Mahdi, *Al-Wāḥidī wa Manhajuhu fī al-Tafsīr* (Cairo: Al-Majlis al-A'lā li al-Shu'ūn al-Islāmiyyah, 1979).

Muhammad Abd al-Rahman ibn Abd al-Rahim al-Mubarakpuri, *Tuḥfat al-Ahwadhī bi Sharḥ Jāmi' al-Tirmidhī*, ed., Abd al-Rahman Uthman, (Beirut: Dār al-Fikr, n.d.).

Muhammad Ajjaj Al-Khatib, *Al-Sunnah Qabl al-Tadwīn*, 2nd edn., (Cairo: Dār al-Fikr, 1971).

Muhammad Ali al-Saboony, *Mukhtaṣar Tafsīr Ibn Kathīr,* new edn., (Dār al-Ma'rifah, 1944).

Muhammad Hashim Kamali, *Principle of Islamic Jurisprudence* (Cambridge: Islamic Texts Society, 1991).

Muhammad Ibrahim Sharif, *Buḥūth fī Tafsīr al-Qur'ān: Tārīkhuhu, Ittijāhātuhu, wa Manāhijuhu* (Cairo: Jāmi'at al-Qāhirah, n.d.).

Muhammad M. Ayoub, *The Qur'an and Its Interpreters* (Albany State University of New York, 1984).

Muhammad Rashid Rida, *Tafsīr al-Qur'ān al-Ḥakīm* known as *Tafsīr al-Mannār* (Beirut: Dār al-Fikr, n.d.).

Nabia Abbott *Studies in Arabic Literary Papyri II: Qur'anic Commentary and Tradition* (Chicago: The University of Chicago Press, 1967).

Al-Nawawī, Abu Zakariyyā Yaḥyā ibn Sharaf ibn Ḥusayn, *Sharḥ Ṣaḥīḥ Muslim* (Beirut: Dār al-Fikr, n.d.).

Al-Qāḍī Muḥammad ibn ʿAbd Allāh Abū Bakr ibn al-ʿArabī al-Ishbīlī al-Mālikī, *Aḥkām al-Qur'ān*, ed., Ali Muhammad al-Bajawi, 1st edn., (Cairo: Dār al-Kutub al-ʿArabiyyah, ʿĪsā al-Bābī al-Ḥalabī, 1975).

Al-Qattan, Manna ibn Khalil, *Mabāḥith fī ʿUlūm al-Qur'ān* (Cairo: Maktabat Wahbah, 1981).

Al-Qurṭubī, Abū ʿAbd Allāh Muḥammad ibn Aḥmad al-Anṣārī, *Al-Jāmiʿ li Aḥkām al-Qur'ān al-Mubayyin li mā Tataḍammanaho min al-Sunnah wa āy al-Furqān* (Cairo: Dār al-Kutub al-ʿArabiyyah li al-Ṭibāʿah wa al-Nashr, 1967/1387).

Al-Qushayri, Abd al-Karim ibn Hawazin ibn Abd al-Malik, *Laṭā'if al-Ishārāt: Tafsīr Ṣūfī Kāzmil li al-Qur'ān* (Dār al-Kutub al-ʿArabiyyah, 1968).

Al-Rāzi, ʿAbd al-Raḥmān ibn Muḥammad ibn Abū Ḥātim al-Tamīmī, *Kitāb al-Jarḥ wa al-Taʿdīl* (India: Mabṭaʿah al-Majlis Dā'irat al-Maʿarifah al-ʿUthmāniyyah).

Safiyyu al-Rahman al-Mubarakpuri, *Al-Raḥīq al-Makhtūm*, 1st edn., (Saudi Arabia: Maktabah Dār al-Salām, 1915).

Al-Salih, Subhi, *Mabāḥith fī ʿUlūm al-Qur'ān*, 2nd edn., (Beirut: Dār al-Malayīn, 1986).

Al-Sarkhasī, Imām Abū Bakr Muḥammad ibn Aḥmad ibn abī Sahl, *Uṣūl al-Sarkhasī*, ed., Abu al-Wafa al-Afghani, (Beirut: Dār al-Maʿrifah .n.d.).

Sayyid Qutb, *Fī-Ẓilāl al-Qur'ān*, 10th edn., (Beirut: Dār al-Shurūq, 1982/1400).

Sezgin, Fuat, *Tārīkh al-Turāth al-ʿArabī: Fī ʿUlūm al-Qur'ān wa al-Ḥadīth*, trans., Mahmud Fahmi Hijazi, (Riyadh: Jāmiʿat Muḥammad ibn Suʿūd al-Islāmiyyah, 1981), vol. 1, part, 1.

Al-Shawkānī, Muḥammad ibn ʿAlī, *Fatḥ al-Qadīr al-Jamiʿ bayn fannay al-Riwāyah wa al-Dirāyah min ʿIlm al-Tafsīr* (Beirut: Maḥfūẓ al-ʿAlī, n.d.).

______, *Irshād al-Fuḥūl ilā Taḥqīq al-Ḥaq min ʿIlm al-Uṣūl.*

Subhi al-Salih, *Mabāhith fī ʿUlūm al-Qūr'ān*, 2nd edn., (Beirut: Dār al-Malāyīn, 1986).

Al-Suyūṭī, Jalāl al-Dīn ʿAbd al-Raḥmān ibn Abū Bakr, *Al-Itqān fī ʿUlūm al-Qur'ān*, 1st edn., (Beirut: Dār al-Kutub al-ʿIlmiyyah, 1987).

______, *Tadrīb al-Rāwī fī Sharḥ Taqrīb al-Rawī*. ed., Abd al-Wahhab Abd al-Latif, (Cairo: Dār al-Kutb al-Ḥadītha, 1966).

______, *Ṭabaqāt al-Mufassirīn.*

______, *Al-Durr al-Manthūr fī al-Tafsīr bi al-Ma'thūr*

The Encyclopedia of Islam. vol.II, E-K (Leiden: E.J. Brill, and London: Luzac and CO, 1927).

Al-Ṭabarī, Abū Jaʿfar Muḥammad ibn Jarīr Yazīd ibn Kathīr ibn Ghālib, *Jāmiʿ al-Bayān ʿan Ta'wīl āy al-Qur'ān*, eds., Muhammad Mahmud Shakir and Ahmad Muhammad Shakir, (Cairo: Dār al-Maʿārif. n.d.).

Al-Tirmidhī, Abū ʿĪsā Muḥammad ibn Sūrah, Sunan al-Tirmidhī. 1st edn., ed., Abd al-Rahman Muhammad Uthman, (Cairo: Dār al-Fikr, 1964-1384).

Von Denffer, Ahmad, *ʿUlūm al-Qur'ān* (Leicester: Islamic Foundation, 1983).

Al-Wāḥidī, ʿAlī ibn Aḥmad, *Al-Basīṭ fī Tafsīr al-Qur'ān al-Majīd*, eds., a group of *ʿUlamā'*, 1st edn., (Cairo: Dār al-Kutub al-ʿIlmiyyah, 1992).

Zaglul, Shahatah al-Sayyid, *Ubay Ibn Kaʿab: al-Rajul wa al-Muṣḥaf*, 1st edn., (Cairo: Al-Haya'ah al-Miṣriyyah al-ʿĀmmah li al-Kitāb, 1978).

Al-Zamakhsharī, Abū al-Qāsim Maḥmūd ibn ʿUmar, *Al-Kashshāf ʿan Ḥaqā'iq Ghawāmiḍ al-Tanzīl wa ʿUyūn al-Aqāwīl fī wujūh al-Ta'wīl* (Cairo: Muṣṭafā al-Bābī al-Ḥalabī wa Awladuh, 1966).

Al-Zarkashī, Abū ʿAbd Allāh Badr al-Dīn Muḥammad ibn ʿAbd Allāh, *Al-Burhān fī ʿUlūm al-Qur'ān,* ed., Muhammad Abu Fadl Ibrahim, (Cairo: Dār Iḥyā' al-Kutub al-ʿArabiyyah, 1957).

Al-Zirikli, Khayr al-Din, *Al-Aʿlām: Qāmūs Tarājim li Ashhar al-Rijāl wa al-Nisā' min al-ʿArab wa al-Mustaʿribīn wa al-Mustashriqīn* (Beirut: Dār al-ʿIlm li al-Malayīn, 1980).

Al-Zurqani, Muhammad Abd Al-Azim *Manāhil al-ʿIrfān fī ʿUlūm al-Qur'ān* (Cairo: Dār Iḥyā' al-Kutub al-ʿArabiyyah, ʿĪsā al-Bābī al-Ḥalabī, n.d.).